How Partisan Media Polarize America

Chicago Studies in American Politics

A SERIES EDITED BY BENJAMIN I. PAGE, SUSAN HERBST, LAWRENCE R. JACOBS, AND ADAM BERINSKY

Also in the series:

CHANGING MINDS OR CHANGING CHANNELS? PARTISAN NEWS IN AN AGE OF CHOICE *by Kevin Arceneaux and Martin Johnson*

THE POLITICS OF BELONGING: RACE, PUBLIC OPINION, AND IMMIGRATION *by Natalie Masuoka and Jane Junn*

POLITICAL TONE: HOW LEADERS TALK AND WHY *by Roderick P. Hart, Jay P. Childers, and Colene J. Lind*

THE TIMELINE OF PRESIDENTIAL ELECTIONS: HOW CAMPAIGNS DO (AND DO NOT) MATTER *by Robert S. Erikson and Christopher Wlezien*

LEARNING WHILE GOVERNING: EXPERTISE AND ACCOUNTABILITY IN THE EXECUTIVE BRANCH *by Sean Gailmard and John W. Patty*

ELECTING JUDGES: THE SURPRISING EFFECTS OF CAMPAIGNING ON JUDICIAL LEGITIMACY *by James L. Gibson*

FOLLOW THE LEADER? HOW VOTERS RESPOND TO POLITICIANS' POLICIES AND PERFORMANCE *by Gabriel S. Lenz*

THE SOCIAL CITIZEN: PEER NETWORKS AND POLITICAL BEHAVIOR *by Betsy Sinclair*

THE SUBMERGED STATE: HOW INVISIBLE GOVERNMENT POLICIES UNDERMINE AMERICAN DEMOCRACY *by Suzanne Mettler*

DISCIPLINING THE POOR: NEOLIBERAL PATERNALISM AND THE PERSISTENT POWER OF RACE *by Joe Soss, Richard C. Fording, and Sanford F. Schram*

WHY PARTIES? A SECOND LOOK *by John H. Aldrich*

NEWS THAT MATTERS: TELEVISION AND AMERICAN OPINION, UPDATED EDITION *by Shanto Iyengar and Donald R. Kinder*

SELLING FEAR: COUNTERTERRORISM, THE MEDIA, AND PUBLIC OPINION *by Brigitte L. Nacos, Yaeli Bloch-Elkon, and Robert Y. Shapiro*

OBAMA'S RACE: THE 2008 ELECTION AND THE DREAM OF A POST-RACIAL AMERICA *by Michael Tesler and David O. Sears*

FILIBUSTERING: A POLITICAL HISTORY OF OBSTRUCTION IN THE HOUSE AND SENATE *by Gregory Koger*

IN TIME OF WAR: UNDERSTANDING AMERICAN PUBLIC OPINION FROM WORLD WAR II TO IRAQ *by Adam J. Berinsky*

US AGAINST THEM: ETHNOCENTRIC FOUNDATIONS OF AMERICAN OPINION *by Donald R. Kinder and Cindy D. Kam*

THE PARTISAN SORT: HOW LIBERALS BECAME DEMOCRATS AND CONSERVATIVES BECAME REPUBLICANS *by Matthew Levendusky*

DEMOCRACY AT RISK: HOW TERRORIST THREATS AFFECT THE PUBLIC *by Jennifer L. Merolla and Elizabeth J. Zechmeister*

AGENDAS AND INSTABILITY IN AMERICAN POLITICS, SECOND EDITION *by Frank R. Baumgartner and Bryan D. Jones*

THE PRIVATE ABUSE OF THE PUBLIC INTEREST *by Lawrence D. Brown and Lawrence R. Jacobs*

THE PARTY DECIDES: PRESIDENTIAL NOMINATIONS BEFORE AND AFTER REFORM *by Marty Cohen, David Karol, Hans Noel, and John Zaller*

SAME SEX, DIFFERENT POLITICS: SUCCESS AND FAILURE IN THE STRUGGLES OVER GAY RIGHTS *by Gary Mucciaroni*

How Partisan Media Polarize America

MATTHEW LEVENDUSKY

THE UNIVERSITY OF CHICAGO PRESS   CHICAGO AND LONDON

MATTHEW LEVENDUSKY is assistant professor of political science at the University of Pennsylvania and the author of *The Partisan Sort*, also published by the University of Chicago Press.

The University of Chicago Press, Chicago 60637
The University of Chicago Press, Ltd., London

Printed in the United States of America
22 21 20 19 18 17 16 15   2 3 4 5

ISBN-13: 978-0-226-06896-1 (cloth)
ISBN-13: 978-0-226-06901-2 (paper)
ISBN-13: 978-0-226-06915-9 (e-book)
DOI: 10.7208/9780226069159

Library of Congress Cataloging-in-Publication Data

Levendusky, Matthew, author.
Partisan news that matters : how cable media polarize politics / Matthew Levendusky.
pages; cm.—(Chicago studies in American politics)
Includes bibliographical references and index.
ISBN 978-0-226-06896-1 (cloth : alkaline paper)—
ISBN 978-0-226-06901-2 (paperback : alkaline paper)—
ISBN 978-0-226-06915-9 (e-book) 1. Television broadcasting of news—Political aspects—United States. 2. Television in politics—United States. 3. Mass media and public opinion—United States. 4. Opposition (Political science)—United States. 5. Polarization (Social sciences)—United States. I. Title. II. Series: Chicago studies in American politics.
P95.82.U6L48 2013
302.230973—dc23

2013005366

♾ This paper meets the requirements of ANSI/NISO Z39.48-1992 (Permanence of Paper).

Contents

Acknowledgments

Writing a book is not an easy task, and in the process, one accumulates debts that are unlikely to be repaid, at least in the short term. This was true of my first book, and in many ways is even truer of this one. At a purely practical level, my first—and greatest—debt is to the University of Pennsylvania's vice provost for research and the School of Arts and Sciences for funding my research. Without their generous support, this work would simply not be possible. I am also very grateful to the staff of the Wharton Behavioral Lab for helping to plan and implement some of the experiments used in this book.

I owe great thanks to the vast numbers of scholars who commented on this project at various stages: Jim Adams, Kevin Arceneaux, Paul Beck, Adam Berinsky, John Bullock, Bob Erikson, Stanley Feldman, John Gasper, Avery Goldstein, Don Green, Greg Huber, Luke Keele, Jonathan Ladd, John Lapinski, Gabe Lenz, Diana Mutz, Lilach Nir, Jeremy Pope, Markus Prior, Rogers Smith, Paul Sniderman, Laura Stoker, Josh Tucker, and many, many others. I am also grateful to a number of seminar audiences for their penetrating comments on this work; parts of this project were presented at the American Political Science Association and Midwest Political Science Association conferences, as well as at Berkeley, MIT, Northwestern, NYU Center for Experimental Social Science, Penn, and Stanford.

Four other groups of people deserve particular accolades. First, I owe a special thanks to my next-door office neighbors: Neil Malhotra and Marc Meredith. Both have heard far, far more about this project that they ever thought they would. I thank them for always being willing to let me discuss one more idea, no matter how half-baked. Second, Jamie Druckman has gone above and beyond the call of duty again and again.

Not only did he help me renavigate the publication process at the University of Chicago Press, he also read the manuscript multiple times and offered detailed and thoughtful advice on nearly every part of it, thereby improving the final product a great deal. I owe him a profound debt that I will never be able to fully repay. Third, Skip Lupia and Matt Baum agreed to serve as discussants at a work-in-progress seminar held at the University of Pennsylvania in the spring of 2012. They both provided incredibly detailed and thoughtful comments on the work, and helped make the final product more persuasive and readable. Finally, I owe the manuscript's referees from the University of Chicago Press a debt of thanks for their helpful and engaged reading of it. Their comments improved the final product a great deal, as did comments on parts of the manuscript from referees and editors at the *American Political Science Review*, *American Journal of Political Science*, and *Political Communication*. To these and many others who I'm forgetting (forgive me!), I extend my deepest thanks.

Oh, and Patrick and Michael: sorry for forgetting about you the first time around. Hope this makes up for it.

CHAPTER ONE

The New Partisan Media Environment

A Tale of Two Frames

In November 2009, U.S. Attorney General Eric Holder announced that Khalid Sheikh Mohammed, the self-proclaimed mastermind of the 9/11 attacks, would be brought to trial in a civilian court in New York City (Finn and Johnson 2009). The decision reflected a long debate within the Obama administration (and before that, the Bush administration) about how to prosecute terrorism suspects, in particular, whether to try them in civilian courts or military tribunals.[1]

Obviously, such a high-profile announcement garnered an extensive amount of coverage and was duly reported in essentially all major television and newspaper outlets. Most of those outlets also discussed both supporters and critics of the administration's decision, giving readers and listeners "both sides" of the story. This type of balanced, objective coverage is consistent with long-standing journalistic norms in the U.S. press (Schudson 2001). Take, for example, the coverage on the *PBS News Hour*, which has been shown to be one of the most balanced and politically neutral news programs on television (Groseclose and Milyo 2005). When covering this story, the *News Hour* reported both on the decision itself and on the Republican criticism of the policy (*PBS News Hour*, 13 November 2009). Likewise, when Holder went to Capitol Hill to face questions from lawmakers about the announcement, the *News Hour* gave equal time to both his supporters and opponents (*PBS News Hour*, 18 November 2009). In all cases, the *News Hour*—like nearly all mainstream news programs—avoided offering an opinion on the day's events and stuck to a strictly objective, fact-based style of reporting.

But on other outlets, the frame for discussing Holder's announcement shunned these norms of objectivity and explicitly endorsed one side of the controversy. On *The O'Reilly Factor*, one of the top-rated programs on the Fox News Network, Bill O'Reilly argued that trying Mohammed in a civilian court was a terrible mistake—such a trial would give Mohammed a platform to promulgate his jihadist message around the globe. Further, the trial would release classified U.S. intelligence procedures, since under disclosure in a civilian courtroom, the government would be forced to hand over these documents to the defense. O'Reilly argued that the decision was a "sorry sordid little petty political maneuver" designed by the Obama administration to embarrass Bush administration officials. The goal was to put President Bush—and the enhanced interrogation techniques used by his administration—on trial (*The O'Reilly Factor*, 13 November 2009). Watching O'Reilly's show, or many other similar programs on Fox News, one would see few reasons to support the Obama administration's decision and far more reasons to oppose it. Indeed, given the flawed logic of the decision, one might wonder how anyone could support it at all.

Other outlets gave a similarly one-sided frame, but from the opposite perspective, defending the administration's decision to try Mohammed in a civilian court. On *Countdown with Keith Olbermann* on MSNBC, the host offered a more liberal perspective, arguing that "our law beats their terror," and the best way to defend the American system of government was to give terrorists trials in civilian courts. This would allow the entire world to see that we treated all of the accused fairly—even self-proclaimed terrorists—thereby offering a profound lesson in America's belief in justice and the rule of law (*Countdown with Keith Olbermann*, 16 November 2009). MSNBC hosts and guests also argued that civilian trials offer a more effective means of convicting terrorism suspects. Senator Richard Durbin of Illinois argued that since 9/11, the United States had successfully convicted 195 terrorism suspects who were tried in civilian courts, but only 3 such convictions were obtained for individuals tried in military tribunals (*The Ed Show*, 16 November 2009). As Rachel Maddow (another MSNBC host) argued, "If you are looking for the tried and true and tested way of delivering justice to terrorists, the federal courts, with the United States prosecutors of the Department of Justice are the proven way to go" (*The Rachel Maddow Show*, 16 November 2009). From this perspective, one might imagine that it is difficult to oppose the Obama administration's decision, in sharp contrast to the inference one might draw after watching Fox.

From Fox News and MSNBC, then, one got vastly different accounts of the same event. They gave quite contrasting perspectives and arguments about why their opinion is the superior one and why their argument should carry the day. Yet for all their striking differences, Fox and MSNBC have two important features in common. First, they both offer primarily one-sided arguments that advantage their own position, with plenty of opinionated commentary from the hosts, leaving no doubt as to where they stand on the issue. While they do discuss the opposing side's arguments, it is mostly to criticize them. The choice of guests only reinforces this tendency. By and large, the typical guest on these shows agrees with the host's point of view: Fox News invites on conservatives like Karl Rove or Liz Cheney, and MSNBC has on liberals like Dick Durbin. While there are obviously some exceptions to this policy,[2] the norm is that hosts and guests agree, making these shows almost like an "echo chamber" of similar opinions (Jamieson and Cappella 2008), offering a particular partisan perspective on the day's news and events.

Second, programs on both Fox and MSNBC offer trenchant critiques of the other side. On Fox, hosts and guests offered stern criticism of President Obama and his decision. Former Bush administration official (and current Fox News commentator) Karl Rove argued that the decision would be "an utter, unmitigated disaster for the security of the United States" (*The O'Reilly Factor*, 13 November 2009). Liz Cheney, daughter of former vice president Dick Cheney, said that Holder's decision was an "indefensible and insufficient way to defend the nation" (*Hannity*, 16 November 2009). Such comments are not only critical of this particular decision, but are used to illustrate a deeper, more fundamental critique of the president, namely, that he is an out-of-touch liberal—Rove argued that the president is "fundamentally way out on the left wing of American politics" (*The O'Reilly Factor*, 24 November 2009) and that while this decision in particular is flawed, it also demonstrates a consistent pattern of poor judgment.

Not to be outdone, MSNBC programs offered strident critiques of the Republicans who were criticizing the president. Keith Olbermann and his guests argued that Republican criticisms of the president were little more than "situational scaremongering" (*Countdown with Keith Olbermann*, 16 November 2009). Commentators here argued that Republican criticisms were motivated by efforts to score political points by frightening the public with the specter of terrorism: "This isn't about security. It's about political gain" (*The Ed Show*, 13 November 2009). Watching the Fox programs above, one would have questioned President Obama's ability to lead. On MSNBC, one would wonder the same about Republicans.

This situation is not unique to this particular case. As I will show in later chapters, on issue after issue, cable news networks, most especially Fox News and MSNBC, present starkly different interpretations of the day's stories. While traditional news outlets still emphasize balance and objectivity, these partisan media outlets provide a more one-sided take on the day's events. Ordinary citizens can align their news consumption with their ideological and partisan leanings by watching these shows—Democrats and liberals can tune in to shows on MSNBC, and Republicans and conservatives can flip to Fox News. Increasingly, more and more Americans choose to do just that: Americans now consume more partisan media than they did in the past (Pew Research Center for the People and the Press 2010), and they are especially likely to consume ideologically congenial media that matches their partisan outlook (Iyengar and Han 2009; Stroud 2011). News is no longer simply information; it can now be a reflection of one's political beliefs.

When subjects consume this sort of partisan media, they primarily hear an echo of their own beliefs and consequently also avoid dissonant information that cuts against their political opinions (Jamieson and Cappella 2008). When Republicans watch Fox News, they hear many conservative and Republican messages but far fewer liberal or Democratic ones; the reverse is true of Democrats who watch more left-wing media. This sort of reinforcing message might make subjects become more extreme, since they hear their own side's messages repeated to them without any countervailing arguments. Such programs, therefore, might potentially polarize the electorate (Sunstein 2009). Further, because these programs harshly criticize the other side, viewers might come to have less respect for the opposition and become less willing to compromise with them, and see them as less legitimate. So viewers watching these shows might come to think the opposition is untrustworthy and merits ridicule rather than respect (Jamieson and Hardy 2013).

Such tendencies potentially have normatively troubling consequences. America's constitutional system, with its multiple veto points and separation of powers, requires compromise. People can be passionate about issues and stand firm in their beliefs, but they have to be willing to compromise for American government to work effectively. Absent such compromise, the system is biased toward the status quo, and society fails to make necessary changes to policy (Gutmann and Thompson 2010, 2012).[3] If partisan media harden citizens' beliefs and make them unwilling to compromise with and listen to the other side, then partisan media have deleterious consequences for American politics. Our contemporary political discourse is filled with claims that Americans—both masses and elites—are increasingly unwilling to compromise. Indeed, some have gone so far as to claim that it is "almost impossible" to achieve consensus solutions on important policy issues in the contemporary political environment (Price 2010). Do partisan media bear part of the blame for this division? Do they make it more difficult to actually govern in America?

To know whether partisan media have these troubling normative consequences, I need to address four related questions. First, do partisan media make citizens more polarized and divided? If citizens become more polarized and extreme, then it becomes harder to bridge the gap between the two sides. As Democrats and Republicans who consume partisan media drift toward the ideological poles, they have less and less common ground, and identifying consensus solutions becomes more difficult (Abramowitz 2010). If partisan media increase polarization in the mass public, then they contribute to gridlock and the difficulty of governing in contemporary America.

Second, do partisan media make citizens less trusting of the other side and less willing to compromise with them? Because partisan media harshly critique the other side and their policies, citizens might come to think the opposition does not have legitimate ideas, and may be less willing to compromise with them. If this occurs, then this has obvious consequences for gridlock and finding common ground on key issues.

Third, do partisan media shape how citizens behave in and understand elections? As President Obama himself has conjectured, partisan media outlets may shape election results because of their slanted discourse about the candidates and issues (Bai 2008). Elections are the most fundamental way for citizens to make their preferences known to elites, so it is vital to understand if—and how—partisan media might shape how viewers' evaluate and select candidates. If these outlets can shape which candidates get elected, this can impact the strategies these candidates pursue to win office, and which policies the winners pursue once in office.

But there is another, equally important way for partisan media to affect elections—they can shape how viewers interpret and understand the election outcomes. In the wake of an election, media outlets offer explanations for why a candidate won or lost: Obama was the candidate of change who benefited from a faltering economy (Holbrook, Clouse, and Weinschenk 2012); George W. Bush won in 2004 because of how he handled terrorism and Iraq (Langer and Cohen 2005). But partisan media, given their perspective, might be especially likely to embrace explanations that offer nefarious rationales for the outcome: "our" candidate lost not because of bad policies but, say, because of media bias (Mutz 2006b). If partisan media lead citizens to accept these sorts of odious interpretations, then it may delegitimize leaders and their policies once in office (Anderson et al. 2005; Mutz 2006b). This would, again, make it more difficult to govern. If an elected official was elected because of illegitimate means, then citizens may not feel compelled to accept his policies, again making common ground and consensus more elusive.

These first three questions explore the direct effects of partisan media on attitudes, willingness to compromise with the opposition, and elections. But even if I find strong effects in each area, a puzzle will still remain. These programs, while they have grown in popularity, still reach a relatively limited audience: the most popular partisan news program—*The O'Reilly Factor* on Fox News—attracts only a bit over three million viewers per evening (Pew Project for Excellence in Journalism 2011). Even if I summed the aggregate prime-time viewership for all partisan media programs, the total would still only come to a few percent of the U.S. population. The final question, therefore, is if only a tiny fraction of the population watches these shows, how can they have such important effects?

I take up these four questions in turn and argue that partisan media contribute to the difficulty of governing in contemporary America. First, I show that partisan media programs polarize attitudes, moving citizens toward ideological extremes. In particular, I show that partisan media increase polarization not by making moderates into extremists, but rather by taking citizens who were already somewhat extreme and making them *even more* extreme. Further, I also document how partisan media make citizens more convinced that their views are the "right" ones, so they become less willing to believe that other points of view have something legitimate to offer. Second, I demonstrate that partisan media make citizens less willing to trust the other party and less willing to support compromise with them, thereby contributing to persistent gridlock. Third, I show that partisan media influence vote choice, as well as how citizens come to understand elections. In particular, partisan media outlets make citizens more likely to accept nefarious interpretations when the other party wins elections, thereby casting doubt on the legitimacy of the winner. Together, these findings suggest that partisan media reify and harden divisions in the mass public, making it more difficult to achieve the compromise and consensus needed to actually govern.

Finally, I take up my fourth and final question—even if partisan media have important effects on their audience, do they matter for the nation as a whole if they only reach a tiny fraction of the mass public? I argue that partisan media *do* matter, in large part because their audience is particularly politically active and influential. Those who do watch partisan media are more involved and invested, and people who are political influential make up a disproportionate share of the audience for these programs (Bai 2009). Further, I explain how partisan media work to influence the agenda and help set the national debate on issues more broadly, which magnifies their effects on the political system. Partisan media have multiplier effects that allow a relatively limited medium that speaks to a narrow segment of the market to have an outsize influence on American politics. Given this, the consequences of such programs extend broadly, even if they only reach a limited fraction of the public.

Obviously, partisan media alone are not to blame for the contemporary spate of gridlock and dissension in Washington DC—forces far beyond partisan media shoulder the lion's share of the responsibility. That said, the sorts of partisan media effects I document here contribute to this problem and help to reify divisions in the mass public, locking down partisans on their side of the aisle and making them less willing to reach across to the other side. From that perspective, partisan media matter, and they contribute to the difficulty of governance in contemporary America.

What Are Partisan Media, and Where Did They Originate?

Simply put, partisan media are opinionated media. Most news outlets strive to report the facts without favoring one side or the other: if they offer a Republican point of view, they also offer a Democratic one (Robinson 1981; Schudson 2001). But partisan media are explicitly different:

they present the facts in such a way to support a particular conclusion. Stories are "framed, spun, and slanted so that certain political agendas are advanced" (Jamieson, Hardy, and Romer 2007, 26). Partisan media fit within a broader narrative: the news is not an end in and of itself, but rather, the news is a vehicle to advancing a particular point of view.[4] They package the news in a way to help people make sense of the world, creating a "self-protective enclave" of consistent messages and a framework to understand the day's events (Jamieson and Cappella 2008, x). These programs help people to make sense of the day's news in light of a particular set of predispositions (Rosensteil 2006, 253; see also Manjoo 2008).

This type of partisan media has a long history in America. Indeed, for most of American history, the news media *were* partisan media. Newspapers and pamphlets (the main sources of news before the twentieth century) took an explicit side and unabashedly promoted a particular partisan viewpoint: Federalist or Anti-Federalist, Whig or Democrat, Republican or Democrat. Around the turn of the twentieth century, however, journalists adopted norms of objectivity and began to report the news rather than advocate a particular point of view (Schudson 2001; Mindich 1998). Opinionated, partisan media largely disappeared from the mainstream of American journalism over the first half of the twentieth century (Groeling 2010). In its place came the more serious, objective journalism, where journalists reported facts without taking a side, the type of journalism that dominated the so-called broadcast era during the middle and latter parts of the twentieth century (Prior 2007).

But in recent years, with the rise of cable television, talk radio, and the Internet, the United States has begun to return to its more partisan roots, with a number of outlets available to viewers that explicitly advocate a particular point of view. Indeed, the partisan style of reporting discussed above certainly has a number of exemplars across these different media, from Fox News and MSNBC on cable TV (Pew Project for Excellence in Journalism 2010) to Rush Limbaugh and Randi Rhodes on talk radio (Berry and Soberiaj 2011; Jamieson and Cappella 2008) to various partisan websites like Town Hall or Daily Kos (Hindman 2008). Partisan media are now an important part of the American media landscape.

Cable television makes for a particularly telling example of the resurgence of partisan reporting. In the early days of cable news, it followed an objective news model. Its main purpose was to allow viewers to get "breaking news," the types of stories that change rapidly in a brief period of time, such as the 1990–1991 Persian Gulf War or the 1992 Rodney King riots in Los Angeles (Pew Project for Excellence in Journalism 2004). But as the Internet grew and expanded, it gradually supplanted cable news as the main source of breaking news. Cable therefore faced an identity crisis and responded by becoming more partisan. Reasoning that viewers had other mechanisms for simply learning the news, cable began to offer more analysis, particularly partisan analysis (Pew Project for Excellence in Journalism 2010).

This shift in reporting style reflects the changing audience of cable news, especially the audience for partisan cable news. Those who watch partisan cable news are (on average) better informed about politics than nonviewers (Jamieson and Cappella 2008; Morris 2005; Stroud 2011). These viewers do not need another source to report the facts but want something different: a partisan interpretation of the day's events. Bill O'Reilly, the most-watched cable news host, put it this way: "People in the United States, now, they know the news already, because they have the Internet, they have talk radio, a lot of vehicles, so they want *analysis and perspective* from a cable network, especially in prime time. They don't want to hear [the news] again" (Pew Project for Excellence in Journalism 2011; emphasis added). MSNBC president Phil Griffin echoes this sentiment, commenting, "You have to stand for something in cable" (Sherman 2010). As the media environment changed, so too did the type of news presented on cable TV.

This shift highlights an important point about the growth and development of partisan media. One might be tempted to ascribe this growth to nefarious motives, but the reality is quite different: these outlets exist because of larger economic, technological, and regulatory shifts in society as a whole (Berry and Sobieraj 2008). First and foremost, partisan media have expanded due to shifts in the media landscape. The rise of the "post-broadcast" media market made these outlets possible, as I argued above; without the growth of cable television (and the changes in cable induced by the Internet), partisan media, at least partisan cable TV news, would not exist in its current form. Further, government regulatory policy also plays a role, with changes like the demise of the fairness doctrine also helping to set the stage for the growth of partisan outlets (Berry and Sobieraj 2008, 2011; Sobieraj and Berry 2011).

Similarly, electoral shifts have contributed to the growth of partisan media outlets, though to a much smaller degree than the sorts of technological and regulatory changes discussed above. While the U.S. population is not deeply polarized (Fiorina, Abrams, and Pope 2005), it has become increasingly well sorted over the past few decades so that voters' policy preferences are more tightly aligned with their partisanship (Hetherington 2009; Levendusky 2009). So today, unlike a generation ago, there is a larger block of the population with a more coherent set of political beliefs. In this sort of an electorate, there is larger market for more ideologically charged news, especially on platforms like cable television (Mullainathan and Shleifer 2005; Polborn, Krasa, and Bernhardt 2008; Gentzkow and Shapiro 2010).[5] Indeed, voters now seem quite willing to seek out information from ideologically congenial sources (Iyengar and Hahn 2009; Stroud 2011). Networks are aware of this and take steps to actually encourage this sort of niche content. While MSNBC was originally a more traditional neutral cable news network, the success of *Countdown with Keith Olbermann* inspired the network to add more left-leaning programming (Steinberg 2007; Stelter 2012b). Indeed, Former President Bill Clinton recently commented that "it [MSNBC] really has become our version of Fox," reflecting the network's shift to a markedly more liberal form of coverage (Stelter 2012b). Former Fox News journalist Major Garrett argues that Fox News pursues the same strategy: "Fox actually wants to keep that [media] polarization and say, look, we're different. We're dramatically different; you can see how we're different. And if you like that difference, you better come over here and you better stay here . . . If you are outraged, this is where you need to be" (Schroeck 2010). Further, highly targeted advertising, while predating cable TV, has become ever more important in the contemporary media environment, leading stations to court a clearly defined audience they can sell to advertisers (Turow 1997, 2012). Partisan TV networks have a vested interest in striking out this sort of ideologically demarcated coverage, suggesting it is unlikely to disappear any time in the near future.

So what outlets, then, constitute partisan media? This is really asking two separate questions: which media types will I study (cable television? talk radio? The Internet?), and what constitutes "partisan" media within or across media types? First, I focus my study here on partisan news programs on cable television. Partisan talk radio has been studied extensively by a previous generation of research (see, among others, Barker and Knight 2000; Jamieson and Cappella 2008), but the literature on the effects of partisan cable television is much less developed, and many questions remain to be answered about their effects. Likewise, while partisan websites are clearly a key part of the future, most Americans continue to get their news from television (Pew Center for the People and the Press 2010), including their political news (A. Smith 2011). Those who consume news online see it as a complement to other sources of news, rather than a replacement for them (De Waal, Schonbach, and Lauf 2005), so the patterns of exposure to websites are likely to mimic the exposure patterns for other outlets. This is not to diminish the role of online news—it will clearly be an important factor in the future—but television news remains dominant for now.[6] I focus here on partisan cable news outlets and leave studies of partisan websites for future research.

When assessing which outlets constitute partisan cable news, I rely largely on two criteria. First, I rely on other sources that have documented biased or slanted coverage on these networks. Second, I use studies of audience demographics, particularly the partisan and ideological demographics, to determine slant, given that press slant and audience preferences are typically in equilibrium (Mullainathan and Shleifer 2005; Gentzkow and Shapiro 2010; Puglisi and Snyder 2011). These two criteria reflect both a demand-side of slant (partisan audiences prefer partisan media), and a supply-side of slant (partisan sources generate partisan content). Together, they should provide a solid basis for determining what constitutes partisan media exposure.

Using these criteria, I focus much of my attention on two main cable news outlets: Fox News, a right-wing outlet, and MSNBC, a left-wing one. Both stations fulfill the criteria laid out above: existing evidence suggests Fox tilts to the Right (Jamieson and Cappella 2008), while MSNBC tilts to the Left (Steinberg 2007; Stelter 2012a, 2012b), a finding confirmed by content analysis by the Pew Project for Excellence in Journalism (see, e.g., the project reports for 2009, 2010, and 2011).[7] For example, former George W. Bush press secretary Scott McClellan admitted that the Bush administration coordinated with Fox News to give them Republican talking points to discuss on air, suggesting a rather overt form of political slant (Dickinson 2011). Further, demographic data from recent media usage surveys suggest the audiences for these networks are heavily skewed by partisanship: the Fox News audience is largely Republican and conservative, and many more liberals and Democrats prefer MSNBC (Pew Center for the People and the Press 2010). By both criteria, then, these two outlets qualify as "partisan" media.[8]

This is particularly true when one examines the main prime-time programs on these networks. On both channels, the main evening and prime-time hours are filled with explicitly partisan shows that are also among the network's most popular offerings. These are the shows that offer the sort of commentary on the news I described above—shows like *The O'Reilly Factor* or *Hannity* on Fox News, or *The Rachel Maddow* Show or *The Last Word with Lawrence O'Donnell* on MSNBC (and *Countdown with Keith Olbermann*, before it moved to Al Gore's CurrentTV). Daytime content on these networks is often less explicitly partisan: Shepard Smith, for example, likely offers fewer personal opinions than, say, O'Reilly or Hannity. But the prime-time opinion shows—which attract the lion's share of the eyeballs—are more explicitly partisan (Pew Project for Excellence in Journalism 2009, 2010). To be clear, then, when I refer to "partisan media," I am really referring to the prime-time opinion programming on Fox News and MSNBC—programs from hosts like Rachel Maddow, Sean Hannity, Bill O'Reilly, and the like.

Who Watches Partisan Television News?

The analysis above explains what partisan media is, but it does not explain who watches these programs. To better understand the audience for these programs, I turn to the 2008 National Annenberg Election Study (NAES) rolling cross-section survey. The Annenberg study included a battery of items about respondents' news-viewing habits that allow me to examine the demographic and attitudinal correlates of watching partisan media sources (for more details on the measures and their construction, see the data appendix at the end of the book). Table 1.1 gives the results of these demographic comparisons.[9]

There are some demographic differences between Fox viewers, MSNBC viewers, and those who report watching neither channel. On average, Fox viewers are slightly older, more likely to be male, white, Southern, or to call themselves born-again Christians, and slightly less likely have postsecondary education; both Fox and MSNBC viewers are slightly more likely to have higher incomes. But on the whole, with the exception of race and religion, these differences are relatively minor, averaging only a few percentage points. Demographically, these viewers are only modestly different from other Americans.

TABLE 1.1 **Demographic and political variables and partisan media consumption.**

Variable	No partisan news	Fox viewer	MSNBC viewer
Demographics			
Average age	53	56	53
Male, %	41	49	46
Caucasian, %	84	93	84
Live in the South, %	26	33	20
High Income (150K+), %	11	14	15
High school graduate, %	94	96	98
Professional degree, %	17	15	24
Political Variables			
Strong Democrat, %	28	6	43
Strong Republican, %	12	44	6
Voted for Obama, %	66	9	91
Iraq was worth the cost, %	26	70	13
No same-sex marriage, %	36	53	18
Following the election "very closely," %	42	61	72
Discuss politics every day, %	28	44	51

Source: 2008 National Annenberg Election Study, rolling cross section dataset.

What makes partisan media consumers are really distinctive are their political beliefs, interest, and engagement. Partisan media consumers are 20 to 30 percentage points more likely to report they are following the election "very closely," and they are likewise nearly twice as likely to report that they discussion politics daily, both of which indicate a higher level of political interest and engagement. Relative to nonviewers, Fox viewers are much more likely to be strong Republicans and much less likely to be strong Democrats; the converse is true of MSNBC viewers. Consistent with this finding, MSNBC viewers are more than ten times as likely to report having voted for Obama in the postelection follow-up survey (a similar finding also holds in the 2010 midterm elections; see Tesler 2010). Similarly, Fox and MSNBC viewers are much more polarized than the remainder of the electorate: Fox viewers show much less support for gay marriage and much higher support for the idea that the war in Iraq was worth the cost to Americans. Relative to the rest of the mass public, Fox and MSNBC consumers have more strongly divided political beliefs. Partisan media consumers' political beliefs, more than their demographics, set them apart from the rest of the nation. This point will be an important one when understanding why a relatively modest audience of partisan media consumers is able to influence the political discourse of the nation as a whole.

Have these Trends Changed over Time?

The analyses above show the correlates of partisan media exposure at a particular point in time (specifically, during the 2008 presidential election). But such results cannot speak to how the correlates of partisan media consumption have changed over time. Given the strongly partisan frames provided on these networks, I am especially interested in whether viewers have increasingly self-selected into the audiences for these shows over time.[10] Is it the case that, over time, more Republicans are watching Fox, and in parallel, more Democrats are watching MSNBC? Given the ideological reputations of these networks, have viewers segregated themselves accordingly?

I turn to the data from the Pew Center for the People and the Press to answer this question. For the past decade, Pew has asked Americans about their media consumption biennially, so I can track the partisan composition of the partisan media outlets over time. Given that Fox has been a consistently conservative source throughout its existence (Jamieson and Cappella 2008), I can study Fox over the 2000–2010 period (during which years Pew asked the relevant questions). Unfortunately, given that MSNBC has only more recently tilted to the Left (Steinberg 2007; Pew Project for Excellence in Journalism 2009), I cannot really meaningfully compare over-time patterns for that network, though I note that the trends there parallel the ones reported below.[11] I therefore focus here on Fox News for the over-time analysis.

Figure 1.1 gives the results of this analysis, showing clear evidence of ideological selectivity over time—Republicans have become much more likely to tune in to Fox News on a regular basis. In 2000, only about 45 percent of Republicans were regular Fox News viewers. But by 2010, nearly seven in ten Republicans (69 percent) reported watching Fox on a regular basis, a 53 percent increase.[12] Democrats show an opposite, albeit somewhat weaker, trend. In 2000, an equivalent percentage of Democrats and Republicans reported watching Fox. But by 2010, only 35 percent of Democrats reported watching Fox, making Republicans approximately twice as likely to tune in to that network. Over time, the Fox News audience became more strongly segregated by partisanship, consistent with the argument above that these networks offer a distinctly partisan take on the news.

This illustrates two important facets of partisan media consumption in the contemporary media environment. First, simply put, parti-

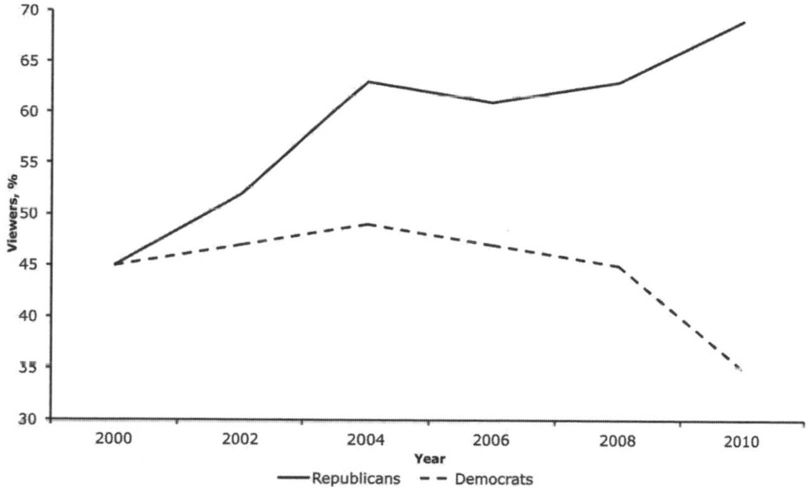

FIGURE 1.1. The percentage of Democrats and Republicans (including leaners) who "sometimes" or "regularly" watch Fox News. (*Source*: Pew Center for the People and the Press Media consumption surveys, 2000–2010)

san selective exposure is real and important, at least on cable TV (see, among others, Garrett 2009, Iyengar and Hahn 2009, Stroud 2011). Increasingly, more Americans are choosing to get at least some of their news from ideologically congenial sources. As Republican strategist Tucker Eskew notes, "People go to their own corners in politics. They go back to their own framework and look for a medium or message that is reinforcing" (Jamieson 2005, 170). People want to find information that's congenial to them to reinforce and reaffirm their beliefs, consistent with Garrett's (2009) argument that selective exposure results from seeking out reinforcing information, rather than avoiding dissonant information. For many Americans, political news is increasingly about seeking out exactly this type of reinforcing content.

Second, while this sort of ideological segregation is real, and politically consequential, it is equally important not to push it too far. The fact that nearly one in three Democrats also report some exposure to Fox shows the limits of partisan selective exposure, even in the contemporary era. Undoubtedly, some Democrats watch Fox News for sport, much like Hillary Clinton does—for the opportunity to yell "You're wrong!" at the TV screen (a story related in Mutz 2006b). Yet other Democrats (and Independents) likely watch it as a legitimate source of news, just as many Republicans do. Americans expose themselves to a varied media diet, consuming sources that reinforce their beliefs, as well as a wider variety of outlets (Rosenstiel 2006). Partisan selective exposure is a real, significant, and important trend, but it is equally important to note that Americans do expose themselves to a variety of sources as well.

Do these Shows Merit Careful Study?

One might still question whether these shows deserve much serious study at all: after all, they reach only a relatively modest audience of a few million viewers on any given night. But this misses the larger picture. First, even if this type of media only affected a narrow segment of America, this is a particularly politically consequential section of the market (see the discussion of table 1.1 above). These are the citizens who have their voices heard by elected officials (Jamieson and Cappella 2008; Abramowitz 2010), and though the cable news audience is small in number, it need not be small in political clout. As *New York Times* journalist Matt Bai notes, "A sizable portion of that paltry cable [news] viewership comprises nearly ever congressional aide, White House official, and assignment editor in Washington, where it is rare to find a political or news office that doesn't have multiple television outlets tuned to the punditry parade. And thus, even more so than [Rush] Limbaugh's radio broadcasts, the cable-news shows take on outsize importance, defining the hourly debate for all those political influentials who, in turn, define it for the rest of us" (Bai 2009). In this instance, small does not indicate unimportant.

Further, the data show that merely looking at audience figures may be misleading. Yes, it is still the case that on any given night, the nightly news programs on ABC, NBC, and CBS have more viewers than even the most popular cable news programs. Somewhere between six and eight million viewers per evening watch the major broadcast news, while even the most popular partisan news programs, like *The O'Reilly Factor*, attract only a bit over three million viewers (Pew Project for Excellence in Journalism 2011). But the over-time trends suggest there is more convergence, with the audience for partisan shows rising and broadcast news falling (Pew Project for Excellence in Journalism 2010). For example, Fox News did not exist until 1996, and only 20 percent of American municipalities had Fox by 2000, but today nearly all markets have access to the station—quite remarkable growth over a fifteen-year period

(Della Vigna and Kaplan 2007). These outlets are also becoming an increasingly important source of political news and information: in a recent Pew study, cable news was cited as the top regular source for campaign news (Pew Research Center for the People and the Press 2012). More generally, these outlets have grown rapidly over the past few years, and show few signs of slowing down into the future (Pew Project for Excellence in Journalism 2009).

Indeed, the trend toward partisan media reflects broad forces in the media environment. Gone are the days of one "mainstream" message coming from the major broadcast networks: today's media environment is characterized by a proliferation of news sources, many matched to viewers' own partisan dispositions (Prior 2007). Partisan media sources are simply one example of this broader trend of seeking out like-minded information, albeit a relatively extreme one (Bennett and Iyengar 2008; Iyengar and Hahn 2009). Given this new reality, scholars need to understand its consequences.

Further, partisan news media outlets are a real and significant part of the broader media environment. While they may not be, as some claim, the "the dominant media force in America,"[13] they do help to shape the contours of political debate in the United States. For example, as I document in later chapters, partisan media outlets have helped to disseminate a number of stories in recent years, such as the charges made by the Swift Boat Veterans for Truth against Senator Kerry during the 2004 election (Shaw 2006) and the ACORN prostitution scandal (Dreier and Martin 2010). These stories then spread to the mainstream media and had repercussions for the broader political debate in the United States—even for individuals who had never watched Fox News or MSNBC. Partisan media, quite frankly, matter.

Studying the Effects of Partisan Media

From one perspective, there might be little reason to be worried about the effects of mass media, even partisan media, on voters' beliefs, attitudes, and behaviors—the classic "minimal effects" paradigm argued that media typically have few effects on viewers, at least as far as we can measure (Klapper 1960). To the extent that mass media impacted viewers at all, it seemed to only reinforce existing beliefs (Berelson, Lazarsfeld, and McPhee 1954; Klapper 1960). But given that such studies all come from the broadcast era of journalism, when a small number of mainstream voices dominated the media, such research might have less relevance for understanding the effects of partisan media. After all, partisan media have a particular slant to the news and favor one side of the debate over the other, and this sort of news might generate very different results from a more balanced, objective presentation of the news.[14]

More recent literature gives some credence to the idea that partisan media have larger effects on viewers. For example, a number of studies have examined the effects of media slant on vote choice and attitudes. When a news source favors one candidate, that changes viewers vote choice, as well as their attitudes. This finding holds across a variety of different media, including newspapers (Dalton, Beck, and Huckfeldt 1998; Druckman and Parkin 2005; Chiang and Knight 2011), talk radio (Barker and Knight 2000; Jones 2002), and television (Della Vigna and Kaplan 2007).[15] Slanted media (broadly defined) impact their audience.

While this work is an important building block for the current study, these findings are limited for at least four reasons. First, while most studies cited above find sizable effects of media slant, others find either quite small or null effects (Meffert et al. 2006; Gerber, Karlan, and Bergan 2009; Gentzkow, Shapiro, and Sinkinson 2012), suggesting the literature is less clear on this point that it might appear at first glance. Second, much of this previous work on the impact of slant focuses solely on the effects of media slant in elections and has much less to say about broader questions about attitudinal polarization, views of the opposition, or other possible effects of partisan media. Put slightly differently, these other works speak primarily to the third question I posed above (on electoral effects) but have less to say about the other topics motivating my analysis. Third, nearly all of these studies have little to say about the key mediators and moderators of these effects. While they might show average effects, they have less to say about what types of media are most effective at changing citizens' attitudes, or which viewers will be most strongly affected by the media. It is simply not enough to know that the media can sometimes shape what viewers think—understanding how these effects vary throughout the viewing public is crucial as well.

Finally, and most importantly, drawing firm causal inferences from these previous studies is extremely difficult. With a few notable exceptions (e.g., Gerber, Karlan, and Bergan 2009), these studies almost all use observational data and suffer from the accompanying limitations. In general, existing designs cannot typically differentiate between media impacting consumers' preferences (e.g., a treatment effect of media slant on attitudes) and consumers selecting media that reinforce their existing preferences (e.g., a selection effect; for more on the general dynamics of this problem with special attention to the problem of opinionated media, see Mutz 2006b). While the slant of an outlet impacts its audience, the audiences' preferences also drive the outlet's slant, so drawing solid inferences from observational data is exceedingly difficult (Mullainathan and Shleifer 2005; Gentzkow and Shapiro 2010). More work is needed to definitively assess how partisan media impact viewers.

Other related work explores the tendency toward partisan selective exposure: who chooses to watch highly partisan media? While the literature on selective exposure generally is enormous and contains a number of conflicting results (Frey 1986; Sears and Freedman 1967; Fischer et al. 2005), there has been renewed interest in recent years in *partisan* selective exposure—selective exposure applied to political topics. In particular, a number of recent studies document that today's viewers are increasingly likely to self-select to watch partisan news outlets (Garrett 2009; Iyengar and Han 2009), especially those who are most politically engaged (Baum and Groeling 2010; Stroud 2011). There is also debate about whether this sort of selective exposure does (Prior 2007; Stroud 2011) or does not (Arceneaux and Johnson 2010, forthcoming) have politically relevant consequences. But note that this is a separate question from the one I pose here. The debate about selective exposure is about asking who watches partisan media. I focus here on the *effects* of partisan media consumption, conditional on watching. I agree that there is indeed selective exposure in the contemporary media environment, much of it driven by partisan and ideological preferences (see figure 1.1), and so not everyone watches partisan media. But for those who do, I show in later chapters that such media consumption is quite consequential. Even with only a limited audience, partisan media can have a large effect on viewers and, in turn, on the broader political environment.

Finally, there is other related literature that examines how partisan slant of different sources changes the credibility of messages (Baum and Groeling 2009, 2010). Because partisan media outlets carry ideological reputations (e.g., Fox is conservative, MSNBC is liberal), subjects use these reputations when evaluating messages from these sources (Baum and Gussin 2008; Turner 2007). So, for example, if Fox News carries a segment that's highly critical of Republicans, that's more informative than seeing that same message on a mainstream or liberal program, precisely because the story runs against Fox's ideological reputation (Baum and Groeling 2009). Such a message provides a costly signal, making it more credible than it otherwise would be (Schultz 2005; Chiang and Knight 2011).[16] Such findings are important but are less directly relevant here. While such counterideological signals provide voters with valuable information, they are valuable precisely because they are rare. As mentioned earlier (and discussed in greater detail in chapter 2), partisan media typically provide exactly the sort of typical ideological cues one would expect: right-wing sources like Fox News support Republicans; left-wing sources like MSNBC support Democrats. The effect of stereotypical messages is a more important component of figuring out how these sources impact viewers.

As a whole then, while much has been learned about the effects of partisan media, much more remains to be done. In the chapters that follow, I draw on a variety of work from the fields of political communication and political psychology to explain why partisan media have relatively wide-ranging effects on viewers' attitudes, beliefs, and behaviors, as well as how a number of important mediators and moderators drive and condition these relationships. I then test these arguments using a series of original experiments and panel data, and document the ability to partisan media to influence viewers in fundamental ways. My analysis offers novel insights into the power and impacts of partisan media.

Outline of the Book

Chapter 2 discusses a series of content analyses I conducted to document how and to what degree partisan media programs slant their presentation of the news. I explore three areas corresponding to the first three empirical questions raised in this chapter. First, I demonstrate how partisan outlets slant their coverage of the issues, selectively presenting facts and interpreting evidence in ways that support their point of view. Second, I show how the programs denigrate and dismiss the other party, discussing them in negative terms, questioning their motives, and so forth. Viewers watching these shows come away with a portrait that the other side is corrupt and incompetent and not a legitimate target for compromise. Not surprisingly, then, these shows also belittle bipartisanship and compromise. Finally, I document how these shows slant their coverage of the issues and candidates during an election season, giving more supportive coverage of their party's candidates and much more negative coverage to their opponents. I also show how, in 2008, Fox News emphasized two delegitimizing explanations for Obama's victory: vote fraud and media bias. These had the potential to make viewers more skeptical of Obama and his presidency. Together, these findings suggest that partisan media's coverage of the day's events has the potential to impact viewers in each of these three key areas.

I build on these insights in chapter 3 to offer a set of hypotheses as to why partisan media shape viewers' behaviors and attitudes. Using theories of motivated reasoning (Taber and Lodge 2006), as well as social identity theory (Tajfel 1970; Tajfel and Turner 1979), I explain the effects of partisan media on attitudinal polarization, attitudes toward the other party and the political process more generally, and vote choice. While I typically expect partisan media to have relatively large effects on all three areas, the size of these effects depends critically on a set of moderating variables, most notably the slant of the media (whether it reinforces or cuts against the viewer's prior beliefs) and the viewer's attributes. This gives me a detailed set of hypotheses to test the power of partisan media in several different areas.

The next three chapters form the empirical core of the book and test the hypotheses laid out in chapter 3. Chapter 4 examines the effects on attitudinal polarization: does watching partisan media make subjects hold more extreme views? Using a series of original experiments, I demonstrate four important empirical findings. First, I show that partisan media do polarize viewers, particularly when subjects watch like-minded media, and that when subjects watch crosscutting media, on average, there is no effect. But this is because crosscutting media polarize some subjects (those with strong prior attitudes), and depolarize others (those who find crosscutting media to be highly credible), highlighting the importance of accounting for moderating variables. Second, I use novel experimental techniques to explore which viewers are most affected by these treatments. I show that the largest effects are concentrated among those who watch partisan media regularly. These viewers come to the experiment somewhat more extreme already, but then watching partisan media makes them even *more* extreme. Thus, partisan media polarize the electorate not by making moderates into extremists but by moving those already somewhat extreme further toward the ideological poles. Third, I show that the polarizing effects of partisan media endure, at least for several days post exposure. While a typical concern with media exposure experiments is that the effects are transitory and ephemeral, my results show that partisan media effects are more stable. Finally, I demonstrate that like-minded media also make subjects more certain that their beliefs are correct—like-minded media increase attitudinal certainty. So not only do subjects become more extreme, they become more convinced that their beliefs are the correct ones.

Chapter 5 shows how partisan media help to breed dislike and mistrust of the other party. Partisan media present a skewed picture of the other party, consistent with their ideological outlook: right-wing shows portray Democrats as unscrupulous, and left-wing shows do the same for Republicans. Using a series of original experiments, I show that this biased portrait of the other party decreases affect for them and makes subjects think that the other party's leaders are incompetent. Watching partisan media further causes viewers to become less likely to trust the opposition and less willing to support compromise and bipartisanship. Partisan media make viewers reject middle-ground solutions and foster distrust and gridlock, making compromise and consensus more difficult to achieve.

Chapter 6 considers how partisan media consumption impacts vote choice. Using panel data collected during the 2008 election, I show that viewers who watch like-minded media are more likely to vote for their party's candidate, and this relationship is quite robust to a variety of different estimation techniques and methods. I also show that this effect is due to partisan media changing how viewers feel about the candidates, consistent with the affect-based findings discussed in chapter 5. This chapter also explains how partisan media influence how citizens interpret the election outcomes. In the aftermath of an election, media and political elites take to the airwaves to explain the outcome. I document how partisan news outlets (specifically, Fox News) made Republicans more likely to accept nefarious interpretations of the 2008 election, claiming that Obama won either because of media bias and vote fraud. These understandings of Obama's victory, in turn, helped to delegitimize the president and his policies for these viewers. Partisan media shape not only how citizens' vote but also why those vote choices and election outcomes matter.

Chapter 7 concludes by pulling together and expanding on these empirical findings and documenting the broader consequences of partisan media for American politics writ large. In particular, I explain how partisan media matter *even those who never actually watch these programs.*

First, partisan media sources help to shape the issues and discourse used to discuss events in the mainstream media. For example, partisan media outlets played a key role in promulgating stories like the Swift Boat Veterans for Truth. This has implications for how scholars think about the role of partisan media in the overall media environment, as well as the how candidates and their campaigns use the media to communicate with citizens. Second, and more importantly, partisan media matter even for nonviewers because of how they affect governance. It is certainly true that partisan media reach only a relatively narrow segment of the electorate, and that given the choice, many viewers will opt out of watching this type of media (Arceneaux and Johnson 2010, forthcoming). But because those who choose to watch are more extreme already and more engaged, involved, and so forth, these are the citizens who will ensure that their voices will be heard in the halls of power. By polarizing viewers, making them more certain of their beliefs, and making them distrust the other side, partisan media make finding consensus solutions more difficult. They engender the "uncompromising mind" that eschews compromise and endorses partisan gridlock, making it more difficult to solve important problems (Gutmann and Thompson 2010). These consequences are felt throughout the political system, so all citizens—even those who never watch partisan outlets—feel the effects of partisan media. Even with a relatively limited audience, partisan media have large, and consequential, impacts on American politics in the twenty-first century.

CHAPTER TWO

What Do Partisan Media Actually Say?

To understand how partisan media shape viewers' attitudes and behaviors, I need to understand how they discuss the news and events of the day. In particular, I need to explore aspects of their coverage that relate to the three main empirical questions raised in chapter 1. First, to know whether partisan media can polarize viewers, I need to understand how they frame, discuss, and slant their coverage of the issues of the day. Second, to know if partisan media can cause viewers to dislike and distrust the other side, as well as breed hostility to compromise and bipartisanship, I need to see how they cover and discuss the other party (as well as compromise and bipartisanship more generally). Finally, to understand how partisan media might impact elections, I need to understand how they cover the candidates and the issues during a campaign. I also need to explore how they interpret the election outcomes. Do they offer conventional rationales that fit with those offered by the mainstream press, or do they instead offer more nefarious rationales that undermine the other party and its candidates? Together, these questions will allow me to document how partisan media cover the news, which in turn will allow me to develop theoretical expectations in the next chapter about how this slanted coverage shapes viewers' attitudes and behaviors.

To uncover the patterns of coverage on partisan media, I draw on two primary data sources. First, I randomly selected fourteen days from the first year of the Obama administration and coded the transcripts of the two most popular programs from Fox News and MSNBC: *The O'Reilly Factor* and *Hannity* from Fox News and *Countdown with Keith Olbermann* and *The Rachel Maddow Show* from MSNBC. All four are opinionated, prime-time shows that form the basis of my study of partisan media (see the discussion in chapter 1), making them appropriate choices for this analysis. Here, I wanted to know what issues they covered, how they covered them, how they talked about the other side, and so forth. To understand the electoral dimension, I conducted a parallel coding of ten days from the fall 2008 presidential campaign. The analysis of these data allowed me to address all three questions about how partisan media cover the news.

Second, I also conducted more detailed case studies of partisan media's coverage of three particular issues—the debate over the 2011 debt ceiling increase, the president's decision to support same-sex marriage in May 2012, and the 2009 resignation of Van Jones from the White House. These analyses were necessarily issue-bound and may not be representative of how these programs discuss issues more broadly. But they allowed me to track the evolution of particular issues over time to explore how partisan media discuss salient issues in more depth. To use a simple analogy, the random set of days provides a wider but shallower view of media coverage, while the case studies give a narrower but deeper perspective. Together, these two data sources allowed me to say something more well-rounded about partisan media's treatment of the day's news and events.

How Do Partisan Media Talk about the Issues?

Simply put, partisan media present a biased view of the day's news. When talking about the day's news and events, they construct this biased account in two distinct but deeply related ways. First, they frame the issues of the day to be consonant with their underlying principles. So when Fox and MSNBC discuss the same story, they provide vastly different accounts of the event—Fox gives the conservative point of view, and MSNBC offers the liberal one. Second (and connected to the first), Fox and MSNBC devote different amounts of time to various news stories, and that attention is not randomly distributed. Fox pays closer attention to stories consonant with conservative talking points, and MSNBC does the same for liberal ones. So by changing the frame, or by changing the amount of coverage devoted to a topic, these outlets shape how viewers see the news of the day.

Take the issue of framing first. Perhaps nothing is more striking about the coverage of the day's news on partisan media than the starkly different ways these shows discuss the same issues. The two sides each provide a coherent frame through which to understand the day's news (Jamieson, Hardy, and Romer 2007). For example, look at the reaction to the release of the Levin Armed Services Report on the use of "enhanced interrogation techniques" (considered by some to constitute torture) during the Bush administration. The Fox News shows, especially *Hannity*, argued that waterboarding and other enhanced interrogation techniques were not actually torture. Even if these methods did constitute torture, it would not matter: they saved American lives. As O'Reilly put it, "The facts are this [waterboarding] worked" (*The O'Reilly Factor*, 22 April 2009). They pointed to the claim that using these techniques prevented an attack on Los Angeles and repeated former vice president Cheney's claim that torture kept America safe (*Hannity* and *The O'Reilly Factor*, 22 April 2009). In contrast, Keith Olbermann emphasized that these documents showed the Bush administration used torture not to prevent another attack, but to find a link between the 9/11 attacks and Saddam Hussein to justify the invasion of Iraq (*Countdown with Keith Olbermann*, 22 April 2009). Rather than engaging with the same set of themes, the shows "talk past" each other in a fundamental way, focusing on separate aspects of the debate that suit their ideological predispositions.

Reaction to Obama's speech at Cairo University in June 2009 drew similarly polarized reactions. The speech was an important one for the president, as he used it to outline his vision for America's place in the world and, in particular, it relationship with Muslim nations, especially Iraq and Afghanistan. Sean Hannity sharply criticized the speech, arguing that he blamed America for the world's problems and gave "9/11 sympathizers a voice on the world stage" by not more strongly denouncing terrorism (*Hannity*, 4 June 2009). In contrast, Keith Olbermann and his guest political analyst, Howard Fineman, argued that Obama's speech was "really brilliantly done," and that Obama had "successfully inserted himself into the ongoing public conversations of the Islamic world." Indeed, the only criticism they had was for Republicans and conservatives—most notably Rush Limbaugh—who attacked the president's speech (*Countdown with Keith Olbermann*, 4 June 2009). I find the same pattern on issue after issue—Obama's budget, the stimulus bill, health care reform, and so forth. It is not a misnomer to speak of a "Fox effect," or more generally, a "partisan media effect," given the way these media frame and present the news in such sharply different ways, both from each other and from the mainstream news stories (Baum and Groeling 2009).

The debate over global climate change highlights how both sides selective use evidence to make their case to the public. Both left- and right-wing sources give a factual but one-sided presentation of the evidence surrounding the controversy. Neither side is being untruthful, per se, but they both carefully pick the facts that support their side and omit the ones that work in their opponent's favor. Discussing the Copenhagen global climate summit, Hannity and right-wing figures argued against efforts to address climate change by touting the "climategate" scandal[1] and decreases in average temperatures, suggesting that global warming is abating (*Hannity*, 9 December 2009). This is consistent with a more general policy by Fox News editors to cast doubt on climate change by indicating there was disagreement in the scientific community (Mirkinson 2010). Indeed, comparing a number of different news outlets, Fox News consistently showed the most skepticism toward global climate change (Feldman et al. 2012). In contrast, Keith Olbermann and other left-wing hosts presented other facts suggesting larger shifts in global temperatures, arguing that this evidence—and the collective judgment of much of the world's scientific community—meant global warming needs to be addressed. Olbermann mentions climategate, but says that it does not change the truth of climate change, and simply represents "massaging of data," and argues that it not a real scandal (*Countdown with Keith Olbermann*, 9 December 2009). Both sides marshal and present the evidence that best reinforces and defends their side, and less consideration to opposing points of view.

To the extent that they present the other side's arguments, they typically do so in a derisive fashion, shooting down or mocking the opposing point of view. So arguments from the other side *are* discussed, but they are usually presented in a straw-man fashion, and are almost always shot down (this has important implications for how viewers perceive the other side, and I return to this point below). Perhaps this should not be terribly surprising: after all, even in ordinary conversation, a committed ideologue typically can (at least to his mind) rebut the arguments from the opposition. Consistent with this, when these shows feature guests, they usually reinforce the hosts' viewpoint. In most circumstances, the guests largely or completely reinforced the host's viewpoints. When politicians appear on these shows, they most typically appear on the program matching their ideological slant: liberals like Bernie Sanders and

Alan Grayson appear on MSNBC; conservatives like Michelle Bachmann and Mike Pence appear on Fox News. The guests serve primarily to reinforce the message offered on these outlets (Feldman et al. 2012). This would fit with claims that politicians are now more likely today to "narrowcast," trying to speak to a more receptive partisan audience (Cohen 2009; Baum 2011a). While the clips of Bill O'Reilly yelling at Barney Frank are legendary (and even generated a popular bumper sticker available at O'Reilly's website), such instances are also relatively rare. Most of the time, hosts and guests agree, and they both reinforce the same message: one side is right, and the other side is wrong (Manjoo 2008).

This also has a more subtle, but important, implication as well. No one would claim that these shows are a model of civility and politesse, but they are also not the "shout shows" decried by many (Mutz and Reeves 2005; Mutz 2007). Indeed, commentators have noted for several years that these shows represent a shift from an argument-based style to a more opinion-driven culture (Rosensteil 2006). The arguing is finished, and one side emerged victorious, at least in the mind of the host and much of the audience. Shouting is not really necessary, because there's no argument (nor any need for it): one side is right, the other side is wrong.

But these shows slant the news in another way beyond framing: they devote differing levels of attention to particular stories. Take, for example, the story of Solyndra, a California company that manufactured solar panels but filed for bankruptcy in September 2011. This case would not be noteworthy except that the company received a loan of more than a half-billion dollars from the Department of Energy, designed as part of a stimulus initiative to support green jobs. Further, internal documents from the Obama administration suggest that administration officials knew that the company had weak finances and might well fail, leading critics to charge that the loan is an example of crony capitalism, since Solyndra executives gave donations to Obama's 2008 campaign (Wilson 2011). As one would expect, Fox and MSNBC used quite different frames when they covered the story. Fox News focused more on the corruption angle to the story, linking the Obama administration's loan to the donations from Solyndra executives, as well as to the personal ties between administration officials and company leaders (see, e.g., *Hannity*, 12 October 2011). In contrast, the discussion on MSNBC focused on how any such venture might be a risk, but the government still needed to invest in alternative energy sources (*The Rachel Maddow Show*, 26 September 2011). But this is not the most striking difference between the coverage on the two stations—the amount of coverage is. Fox News broadcast more than two hundred stories discussing Solyndra during August, September, and October 2011, while MSNBC only aired four stories over this period.[2] Fox News had more than *fifty times* the coverage of this topic, and it was sharply negative, criticizing the president for his failed judgment and crony capitalism. The differences in coverage (which tend to reflect the differences in ideological reputation across networks) given to a particular story can help to magnify the effects of any particular frame.

When these shows discuss a story repeatedly, they do two important things to draw in the audience, both of which have broader political implications. First, while they repeat the same basic charge over and over again (in case a viewer missed it or forgot it), they also offer something new over time so that the story evolves. From a business standpoint, this makes perfect sense: it allows viewers to hear the original story (so viewers who missed an earlier episode can learn it, and earlier viewers can have the lesson reinforced), and it also offers viewers something new and tantalizing to keep them tuning in—viewers have to watch to see where the story will go next. Second, these shows also use these charges to discuss more general flaws in the opposition. The story of Solyndra nicely illustrates both properties. Not only as the Obama administration guilty of this offense in the Solyndra case, but they also offered loans to other politically connected but financially fragile firms, such as Sun Power (*Hannity*, 12 October 2011). The story was not just Solyndra, but it was broader and evolving, so viewers needed to tune in every day (or at least a few times a week) to see how the story evolves. The Solyndra scandal was also used on these same broadcasts as evidence of Obama's more general pattern of corruption and cronyism, so this one case became the exemplar of a broader trend. Politically, these patterns have important ramifications. The repetition and slightly changing story line set up incentives for viewers to return for more reinforcement and exposure, helping to ensure viewers receive multiple does of the partisan media effect. Also, by linking this to general concerns, they helped the story fit within broader partisan schema about the other side, making it easy for viewers to know how to use this information to update their prior not just about this one story, but about political elites more generally. In short, these outlets influence viewers not only with tone of coverage, but with the volume as well.

More broadly, not only do they devote different amounts of coverage to the same story, but these differing political agendas between networks lead them to cover entirely different stories altogether. One story discussed on MSNBC may not be mentioned at all on Fox, and vice versa. While they have the same potential universe of stories, given their priors, they select very different ones to cover. For example, on 4 May 2009, *Hannity* discussed several stories relating to left-wing bias in the mainstream media, Obama's first Supreme Court nominee, climate change, the life of Jack Kemp, and Elizabeth Hasselback's new diet. In contrast, *The Rachel Maddow Show* discussed a totally different set of topics on that same day, covering tax havens in the Cayman Islands, efforts by the Republican Party to rebrand itself, Obama's policy on military tribunals, and a discussion of allegations that Republican Senator Jeff Sessions had made racist comments in the past. The *PBS News Hour* that evening discussed swine flu infection, President Obama's tax policy (and the U.S. economy more broadly), the U.S. drawdown in Iraq, the death of Jack Kemp, President Obama's first Supreme Court nominee, and a report on ethnic conflict and cooperation in Rwanda. This is not a terribly atypical case. While there is often some topical overlap, it is usually far from complete. The choice of stories, moreover, reflects the point above about how they treat the opposition. So left-wing sources cover the allegations of racism against a Republican senator, while right-wing ones discuss liberal media bias. The shows talk past each other (and much of the mainstream press), each one focusing on the stories that best support their position.

But there is at least one topic where both Fox and MSNBC give disproportionate coverage to an issue relative to the mainstream media: the question of media bias. This is particularly true of Fox News, where liberal media bias is a perennial topic (see also Jamieson and Cappella 2008). For example, *Hannity* highlighted this theme on 3 February 2009, when he discusses how the mainstream media treats Obama favorably, in no small part because they built him up during the 2008 election. The 22 April 2011 episode prominently featured "The Invisible Narrative," a detailed discussion of the left-wing media bias in America. Indeed, the phrase "liberal media" was used on over a hundred stories on Fox News during 2009. While media bias is a more frequent topic of conversation of Fox News, left-wing shows discuss it as well, though they focus on the alleged right-wing tilt to the media. Keith Olbermann, for example, charged that the media was far too complacent in accepting the

Bush administration's march to war in the run-up to the invasion of Iraq (*Countdown with Keith Olbermann*, 14 December 2009; see also Olbermann's "Special Comment" segment that aired during the 15 November 2010 show). These programs paint themselves as offering an alternative to flawed presentations elsewhere, thereby differentiating themselves from the rest of the news market. This has an important consequence for these types of shows: to the extent that the rest of the media is biased, watching an "objective" show on Fox or MSNBC becomes all the more important for the audience, because that becomes the source for the "real" news. By highlighting examples of media bias, and then claiming to offer an alternative, the shows help to maintain their audience (Jamieson and Cappella 2008). Despite their partisan tenor, these shows paint themselves as the more "objective" sources because they avoid the bias seen in the mainstream news or other outlets.

Overall, then, the evidence suggests partisan media's coverage of the issue is quite slanted and biased. When both Fox and MSNBC cover the same story, they do so in fundamentally different ways, framing the story uniquely, emphasizing disparate pieces of evidence, and generally fitting it within their larger ideological narrative. Further, they also choose different stories to cover, with Fox devoting more attention to stories that emphasize and underline conservative themes, and MSNBC doing the same for liberal ones. The news is used to advance a larger agenda.

How Do Partisan Media Talk about the Other Side?

The discussion above demonstrates how partisan media outlets frame and slant their coverage of the issues of the day. Perhaps not surprisingly, these shows also offer a slanted look at the two major political parties. Generally speaking, they do spend some time supporting their own party and its leaders, but they also spend a great deal of time criticizing the opposition.[3] So when watching these shows, one hears not only that the other side's arguments are flawed but the leaders of the opposition are also similarly flawed. Two techniques used on these shows illustrate these patterns. First, when hosts are discussing a particular issue, they link the opposition's flawed position on the issue to a more general flaw in the opposition party, as I showed above in the Solyndra case. So Obama's position on climate change is not simply wrong on its own, but it also represents his flawed liberal, statist approach to problems more generally; his support of Solyndra is just another example of his (and the Democrats') support of crony capitalism. The Republicans' support for tax cuts for the wealthy is not only wrong on its own but also shows how Republicans are in the pocket of the rich more generally on deregulation, financial reform, and so forth. This one particular issue becomes an exemplar of the more general flawed logic from the other side.

Second, these shows also highlight errors and gaffes from the other side, emphasize their most outrageous comments, and generally mock and ridicule the opposition. Sean Hannity frequently refers to President Obama as "the anointed one," even calling him "the Messiah" to mock the reverence shown to Obama by members of the (allegedly) liberal press (*Hannity*, 24 March 2009). Not to be outdone, Keith Olbermann refers to O'Reilly as "Bill O the Clown" (*Countdown with Keith Olbermann*, 9 March 2009) and uses similarly derisive language to refer to various Republican officials and other right-wing figures. Similarly, partisan media programs love to point out when there are internecine squabbles in the other party, such as when liberal Democrats opposed the president's plan to send more troops to Afghanistan (*The O'Reilly Factor*, 7 October 2009) or when Republicans split over whether America should directly support the Iranian protesters who took to the streets opposing the reelection of President Ahmadinejad (*The Rachel Maddow Show*, 22 June 2009). While even mainstream outlets focus a great deal of attention on within-party disputes (Baum and Groeling 2009, 2010; Groeling 2010), this trend is arguably even more pronounced in partisan media.

The flaws in the other party highlighted by these shows are not simply minor offenses; rather, they reflect why it could be dangerous (in the eyes of the host) to have the other party in power. The opposition is not simply wrong, but dangerously so. Sean Hannity, commenting on the Obama administration's foreign policy, argued that "Barack Obama is so weak on defenses [*sic*] in every regard and sucking up to the world's dictators that people are going to die because of what Barack Obama is doing right now" (*Hannity*, 22 April 2009). Not to be outdone, left-wing figures often take similarly sharp stabs at Republicans and conservative commentators. For example, Keith Olbermann frequently chastises leading Republicans and conservative figures, such as Glenn Beck and Sarah Palin, in harsh terms. During his 28 June 2010 broadcast, he lashed out at Palin's "imbecility" and her "endorsement of stupidity," a typical theme in his discussion of her. Both sides discuss the other side using negative language.

This carries over more generally into the tone of stories about the opposition. Looking across shows, the vast majority of stories about the other party have a negative tone. So Democrats are painted in a negative light in most stories on Fox News, and the same is true of Republicans on MSNBC. This is consistent with the finding that these shows spend more time criticizing the opposition than they do supporting their own party (Chalif 2011; Smith and Searles, forthcoming). Watching these shows is more about learning why the other side is wrong rather than your own side is right (Holbert, Garrett, and Gleason 2010). This reinforces the selective attention noted earlier: these shows highlight stories where the other side looks bad, thereby reinforcing the prior predispositions of their audiences.

These shows also love to discuss instances of hypocrisy and double standards from the other party (see also Jamieson and Cappella 2008). For example, O'Reilly pointed out that liberals claim that everyone should be tolerant, but liberals themselves do not tolerate conservatives opposed to gay marriage. O'Reilly remarked that Sean Penn's remarks at the 2009 Oscars supporting gay marriage were "the epitome of intolerance" (*The O'Reilly Factor*, 23 February 2009). Likewise, Olbermann and Maddow pointed out examples of right-wing hypocrisy, arguing that Republicans claims to be antispending during the Obama administration are hypocritical in light of their policies during the Bush administration (*The Rachel Maddow Show*, 22 April 2009), or that many Republicans who rallied against the 2009 stimulus bill then boasted about the job-creating impact of the stimulus funds to their constituents (*The Rachel Maddow Show*, 9 February 2010). This reinforces the perfidious and nefarious image painted of the other side: they not only support flawed policies, they are duplicitous and deceptive.

Perhaps not surprisingly, these shows typically do not support efforts to find bipartisan compromise and centrist solutions to problems. Instead, these shows denigrate bipartisanship, compromise, and the like. This should not be shocking: if the other side is so deeply flawed and duplicitous, why should our side compromise with them? For example, during the debate over health care reform, left-wing hosts from MSNBC argued that the president and congressional Democrats should abandon the quest for bipartisanship, given that Republicans are not seriously willing to negotiate on these issues. As Keith Olbermann put it, "So, why push health care bipartisanship in the face of Republican brinksmanship?" (*Countdown with Keith Olbermann*, 5 August 2009). Bipartisanship is not an effective strategy, because the other side is duplicitous, and they're playing politics. Because they're flawed, "our side" cannot negotiate with them. And when the other side will not negotiate with our side, then we need to stand up for our own policies: "When did it become a bad thing to stand on your principles?" (*Hannity*, 29 July 2011; see also *Hannity*, 17 December 2009). Standing on principle—rather than engaging in flawed bipartisanship with a duplicitous opposition—is the more important strategy.

Again, the pattern is relatively clear: these shows attack the other side, highlight their flaws and foibles, and paint them as duplicitous and corrupt. They also attack and criticize much of the effort to reach out and compromise with the other party, instead preferring to stand firm on principle. So these shows not only slant their coverage of issues, they also slant their coverage of the other party (and efforts to compromise with them) as well.

How Do Partisan Media Cover Elections?

The same patterns of hostility toward the opposition and their policies occur again and again during the election season. First, while partisan shows defend their ticket of choice, they spend just as much—if not more—time attacking the other one. Fox News defended McCain (at least once he becomes the nominee), but they also attacked Obama and explained why he would not be a good president. In effect, they remind their audience why they want one side and—just as importantly—why they do not want the other party (Smith and Searles, forthcoming).

During the election, these shows also stressed negative themes and narratives about the opposition, consistent with their more general negative tone toward the other party. Right-wing sources spent a great deal of time discussing how Obama was a tax-and-spend liberal, how he showed flawed judgment by associating with Bill Ayres and Jeremiah Wright, and how Democrats might use ACORN (a low-income advocacy group) to perpetuate voter fraud (on this last point, see Dreier and Martin 2010). Left-wing shows reciprocated by discussing Sarah Palin's lack of intelligence, her lack of preparation for national office, and the fact that she stretches the truth (i.e., her discussion of the Bridge to Nowhere, the state plane sold on eBay, etc.). While many of these themes were also discussed in the mainstream media (Kenski, Hardy, and Jamieson

2010), the partisan media pushed them with a particular vehemence, and the discussion was asymmetric: Fox News defended Palin from many of these charges, but they did not offer rebuttals to their claims about Obama. Watching partisan media, it was hard to escape these sorts of negative themes about the other side.[4]

But the slant on these networks does not stop when the election is over. Partisan media outlets, like all media outlets, construct a narrative to explain the election outcomes. In 2008, most media outlets and commentators argued that Obama won because of Bush's relative unpopularity and poor economic performance (Holbrook, Clouse, and Weinschenk 2012; Sabato 2009), as well as Obama's considerable skill as a campaigner (Heilemann and Halpern 2009). But what about Fox News? The case of this channel is particularly interesting, since it slanted its coverage toward the losing candidate (Senator McCain), making them the more likely network to endorse a delegitimizing narrative about the Obama victory. Like much of the rest of the media, Fox focused on the factors cited earlier, but they also advanced two more nefarious explanations for the 2008 election outcome. First, they argued that Obama won (at least in part) because of left-wing media bias. The mainstream media *wanted* Obama to win, so they slanted their coverage to achieve the desired outcome (Goldberg 2009). Consistent with these arguments, during the 2008 campaign, Fox News devoted much more coverage to media bias than other outlets,[5] a pattern that continued into the first years of the Obama presidency (see the discussion above). So Obama's victory, then, according to Fox, reflected (at least in part) the desires of the liberal media.

Fox also discussed another potential explanation for Obama's victory: vote fraud and corruption. The coverage of this topic was less extensive than the discussion of media bias, but there were a number of stories on Fox discussing ACORN and its fraudulent efforts at voter registration. While the story was discussed on the mainstream media as well (Dreier and Martin 2010), the coverage on Fox was notably more extensive.[6] Together, these two explanations helped suggest to Fox News viewers why their candidate lost and Obama won: because liberal elites in the media and left-wing groups helped him steal the election. This message has a potentially powerful effect on how these viewers might view the president and his policies (Anderson et. al 2005; Mutz 2006b).

But overall, the main pattern is clear: as in its more general coverage of the day's news, the news during an election season reflects the slant of these programs. Right-wing sources denigrate Democratic candidates and policies, left-wing shows do the same for Republicans and their ideas. As is the case more generally, these outlets fit the news within their broader ideological narrative.

Case Studies of Partisan Media Coverage

The discussion above highlights how partisan media covers a wide variety of issues over the past few years. But it suffers from an important limitation: while it covers a great deal of ground, it does not allow me to explore how any given story evolved and emerged over time. To help supplement my earlier analysis, in this section, I explore partisan media's coverage of three issues in greater depth: the debate over raising the federal debt ceiling in the summer of 2011, President Obama's announcement in 2012 that he supported same-sex marriage, and the allegations against Van Jones that eventually led to his resignation from the White House in 2009.

These three issues have several attractive features that make them well suited for my purposes. Both the debt ceiling debate and the gay marriage decision garnered significant attention on both Fox and MSNBC, allowing me to actually analyze what both networks said about the issue. Further, one is a detailed policy debate that raged for months, the other is a presidential announcement that came and went from the news cycle relatively quickly, allowing me to understand how these networks cover different types of news stories. Finally, one is an economic issue, focused primarily on questions of taxes and spending, and the other is a social issue, and a particularly controversial one at that. While no two issues could ever span the wide range of issues that could be discussed in the media, these two allow me to cover quite a bit of that range.

The Van Jones story, while much less prominent than the other two decisions, highlights an important feature of partisan media. This is a story that began on partisan media and then spread to the mainstream news, and eventually led to Jones's resignation from the White House staff. This story helps to illustrate the "downstream" power of partisan media: even if the audience for these outlets is rather narrow, they can have larger effects for American politics because of how they influence the broader media agenda.

The 2011 Debt Ceiling Debate

To finance it expenditures that are in excess of current tax revenues, the federal government issues debt, largely in the form of bonds. Before the twentieth century, Congress individually approved the duration, amount, and interest rate of each bond, typically issuing bonds to fund a particular project, such as the Panama Canal. But during World War I, this simply became too time intensive given the amount of money that needed to be raised to fund the overseas military campaigns. To help expedite funding the war effort, Congress delegated the power to issue bonds and other debt instruments to the Treasury Department. But because there were fears that this was abrogating Congress's power of the purse, in 1917 Congress imposed a limit on how much debt the Treasury Department was authorized to sell, hence, the federal debt ceiling.[7] This freed Congress from the responsibility of having to approve each bond individually, but gave it some control over how much debt was issued by the federal government. Note, however, that the debt ceiling is separate from decisions about taxation and spending (Austin and Levit 2012).

For much of the twentieth century, the debt ceiling was largely uncontroversial. Since 1962, Congress has voted seventy-four times to raise the debt ceiling, including sixteen times between 1993 and 2010—ten of those between 2001 and 2010. While politics had intruded in on previous efforts to raise the debt ceiling, the debate in 2011 would be unusually protracted (Austin and Levit 2012). Several factors undoubtedly played a role here: the continued economic downtown following the 2008 financial crisis, which raised the salience of budget and tax issues throughout the nation, as well as the emergence of the Tea Party caucus, which took a strong stance against increasing government debt. Having campaigned against federal spending and deficits in 2010 (Skocpol and Williamson 2012), the Tea Party decided to hold a firm line on increasing the debt ceiling in 2011. This put Republican leaders, especially in the House, in a very difficult position, given that few Tea Party members were willing to vote for a deal that would increase the debt ceiling (Cillizza and Blake 2011). While a deal was eventually reached, it was only after months of intense debate in Washington between the president and legislative leaders (Silverleib and Cohen 2011).

For the present purposes, however, the key issue is how partisan media (specifically, Fox and MSNBC) covered this issue. I began my analysis with the May notice from the Treasury Department that it would soon hit the debt ceiling, and concluded it when President Obama signed the debt deal into law in early August.[8] I then sampled fifteen stories from popular shows on Fox and MSNBC during this period, paying attention to how these shows discussed the policy itself and how they discussed the other party and treated efforts at bipartisanship and compromise.[9] The specific programs I used from Fox News were *The O'Reilly Factor* and *Hannity*, which were the network's most popular options; on MSNBC, I used *The Rachel Maddow Show* and *The Ed Show*, again, two popular offerings from that network (note that *Countdown with Keith Olbermann* was no longer airing on MSNBC during the debt ceiling debate). This gave me a sense of how the key prime-time hours of partisan television covered this debate.

Both networks presented a one-sided interpretation of the controversy that fit with their general ideological narrative, consistent with the pattern seen above. On Fox, the debt ceiling controversy was portrayed as a reflection of the Obama's administration's spendthrift ways: too much money was spent on social programs, the stimulus, and so forth. What was needed was a sense of fiscal discipline: spending should be cut, and Republicans should insist on holding the line on taxes. If any taxes were raised, it should be taxes on lower-income individuals, those who currently have little to no federal tax burden (*Hannity*, 21 July 2011). The solution was to "let the private marketplace be unleashed" by reducing federal regulation and spending, and allowing the private sector to flourish (*The O'Reilly Factor*, 13 July 2011). MSNBC presented a one-sided interpretation of the debate consistent with their prior beliefs. Here, the problem was that Republican policies moved us away from a model of "shared sacrifice:" what was needed was to raise taxes on the wealthy and corporations without asking the middle class (or poorer citizens) to cut back on social programs (*The Ed Show*, 29 July 2011). MSNBC argued that we could not cut our way out of the debt ceiling debate, because further spending cuts would harm the fragile economic recovery (*The Rachel Maddow Show*, 5 July 2011; *The Ed Show*, 23 June 2011). Instead, MSNBC hosts argued that more revenues (i.e., tax increases) were needed to resolve the issue. Neither side's arguments should be terribly surprising in light of what I discussed earlier: each presented a view of the facts that fit with their prior beliefs about the proper balance of spending and taxes.

The two programs also offer sharply different interpretations of the consequences of failing to reach a deal to resolve the impasse (i.e., what would happen if the United States were to default on its debt). Fox News argues that President Obama, who consistently argued that the failure to reach a deal would have dire consequences both at home and abroad, was using "scare tactics" to pressure members into making a deal (*Hannity*, 20 July 2011). If there were no deal to raise the debt ceiling, the government would still be able to pay some bills, and fund some programs. The conservative argument is that the United States could use incoming revenues to pay for essential services, such as the interest on existing debt, social security, and salaries for active duty military personnel. Other programs—like the IRS, EPA, and so forth—would then have to be cut back (*Hannity*, 13 July 2011). This is consistent with broad, and long-standing, conservative arguments about reducing the size and scope of government.

In contrast, MSNBC emphasized that without a deal over the debt ceiling, the government would potentially have to cut back on popular social programs: not only Social Security and Medicare, but also highway spending, Pell grants, education aid to states, food assistance for women and children, and so forth (*The Rachel Maddow Show*, 28 July 2011). There is no easy way to adjudicate between the competing visions proffered by Fox and MSNC on the implications of the debt ceiling: faced with a revenue shortfall, there are many potential solutions to bring outflows and inflows in line with each other. The more interesting and important point is how both sides paint a picture of the consequences consistent with their general ideological disposition. Fox talks about how the failure to reach a debt ceiling deal could force the government to shrink, consistent with a long-standing conservative argument that a smaller government is a better government. MSNBC, in contrast, focus on a variety of popular, middle-class programs that could be threatened by the lack of a deal, consistent with its defense of these entitlement programs.

Not only do these shows paint a one-sided picture of the facts, they also use this debate to criticize the other party. Fox is certainly concerned about the debt ceiling itself, as well as offering more general indictment of Democratic overspending, but they also used the debt ceiling as a mechanism for talking about Obama's lack of leadership on the economy. Again and again, they railed against Obama's failure to take a leadership role in directly negotiating to end the crisis, especially early in the crisis when Vice President Biden was helping to negotiate a deal (*The O'Reilly Factor*, 27 June 2011; *Hannity*, 13 July 2011). Further, the failure on the debt ceiling deal was symptomatic of Obama's failure to lead on the economy more generally (*Hannity*, 9 August 2011). As I discussed earlier, these types of specific issues become a vehicle for attacking the other side on more fundamental grounds.

MSNBC similarly talked about a failure of leadership, but from Republicans. Here, the issue is that Republican leaders—especially Speaker of the House John Boehner—could not be responsible and come to the table to negotiate a compromise. They were trapped because of the extremist Tea Party members who insisted on no compromise over the debt ceiling (*The Ed Show*, 28 July 2011; *The Ed Show*, 29 July 2011). Because Boehner could not exercise leadership and control the Tea Party caucus, the problem was primarily a Republican one. Indeed, Republicans received nearly all of the blame for the entire debt ceiling debate on MSNBC. One commentator—political science professor Melissa Harris-Perry—argued that the debt ceiling crisis was "totally, 100 percent, a manufactured crisis that for some reason Republicans in Washington have decided to burden us with" (*The Rachel Maddow Show*, 28 July 2011). The crisis as the result of Republican—particularly Tea Party—intransigence: they were "invincibly ignorant" and simply refused to listen to reason and see the dire consequences of failing to increase the debt ceiling (*The Rachel Maddow Show*, 21 July 2011). Again, both sides laid the blame with the other party, and they used the debate to disparage and criticize the opposition.

Both networks also used the past increases to the debt ceiling to emphasize themes of hypocrisy and double standards from the other side. On a number of shows, MSNBC drew on the fact that former presidents Bush and Reagan both repeatedly raised the debt ceiling during their presidencies. Republicans never complained then about profligate spending, only making it an issue under a Democratic administration (*The Rachel Maddow Show*, 19 July 2011). Similarly, Fox argued that Obama too was guilty of a flip-flop on this issue, given that he opposed raising the debt ceiling back in 2006 during the Bush presidency (*Hannity*, 20 July 2011).

Both networks also offer a slanted view on bipartisanship and compromise. Hosts and guests on these programs—especially Sean Hannity on Fox News—railed against bipartisan compromise. Republicans should stand firm and not compromise with the Obama administration on tax increases, instead insisting on a debt ceiling deal built on spending cuts. Arguing against calls for bipartisanship and compromise, Hannity argued, "When did it become a bad thing to stand on your principles?" (*Hannity*, 29 July 2011). Similarly, former Alaska Governor Sarah Palin argued that "we [Republicans and conservatives] cannot afford to retreat right now. . . . Now is not the time to retreat. This is the time to reload" (*Hannity*, 13 July 2011). Bipartisanship and compromise is to be avoided; instead, members should stand firm on their principles. Fox's treatment of the House and Senate Republicans offers an interesting window into this debate over bipartisanship. Fox praised House Republicans, who consistently pushed for deep spending cuts to get a debt ceiling deal. Senate Republicans, in contrast, were roundly criticized, because they were working to try and achieve a bipartisan deal that included some revenue increases (*Hannity*, 29 July 2011).[10] Senate Republicans were being too accommodating, and instead should take a page from their House counterparts, insisting on standing firm for conservative principles. This also underlines the general pattern about how these shows talk about their own party: in general, they support their own party, expect when they are being too accommodating or violating too many principles. Bipartisanship and compromise with the other side become dirty words in the partisan media lexicon.[11]

Overall, then, the treatment of the debt ceiling debate on these networks was remarkably consistent with the more general tenor of their coverage of issues. Both networks presented a sharply one-sided view of the facts consistent with their general partisan and ideological predisposition, and they used the opportunity to criticize the other side, blaming them for the crisis and arguing that they were guilty of hypocrisy. Further, this disparaging treatment of the other side also spills over into more general criticism of bipartisanship and compromise.

Obama's Support for Gay Marriage

Few issues in American politics have been as controversial in recent decades as gay rights. While Americans, especially younger Americans, have become markedly more tolerant of gays and lesbians over time (Fiorina, Abrams, and Pope 2005), no president or major party presidential nominee has ever publically supported same-sex marriage. That all changed on 9 May 2012, when President Obama formally announced that he supported gay marriage: "I've just concluded that for me personally, it is important for me to go ahead and affirm that I think same-sex couples should be able to get married" (Memoli and Hennesy 2012). The decision followed Vice President Biden's announcement on 6 May 2012 that he was "absolutely comfortable" with gay marriage (Knowlton and Barbaro 2012), which put pressure on Obama to clarify his stance.

To analyze the reaction to this announcement, I coded all stories from the same sets of programs (*Hannity* and *The O'Reilly Factor* on Fox News; *The Rachel Maddow Show* and *The Ed Show* on MSNBC) between 9 May 2012 and 16 May 2012 (the week following the president's announcement).[12] Doing so allowed me to see the reaction to the president's decision on these programs.

Interestingly, these programs featured effectively no debate over the issue of gay marriage itself. On both Fox and MSNBC, no one really debated the merits of the decision (though, as I show below, the decision is seen in a more positive light on MSNBC). Instead, the discussion focused on two related questions. (1) Why did Obama make this decision: principle or politics? (2) What will the electoral effects be? These correspond closely to the second and third questions I raised at the beginning of this chapter: how do partisan media outlets talk about the other side and their motives, and how do partisan media discuss candidates and issues in an election season.

Take first the issue of Obama's motivations for supporting gay marriage. On Fox News, the answer was clearly that Obama came out in support of gay marriage for political reasons—this was about politics, not principle. Obama's decision was presented as a political move designed with two goals in mind: to pander to his base and help mobilize liberals for the upcoming 2012 election (*The O'Reilly Factor*, 11 May 2011; *The O'Reilly Factor*, 9 May 2011), and, more importantly, to raise money from gay donors and Hollywood liberals who agree with President Obama's decision. Fox's hosts pointed to the fact that the day after Obama's announcement, he headed to a star-studded fundraised at George Clooney's home, which took in upward of 15 million dollars for his reelection campaign, and the following week, he held a fundraiser at the home of openly gay singer Ricky Martin in New York (*Hannity*, 10 May 2011). Put succinctly, Fox portrays Obama's announcement as a "pure money play" (*The O'Reilly Factor*, 16 May 2011). The gay marriage shift, in other words, is just another political stunt.

But the president's support for gay marriage was also used on Fox to highlight a broader theme: Obama is a serial flip-flopper, always changing his position to pander to the public. Obama is a "perpetually pandering feature of political expedience" whose positions are like "silly putty" because he changes them so much (*Hannity*, 9 May 2011). This is true not just of gay marriage, but also on other issues, like lobbying reform, deficit reduction, and so forth. This one issue (the position shift on gay marriage) was used to illustrate a more general point, namely, that Obama continually changes his positions and has no principles.

Fox News also used this shift in Obama's position to draw a link to another perennial theme on partisan media outlets: media bias. Fox commentators argued that the media favors gay marriage, so they give more positive coverage to Obama's decision, given that it fits with their priors (*The O'Reilly Factor*, 15 May 2011). The media is effectively functioning not as reporters on this issue, but rather as "stenographers for Barack Obama" (*Hannity*, 10 May 2011). Further, Fox also claimed that the media is guilty of a double standard in how they covered the president's shift on this issue. When the president changes his position on the issue, he evolves, but when Mitt Romney changes his position, he's a flip-flopper: "liberals evolve, and conservatives devolve" (*Hannity*, 10 May 2011). Again, the particular issue became a tool for connecting to broader and recurrent themes on these outlets.

Not surprisingly, MSNBC gave a very different explanation of why the president changed his position on gay marriage: the narrative here was about principles, not politics. The emphasis was on the courage behind the president's decision (*The Ed Show*, 11 May 2011), highlighting the fact that his decision shows leadership (*The Ed Show*, 9 May 2011). Rather than reflecting political calculations, it reflects his personal experiences knowing same-sex parents, as well as conversations with Michelle Obama and other key advisors (*The Ed Show*, 9 May 2011; *The Ed Show*, 10 May 2011). The MSNBC hosts and guests also echoed the president's "evolution" rhetoric, contrasting sharply with the "flip-flop" characterization on Fox.

Indeed, on MSNBC, the only one flip-flopping was Mitt Romney, who initially strongly backed gay rights when he ran for the Senate in 1994, but now was sharply opposed to same-sex marriage and other gay-rights issues (*The Ed Show*, 10 May 2011). MSNBC hosts and guests also connected this to a broader pattern of Republican elites becoming increasingly hostile toward gay-rights issues (*The Rachel Maddow Show*, 10 May 2011). This connects to two broader themes discussed above. First, it serves to paint Republicans in an unfavorable light, given that they were taking a position increasingly discordant with public opinion. This is consistent with the general pattern that these programs try to paint the other side as extremists who are out of step with the American public. Second, it also highlights how these shows emphasize what their own side does right, while simultaneously emphasizing what the other does wrong. Note that on both Fox and MSNBC, there was a good deal of discussion of how the "other side" as doing something wrong: Obama is a political waffler on Fox, and Republicans are not in agreement with mainstream opinion on MSNBC. These shows are as much about why the opposition is wrong as they are about why their side is right.

Both networks also explored the ramifications of this decision for the 2012 elections. On Fox, one of the major themes was how Obama's move was simply a political ploy to raise money from gay donors and liberals. But these programs also argued that the move would hurt Obama's changes in the fall election, given that gay marriage is unpopular in a number of key states, such as Virginia and North Carolina. Further, this move would also help mobilize evangelicals, which would be a boon for Romney, given that these groups are skeptical of him due to his Mormon faith (*The O'Reilly Factor*, 16 May 2011). In contrast, MSNBC argued that the decision will have little effect on Obama's reelection prospects, given that the issue was very low salience for the vast majority of voters (*The Rachel Maddow Show*, 9 May 2011). If anything, the political effect of Obama's decision would be largely symbolic: other officials who privately supported gay rights but had been afraid to public embrace them may now feel they can support them (*The Rachel Maddow Show*, 9 May 2011).

Overall, then, results of this case study reinforce the general patterns seen above. Even when debating a presidential announcement rather than a more general policy issue, the story can be fit within a broader political narrative about the other side, casting doubt on them and their motivations. The news on these outlets fits within a larger political narrative about American politics.

The Van Jones Story and the Agenda-Setting Power of Partisan Media

Van Jones was initially appointed in March 2009 to be special White House advisor on green jobs, enterprise, and innovation, working with the Council on Environmental Quality to help promote environmental efforts in the Obama administration. Jones, a long-time activist, was known for his advocacy on both environmental and civil rights issues. Like many such appointments, Jones initially garnered little controversy or even attention, with only a handful of news stories about him appearing in his first few months in office. That all changed during the summer of 2009, when Fox News hosts began to criticize Jones on the air. The attacks eventually spread to the mainstream media—and into the talking points of congressional Republicans—and forced Jones to resign from his post. This case study shows how partisan media cover a relatively low salience issue and turn it into a larger, more consequential issue. This case shows how partisan media's agenda can spread to the mainstream press, which has important consequences for the power of partisan outlets.

To study the Van Jones case in more detail, I tracked the discussion of the case on Fox News, and then covered how it spread to other outlets, including the broader mainstream press. This allowed me to examine the agenda-setting power of partisan outlets.[13]

The first discussion of Jones on Fox came on 15 July 2009. That night's *Hannity* featured a brief mention of Jones, discussing his previous arrest record and the fact that Jones previously admitted he had been a Communist. Hannity used this as a way to take a jab at the president, arguing that (self-avowed) Communist Jones "should feel right at home in the 'land of the czars,'" repeating a theme from previous shows that the president surrounded himself with left-wing radicals.[14] The following week, Glenn Beck made similar claims, and argued that Jones was part of a larger plot by Obama to use government policy to achieve racial justice—in effect, reparations via other means (*Glenn Beck*, 23 July 2009). Beck continued to address the Jones story over the next few weeks on his show, spending increasing amounts of time on it by late August 2009. At this point, however, no other media outlets were really reporting the story: before late August, no other network, major newspaper, or magazine cataloged by LexisNexis mentioned Jones in connection with the allegations suggested by Fox News (see figure 2.1). For the first few weeks, the issue was simply a Fox News story promulgated by Beck and Hannity.

The first outlet outside of Fox where I found a mention of the Van Jones story was *Countdown with Keith Olbermann* on MSNBC. Olbermann claimed that Beck's discussion of Jones as motivated by personal vengeance: Jones was founder and part of a group (Color of Change) that lead the boycott of Beck for calling the president a racist, a boycott that cost Beck a number of sponsors (*Countdown with Keith Olbermann*, 25 August 2009). This exchange continued for several weeks, with

Fox News arguing that Jones was a radical/Communist who wanted to effect radical change in the United States, and Olbermann repeating his counterclaim that Beck's attack on Jones was motivated by the attack on Beck.

On 2 September, however, Fox News unveiled a new charge against Jones: that he used an expletive to refer to Republicans in a public forum, and that he expressed solidarity with Muslims after the 9/11 attack (*Hannity*, 2 September 2009). The following day, Fox reported that Jones signed a letter alleging that the U.S. government may have had advance knowledge of the 9/11 attacks and claimed that Jones was a racist because he said that there was a racial dimension to pollution/environmental issues, namely, that white polluters often targeted poor or minority neighborhoods (*Hannity*, 3 September 2009). Now there were four separate lines of attack on Jones, up from the original one: Jones was a self-avowed Communist, he was racist, he referred to Republicans using expletives, and he was a 9/11 "truther."

Several things began to shift in the story around this point. First, the story became not just about Van Jones *qua* Van Jones, but became about the larger question of the Obama administration. Though Beck linked Jones to a broader progressive movement trying to dramatically change America with the help of the Obama administration from the beginning, the story to subtly shifted to focus on the implications of Jones's appointment for the Obama administration: either Obama's vetting process was broken (because they failed to notice that Jones made these controversial remarks), or Obama knowingly employed radicals. Indeed, after exposing Jones, Fox turned its attention to other so-called czars in the White House with controversial views, making the case that Jones was not an isolated case, but rather part of a larger trend of nonmainstream views inside the Obama administration (*Hannity*, 3 September 2009). Note how this fit nicely with the discussion earlier in the chapter: partisan media outlets use this particular individual story to highlight a larger trend that is indicative of a flaw in the other side. So Obama did not just make a mistake with this one individual; this was part of a broader trend of associating with radicals. The story became about the larger ideology of the Obama administration.

Second, in late August and early September, the story began to filter out into the mainstream media beyond Fox News and MSNBC, with stories appearing on CNN and in major papers, such as the *Washington*

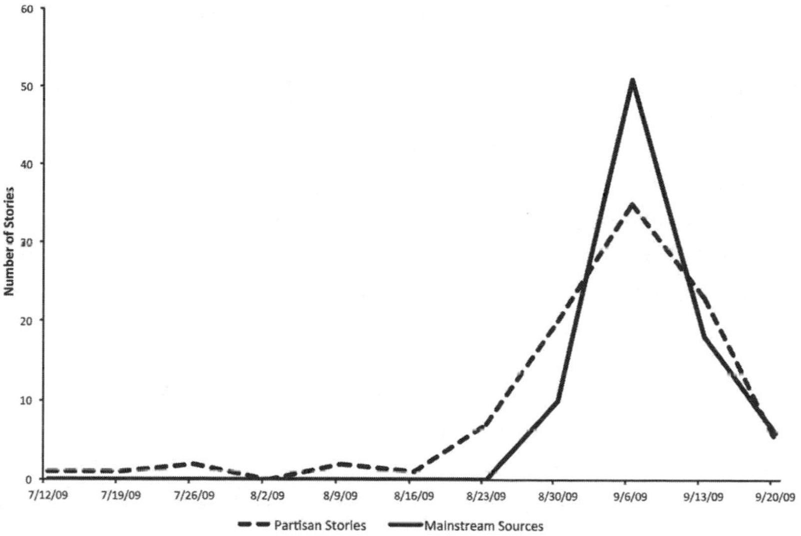

FIGURE 2.1. Number of stories about Van Jones per week in partsian and mainstream Outlets.

Post. Figure 2.1 plots the number of stories (by week) about Van Jones in both partisan and mainstream outlets.[15]

While there were only two mainstream news stories about Jones before late August, the story began to quickly spread after that. As the story spread, so did the allegations against Jones initially promulgated by Fox News and other right-wing outlets. So now, even viewers who never would have watched Fox News—but might have read their local paper—saw the charges against Jones. On 5 September, the *Washington Post* reported on Jones's apology for signing the 9/11 petition, as well as for using expletives to refer to Republicans (Franke-Ruta and Kornblut 2009). As the allegations against Jones spread, there was also increasing pressure on the White House to remove Jones. Republicans in Congress, including Representative Mike Pence of Indiana, called for Jones to resign, and Senator Bond of Missouri called for hearings on Mr. Jones's appointment, as well as the broader question of how policy "czars" were appointed. Such calls led Jones to resign via a written statement over the Labor Day weekend (Broder 2009). The spread of the news story to the mainstream media—and to the talking points of congressional Republicans—seems to have doomed Jones's position within the administration.

But as figure 2.1 also makes clear, Jones's resignation did not end the story. Indeed, the story continued on for several weeks, focusing on a few themes: the issue of "media bias" given that the story began on Fox News and took over a month to spread to the mainstream media and the general issue of "czars" and how much power they have within the Obama administration. Both became important topics on both partisan and mainstream sources. The first is a major theme on partisan media, as I discussed above, and helps to fuel suspicion of the mainstream media among partisan viewers. The second theme—the power of "czars" within the White House—ultimately became the story. Such themes fit within broader right-wing attacks on the president (for his elitism, his support of experts, etc.), and Beck and others used the Van Jones incident to push for a broader investigation into other Obama administration appointees, such as Cass Sunstein (*Glenn Beck*, 22 September 2009).

More generally, this story highlights how the partisan media agenda can bleed over into the mainstream news agenda. What began as a relatively minor news story on Fox spread to the mainstream press and eventually forced a White House staffer to resign. So partisan media, at least in some circumstances, can help to set the nation's agenda. These shows and their talking points have important downstream implications for the nation's politics as a whole; I will return to this point at some length in the concluding chapter. The limitation of this case study, of course, is that I do not know how frequently cases like the Van Jones resignation occur. While there are certainly other examples of partisan news stories that become mainstream news items—such as the ACORN scandal or Shirley Sherrod—it is difficult know exactly how common such items are. In particular, it is difficult to know how frequently partisan media attempt to promulgate a news story that fails to jump to the mainstream press (which is crucial to judging the influence of partisan outlets).[16] Future scholars can take up the more general question of the partisan media agenda's influence on the mainstream press; for my current study, it is enough to know that partisan media outlets can—and do—sometimes shape the broader national talking points.

Summing Up

Looking across both data sources (the sample of days and the case studies), the general pattern is remarkably clear: partisan media outlets give a particular and distinct slant to the day's news and events. They do so in three key ways. First, they slant how they talk about the issues of the day, offering one-sided coverage of political controversies and debates and devoting disproportionate coverage to topics and issues that favor them. Second, they talk about the other side in consistently negative terms, criticizing not only their policy positions but also their motivations for enacting policies, and particular issues are used to illustrate a more systematic pattern of flawed behavior from the other side. These sharp attacks and criticisms of the other party are, unsurprisingly, accompanied by a marked denunciation in most circumstances on bipartisanship and compromise. Finally, with respect to elections, these programs make it clear which candidate viewers should support, not only supporting their own candidate but also denouncing the opposition. In short, across all three areas, partisan news is one-sided; it is the type of news that helps to reinforce a particular political vision of the world. The task now to unpack why and how this type of slanted coverage affects viewers. The next chapter turns to that task.

CHAPTER THREE

Why Do Partisan Media Affect Viewers?

Chapter 2 documented how partisan media slant their coverage of the parties and the issues, explicitly favoring one side of the debate and one party over the other. This should have wide-ranging implications for partisan media's ability to polarize viewers, discourage support for bipartisanship and compromise, and shape how viewers behave in and understand elections. This chapter explains *how* that these effects occur, and I derive a series of hypotheses that can be tested in the subsequent empirical chapters.

Why Do Partisan Media Polarize Attitudes?

Partisan media's biased presentation of the news impacts viewers' attitudes, their willingness to compromise, and their vote choice (and interpretation of elections) because of how it interacts with fundamental tendencies in human cognition. Humans are motivated reasoners (Kunda 1990). We have two broad classes of goals: accuracy goals (the desire to reach the correct conclusion), and directional goals (the desire to reach the preferred conclusion, the one that supports our existing beliefs). Human reasoning relies on both of these, but our directional goals are particularly strong: we process information so that it fits with our existing beliefs, especially on an affectively charged topic like politics. When citizens hear a news story about, say, President Obama, simply on hearing his name, their attitudes and feelings toward him come to the fore, even without any conscious thought (a process known as "hot cognition";

see Lodge and Taber 2005; Morris et al. 2003). These thoughts and feelings about the president then shape how citizens interpret the evidence provided in the story. If the information suggests President Obama is ably handling his job, supporters of the president will uncritically accept the news while his critics will counterargue and challenge it (a process known as "disconfirmation bias"; see Ditto and Lopez 1992). As a result, even balanced sets of arguments can generate attitudinal polarization (Taber and Lodge 2006; Taber, Cann, and Kucsova 2009).

Partisan media programs intensify this motivated reasoning because of their slanted presentation of the news. Consider first how this process occurs when subjects watch like-minded media—that is, pro-attitudinal media that reinforce their existing beliefs, such as when a conservative Republican watches Fox News. Such programs heighten motivated reasoning (and hence polarization) for two reasons. First, these programs broadcast one-sided, pro-attitudinal messages to viewers, which they will uncritically accept (Taber and Lodge 2006). But absent any competing message, this general tendency to accept pro-attitudinal information becomes even stronger: because it lacks a counterargument of any sort, this information (implicitly) seems stronger and even more persuasive (Klayman and Ha 1987; Lodge and Taber 2001; Zaller 1996). Subjects will therefore move in the direction of the evidence and become more extreme (Moscovici and Zavalloni 1969). The type of "echo chamber" environment found in like-minded media will push viewers toward the ideological extremes. Subjects who used to agree or disagree with a policy will now strongly agree or strongly disagree with it, thereby polarizing the electorate.

But the slanted presentation of the news on like-minded partisan media will engender attitudinal polarization for a second reason: these programs powerfully invoke viewers' partisan social identities. Humans naturally perceive the world in terms of in-groups (the group to which they belong) and out-groups (all other groups). As a result of this classification, humans show a marked tendency to prefer members of the in-group to out-group members (Tajfel and Turner 1979). While there are a host of potentially relevant political group identities (Huddy 2001), arguably none is more significant than one's partisan (social) identification, at least in the United States (Greene 1999; Green, Palmquist, and Schickler 2002). Given this, appeals to partisanship should have an especially strong impact on how viewers process the messages from partisan media outlets.

Partisan media's framing of the news primes and activates viewers' partisan identities. These shows frame the news as a struggle between the two major parties (see the discussion in chapter 2), which in turn cues voters that they should understand these issues through the lens of partisanship (Price 1989; Goren, Federico, and Kittleson 2009; Yzerbyt et al. 2006). When such identities are made especially salient, as they are on partisan media, this exacerbates in-group/out-group thinking (Mullen, Brown, and Smith 1992), especially when in-groups are depicted as being in conflict with out-groups (Brewer 1991). So while partisans should generally be susceptible to in-group/out-group thinking in politics (Greene 1999), the depiction of the news on these programs strengthens this tendency.

Priming this sort of salient partisan identity increases viewers' directional goals—it heightens their desire to reach a conclusion in line with their partisanship, thereby strengthening their biases toward attitudinally congenial information. Simply put, cueing partisanship increases its ability to slant how subjects see the world by strengthening the desire to engage in motivated reasoning. This is consistent with work in social psychology demonstrating that priming relevant group identities, such as partisanship, increases attitudinal polarization (Abrams et al. 1990; Lee 2007). So while there is a general tendency toward attitudinal polarization in political settings simply because humans are motivated reasoners, the unique environment of like-minded partisan media—with its one-sided content and partisan primes—should be especially likely to generate attitudinal polarization. This leads me to state my first hypothesis.

<u>The Like-Minded Attitude Hypothesis (H1)</u>: On average, exposure to like-minded partisan media will polarize attitudes (i.e., increase attitudinal extremity).

But what happens when subjects watch crosscutting partisan media that presents them with counterattitudinal messages (for example, when a Democrat sits down to watch Fox News)? Here, subjects' preferences are challenged rather than reinforced. When presented with information running counter to their prior beliefs, subjects will attempt to discredit and counterargue it (Ditto and Lopez 1992; Taber and Lodge 2006; Taber, Cann, and Kucsova 2009). Subjects will believe they have refuted this information, which makes the evidence supporting their own position seem even more persuasive by comparison, pushing them toward greater attitude extremity (Redlawsk 2002; Taber and Lodge 2006). Crosscutting media will therefore increase attitude extremity and polarization: a "boomerang" effect.

The Crosscutting Attitude Hypothesis (H2): On average, exposure to crosscutting political media will polarize attitudes.

Moderators of these Effects

The like-minded and crosscutting attitude hypotheses predict that, on average, partisan media exposure will polarize subjects' attitudes. But not all subjects should polarize equally, because not all subjects are equally well equipped to be motivated reasoners—motivated reasoning takes effort and skill. Citizens with stronger directional goals and more cognitive resources are more likely to demonstrate the biased processing characteristic of motivated reasoners (Taber and Lodge 2006). Here, strong directional goals come from having strong partisan and ideological identities—subjects who are more strongly partisan and ideological have greater incentives to respond to the partisan primes embedded in these cues. Having more cognitive resources translates to having more political knowledge, engagement, interest, and so forth—having more of the skills that help subjects respond to and process political arguments. So more partisan/ideological viewers with more political knowledge, interest, and so forth, will show the greatest tendency to engage in motivated reasoning, and hence be the most likely to polarize in response to partisan media messages.

The Differential Motivation and Ability Hypothesis (H3): Subjects with stronger directional goals and more cognitive resources should be more likely to polarize in response to partisan media messages.

Crosscutting media affords a particular example of this type of differential motivation and ability. Polarization from crosscutting messages stems from counterarguing the messages from these programs, but not all viewers are equally equipped to do this—subjects need to be informed about the issue, and to care deeply about it, to effectively generate these counterarguments (Taber and Lodge 2006). The ability to do this comes from holding strong attitudes. Strong attitudes are ones where the subjects know more about the issue, and hence can more easily generate counterarguments, and the issue is more central and important to them, so they will be more motivated to generate counterarguments (Petty and Krosnick 1995). Strong attitudes therefore help subjects polarize in response to crosscutting media (Pomerantz, Chaiken, and Tordesillas 1995; Taber and Lodge 2006; Zaller 1992).[1]

The Strong Attitudes Hypothesis (H4): Exposure to crosscutting media will especially increase attitude extremity for viewers with strong prior attitudes.

The crosscutting media hypothesis (H2) and the strong attitudes hypothesis (H4) predict that many subjects, especially those who hold strong attitudes, will polarize in response to exposure to crosscutting media. But not *all* subjects will polarize in response to crosscutting media. Theories of persuasion and attitude change argue that persuasion stems the message itself, the receiver of the message, and the sender of the message (O'Keefe 2002). My hypotheses so far depend on the features of the message (the like-minded and crosscutting hypotheses) and the receiver of the message (the differential motivation/ability and strong attitudes hypotheses). But the sender also matters: in particular, her credibility matters. High-credibility sources persuade listeners, low-credibility sources do not and are generally ignored (the *locus classicus* is Hovland and Weiss 1951; for examples in political science, see, among others, Baum and Groeling 2010; Druckman 2001a, 2001b; Kuklinski and Hurley 1994; Lupia and McCubbins 1998).

So *credible* crosscutting sources will persuade listeners, thereby moderating their attitudes. So, for example, if a Democrat watches Fox News, and he finds Fox to be a credible source, he should move in the direction of Fox; that is, he should moderate his opinion and move toward the center of the ideological distribution (consistent with the hopes of deliberative theorists who argue for the moderating effects of exposure to crosscutting voices, see Mutz 2006a).

But which viewers will see crosscutting sources as credible? The answer is not terribly clear, given that much prior work argues that source credibility stems from perceived common interest (Lupia and McCubbins 1998; Kahan, Jenkins-Smith, and Braman 2011).[2] While most viewers do not think crosscutting sources are credible, that belief is not universal: in 2010, 21 percent of Democrats saw Fox News as a credible source, and

13 percent of Republicans saw MSNBC as a credible outlet (Pew Research Center for the People and the Press 2010). For these subjects, I expect to find a moderating effect of crosscutting media exposure.

Why subjects find crosscutting sources to be credible is not especially important for my argument here; the key point is simply that, conditional on finding crosscutting sources to be credible, viewers should moderate their opinions when exposed to them. Future work can determine the roots of these credibility judgments; for now, knowing whether or not they exist is sufficient.

<u>The Source Credibility Hypothesis (H5)</u>: Viewers who perceive crosscutting sources to be credible will moderate their opinions after exposure to them.

What Happens Over Time?

Hypotheses 1 through 5 outline what will happen immediately after exposure to partisan media. But what happens to these effects over time? One enduring concern with media persuasion studies is that such effects rapidly fade away (Druckman and Nelson 2003). But given a motivated reasoning process, there is good reason to suspect that these effects endure, at least in the short term. While citizens use both memory-based and online processing to update their beliefs (Redlawsk 2001), online processing is especially important when relying on affectively laden motivated reasoning processes (Lodge and Taber 2001). So, for example, when citizens watch a partisan media program about gun control, they bring to mind their attitude toward gun control, update it on the spot using the new information in the segment, and then store this updated attitude in long-term memory (Lodge, McGraw, and Stroh 1991). Later on, viewers may not remember the specific arguments from the partisan media host that caused them to update their opinions, but they should remember their overall attitude—the details fade away, but the summary attitude remains (Lodge, Steenbergen, and Brau 1995). Attitudes updated in response to partisan media, then, should not immediately fade away, but should temporarily endure.

<u>The Duration Hypothesis (H6)</u>: The polarizing power of partisan media will endure for several days postexposure.

Relatedly, what happens when subjects are exposed to multiple doses of partisan content over time? This is a particularly important question, given that most viewers who watch partisan outlets do so repeatedly over time: most viewers get a regular dose of partisan media (Pew Research Center for the People and the Press 2010). For the initial exposure, subjects' will respond as I argued above: on seeing the biased content of like-minded media, they will process the arguments in light of their prior beliefs and either polarize or moderate their attitudes. But what happens if they hear a partisan media source talk about the issue again? What if Sean Hannity talks about the importance of tax cuts on Monday, and then again on Tuesday? What is the effect of the second dose of the treatment? There should still be an effect: subjects will still process the message in light of their prior beliefs, and the underlying motivated reasoning process will be the same. But the effect of the second dose will almost necessarily be smaller than the first: subjects polarized or moderated in the first instance, so they have less room to adjust further on subsequent viewings—this is the logic of "pretreatment" effects (Druckman and Leeper 2012). Given this, exposure to partisan media outlets will continue to affect viewers over time, though the marginal effect of each additional exposure will decrease.

The Repetition Hypothesis (H7): Repeated exposures to the treatment will continue to affect subjects' attitudes, though the marginal effect of each additional exposure will decrease.

Not only will partisan media increase attitude polarization, they will also increase attitude *certainty* as well. Attitude certainty is a subject's subjective sense that his attitude is correct; it is the "sense of conviction or validity about one's attitude or opinion" (Gross, Holtz, and Miller 1995, 215). Subjects with certain attitudes "know" their attitudes are the correct ones.[3]

Such increases in attitude certainty are important, because certain attitudes are consequential attitudes. For example, certain attitudes are more stable over time, more resistant to persuasive appeals, and more likely to shape how subjects behave (Tormala and Rucker 2007). Certain attitudes are also given more weight when choosing between candidates in elections (Alvarez 1997; Miller and Peterson 2004). They are the sorts of stable, consequential attitudes long sought by public opinion researchers as being central to democratic theory (Zaller 1992). If partisan media can in fact make subjects more certain of their attitudes, then this has important implications for American politics.

Like-minded media should increase attitude certainty because of the reinforcing content they provide to viewers. Previous work in social psychology argues that subjects become more certain and confident of their beliefs when they encounter reinforcing content. Indeed, studies often manipulate attitude certainty by having subjects read attitude reinforcing material, given that reinforcing content tends to make subjects more convinced that their own attitudes are correct (Tormala and Petty 2002; Tormala and Rucker 2007).

This should be especially true when subjects hear the arguments repeatedly over time. As subjects hear arguments about taxes, or defense spending, or national security repeatedly over time (as they tune in to these shows over days and weeks), they hear the same sorts of like-minded arguments again and again. This sort of repetition increases the persuasiveness and effectiveness of messages (Cacioppo and Petty 1989) and makes subjects more confident in their positions (Druckman and Bolsen 2011; Druckman, Fein, and Leeper 2012). Over-time exposure fosters greater confidence and certainty in one's attitudes.

Likewise, as above, crosscutting media should have a similar effect on increasing attitudinal certainty. Because subjects' are rejecting and counterarguing the crosscutting arguments on these programs, they are implicitly resisting persuasion from these sources. This should increase the certainty with which they hold their attitudes (Tormala and Petty 2002).

The Attitude Certainty Hypothesis (H8): Exposure to partisan media, especially repeated exposure, will increase attitude certainty.

Effects on Viewers' Willingness to Compromise and Support Bipartisanship

Not only does the slanted coverage on partisan media polarize viewers' attitudes, it also shapes how they perceive the other party, and in turn, influences their willingness to compromise and support bipartisanship. Because these programs prime viewers' partisan social identities, and engender (partisan) motivated reasoning, the same types of processes will shape viewers' attitudes in this domain as well.

Consider first what happens when a subject watches like-minded media. Such shows will decrease affect toward the other side for three reasons. First, these shows prime (partisan) group identities, as I argued above. Heightened group identities shape attitudes and emotions, especially attitudes toward the out-group. In particular, viewers should be more likely to feel negatively toward the out-group, and prescribe negative traits and attributes to them (Ray et al. 2008; Klein and Ahluwalia 2005; Iyengar, Sood, and Lelkes 2012). Second, the motivated reasoning processes engendered by these shows makes viewers dislike and distrust the opposition. Because motivated reasoning makes subjects think their own side's arguments are stronger and more persuasive (and the opposing side's arguments as weaker and less persuasive), individuals on the opposing side seem biased, self-serving, and deeply flawed. As a result, affect for them decreases (Pronin, Puccio, and Ross 2002).[4] Finally, because the like-minded media host and the viewer share a common social identity (partisanship), the host's message becomes especially compelling to the audience—the host serves as an in-group cue giver. Messages from in-group members are especially persuasive (Mackie 1986; Mackie, Worth, and Asuncion 1990), so individuals will be more likely to accept these in-group messages.[5] Given that these programs typically vilify the opposing party (as I discussed in chapter 2), this suggests affect for the other side should decrease when subjects are exposed to like-minded partisan media.

But like-minded media should also increase affect for one's own party as well. Like-minded media do criticize and critique the opposing party, but they also support the viewers' party as well. So if a Republican watches Fox News, they should like Democrats less (because Fox portrays them as scheming, dishonest, and so forth), and like Republicans more. Hearing about a liked object should increase the viewers' affect for it. That said, however, because like-minded media spend more time criticizing the opposition than they do supporting their own party (Chalif 2011; Smith and Searles, forthcoming), I expect the effects on opposite-party affect to be larger than the effects on same-party affect.

The Like-Minded Affect Hypothesis (H9): Exposure to like-minded partisan media will decrease viewers' affect for the other party and increase their affect for their own party.

What happens when viewers watch crosscutting media: what does this do for their feelings toward the opposing party? Subjects will again engage in motivated reasoning when they watch crosscutting media and will attempt to counterargue and refute the material presented to them on this program. In so doing, they will come to perceive their own party's arguments as stronger and more persuasive and the other party's as weaker and less compelling. They should come to like the other party less as well; after all, the other party actually believes these specious arguments given on crosscutting media. Refuting the other side's arguments will make viewers like the opposition less (Pronin, Puccio, and Ross 2002).

Crosscutting media also spend time criticizing the viewers' own party: when a Democrat watches Fox News, he not only hears Republican arguments and praise for Republicans (which he counterargues and rebuts), but he also hears criticism of the Democrats and their ideas. This sort of critique coming from the out-group will prime his partisan group identity and lead him to psychologically defend his own party. So after watching crosscutting media, viewers should not only like the other party less—they should like their own party more.

The Crosscutting Affect Hypothesis (H10): Exposure to crosscutting partisan media will decrease viewers' affect for the other party, and increase affect for their own party.

But as above, there will be some viewers who will be inclined to accept rather than counterargue the messages from crosscutting sources—those who find crosscutting sources to be highly credible. Again, while most viewers will not find crosscutting sources to be credible, some viewers will do so. If viewers find these sources to be credible, as I argued above, they will accept the messages from these shows, which here implies that they will like the opposing party more and their own party less.

The Credibility and Affect Hypothesis (H11): For viewers who find crosscutting sources to be credible, exposure to crosscutting media will increase their affect for the opposing party and decrease affect for their own party.

These partisan media programs should not only change how viewers feel about the other party, but they should also have consequences for viewers' willingness to engage with them in the political process. In particular, they should lower levels of trust in the other party, and viewers' willingness to support bipartisan compromise with them. Take the case of trust first. Judgments about trust are implicitly rooted in have some positive assessment of the authorities in question. To trust a party is to believe that they will do what is right for the nation, even absent scrutiny (Levi and Stoker 2000; Miller and Listhaug 1990). So a failure to trust the other party implies a belief that they cannot (or will not) act in the nation's best interest, but rather will act in their own more narrow partisan interest. Because partisan media programs make viewers more suspicious of the opposing side and its leaders (as I argued above), viewers should be less willing to trust the opposing party after exposure to partisan outlets. Further, because distrust is a negative trait, subjects should also be willing to assign it to the other party as an out-group (Ray et al. 2008). Like-minded media remove the positive assessments of the other party that underlie trust, and therefore, should lead viewers to distrust the other side.

This partisan-specific trust, while distinct from the more typical measure of generalized trust in government, still plays an important role in a mass democracy. Trust in government is shaped by trust in the parties (Keele 2005), and in particular, trusting that the opposition party to do what is right (Anderson et al. 2005). One need not like the other party or their policies, but one has to believe they will act in the best interest of the nation (Mutz 2007). Otherwise, the trust that is crucial to actually solving social problems becomes all the more elusive (Hetherington 2005).

<u>The Trust Hypothesis (H12)</u>: Partisan media exposure will make viewers less likely to trust the opposing party.

This same process should likewise lower support for bipartisan compromise with the other party. Bipartisanship rests on the (implicit) idea that both parties have legitimate policy proposals, and the best policies are the ones that combine approaches from Democrats and Republicans (Gutmann and Thompson 2010). Partisan media, however, diminish the belief that the other party offers some legitimate policy solutions. First, once again, the in-group message that the other party's policy positions are deeply flawed will be highly persuasive. Second, priming partisanship should lead viewers to see their party's proposals as stronger and more credible (since they come from the in-group), and likewise to see the opposing party's proposals as being less so (since they come from the out-group). This should lead viewers to be less willing to support the bipartisan approach that involves trading in-group ideas for out-group ones (Shea 2013). Further, the negative emotions about the opposing party (as the out-group) generated by partisan media will also lower support for compromise with them (MacKuen et al. 2010).

The Bipartisanship Hypothesis (H13): Partisan media exposure will make viewers less likely to support bipartisan compromise with the other party.

The logic of the bipartisanship hypothesis also suggests why these programs should have an effect on support for policies attributed to the other party. As I argued above, the priming of partisan group identities on these shows means that individuals will come to prefer policies from their own party (since they come from in-group sources) and will dislike policies from the opposing party (since they come from an out-group source). Given this, after exposure to partisan media, subjects should be less willing to support policies if they are attributed to the opposing party. Note that the key point here is not simply that viewers dislike policies attributed to the other party—that is well known (Rahn 1993; Cohen 2003). The key point here is that holding attribution to the other party constant, viewers should be less likely to support the policy after partisan media exposure.

The Policy Support Hypothesis (H14): Partisan media exposure will make viewers less likely to support policies attributed to the other party.

Electoral Effects

These same theoretical mechanisms explain why partisan media will shape viewers' electoral choices. For example, when subjects watch like-minded partisan media programs, they hear messages that support their candidate and vilify the opposition (see the discussion in chapter 2 about partisan media's coverage of the 2008 election). So watching Fox News in

2008, viewers saw a discussion of Obama's ties to Reverend Wright and ACORN and a discussion of Obama's tax-and-spend liberal tendencies, while also hearing messages supporting McCain and Palin's credentials. Likewise, on MSNBC, one would have seen repeated discussion of Palin's ineptitude and general support for Obama. Such messages reinforce viewers' prior beliefs, so they will tend to accept them without scrutinizing them, consistent with the logic of motivated reasoning. Further, because these messages prime partisan social identities, the message from an in-group like-minded host criticizing an out-group presidential nominee will be an especially persuasive message. This should polarize affect for the candidates and lead viewers to be more likely to support their own party's nominee. Partisan media messages function as "red meat," helping excite viewers' passion for their party's nominee and their antipathy for the other party's candidate, thereby strengthening their commitment to their party and its candidate (much like campaign advertising; see Arceneaux and Huber 2007). Like-minded media acts like a reinforcement mechanism: while party voting is quite high among all voters in the contemporary era (Bartels 2000), like-minded media exposure should exacerbate and strengthen this trend.

I expect crosscutting media exposure to work much as in the other areas discussed above. Watching crosscutting media, viewers see a barrage of rationale explaining why they should support the opposing party candidate. But as before, because subjects are motivated reasoners, this should, if anything, reinforce subjects' desire to support their same-party nominee. As before, subjects implicitly rebut and counter these arguments, and as a result, become even more strongly attached to their same-party nominee, even above and beyond the tendency toward party-line voting.

The Vote Choice Hypothesis (H15) : Exposure to partisan media will increase viewers' support for their party's presidential nominee.

But partisan media should not only affect vote choice; they should also affect how viewers interpret and understand the election. In the aftermath of every election, media and political elites offer a variety of different explanations for why one candidate won the election and what this means for our politics (e.g., does the winner have a mandate, and if so, for what policies?). These interpretations matter for at least two reasons.

First, political leaders use these interpretations as evidence that the public wants them to pursue a particular policy (Hershey 1992; Thomas and Bass 1996). This gives rise to a leader's agenda, and can in fact shape public policy outcomes (Grossback, Peterson, and Stimson 2006). Second, on a more micro level, these interpretations shape voters' views of the winner, his legitimacy, and the legitimacy of the process. If voters supporting the losing candidate think the other candidate won because of fraud, or media bias, or some other illegitimate reason, this will negatively influence how they perceive the winning candidate, his policies, and indeed, the entire political system (Mutz 2006b). How voters understand an election, therefore, has potentially far-reaching consequences for attitudes toward the political system more generally.

The explanations constructed by electoral "losers"—those whose party lost the election—are particularly important. Electoral winners tend to interpret their victory as evidence of their candidate's superior policies, campaign strategy, and so forth (Mutz 2006b). But the explanations by losers, especially those constructed by partisan media, are potentially more consequential, because they have the potential to delegitimize the winner. Delegitimizing explanations explain the loss not in terms of candidate skill or circumstances, but rather in terms of factors like strategy ("we had the right message, we just ran the wrong ads"), media bias ("the media wanted the other guy to win, so they tilted coverage in his favor"), vote fraud ("the other side had to cheat to win"), and so forth (for more discussion of these sorts of rationales, see Mutz 2006b). These delegitimizing explanations claim that our side *should* have won, but in effect was cheated out of the win. For example, as I discussed above with respect to the 2008 election, Fox News attributed Obama's victory not just to Bush's unpopularity and the economic collapse, but also to factors like media bias and vote fraud from groups like ACORN. So Republicans who watched Fox in 2008 would have been more likely to attribute Obama's victory to these sorts of delegitimizing factors. More generally, however, I expect that electoral losers who watch like-minded media will be more likely to attribute their loss to delegitimizing factors.[6]

<u>The Election Interpretation Hypothesis (H16)</u>: Electoral losers who watch like-minded media will be more likely to attribute their side's loss to delegitimizing factors.

Summarizing the Theoretical Predictions

Throughout this chapter, I have explained how the unique structure and content of partisan media programs interact with human's tendency to be motivated reasoners to polarize attitudes, decrease subjects' willingness to compromise and support bipartisanship, and shape how viewers vote in and understand elections. In short, I offer a variety of different predictions that help to answer three empirical questions I set out in chapter 1: (1) can partisan media polarize, (2) can they shape subjects willingness to compromise and support bipartisanship, and (3) can they shape viewers' vote choice and understanding of elections? Table 3.1 offers a summary of the predictions, how they line up with these three broad questions, and the chapter where I test each of these hypotheses.

As the reader will note, each of the questions lines up with a chapter: so chapter 4 tackles the first question about polarization, chapter 5 tackles the second question about support for bipartisanship, and chapter 6 tackles the third question about electoral effects. These chapters allow me to test the empirical predictions I laid out in this chapter, so I now turn to that task.

TABLE 3.1. **Summary of theoretical predictions, organized by question and chapter.**

Hypothesis name (number)	Statement of hypothesis	Chapter
Do partisan media polarize viewers' attitudes?		
Like-minded attitude hypothesis (H1)	On average, exposure to like-minded partisan media will polarize attitudes (i.e., increase attitudinal extremity).	4
Crosscutting attitude hypothesis (H2)	On average, exposure to crosscutting political media will polarize attitudes.	4
Differential motivation and ability hypothesis (H5)	Subjects with stronger directional goals and more cognitive resources should be more likely to polarize in response to partisan media messages.	4
Strong attitudes hypothesis (H4)	Exposure to crosscutting media will especially increase attitude extremity for viewers with strong prior attitudes.	4
Source credibility hypothesis (H5)	Viewers who perceive crosscutting sources to be credible will moderate their opinions after exposure to them.	4
Duration hypothesis (H6)	The polarizing power of partisan media will endure for several days postexposure.	4
Repetition hypothesis (H7)	Repeated exposures to the treatment will continue to affect subjects' attitudes, though the marginal effect of each additional exposure will shrink.	4
Attitude certainty hypothesis (H8)	Exposure to partisan media, especially repeated exposure, will increase attitude certainty.	
Do partisan media decrease viewers' willingness to support bipartisanship and compromise?		
Like-minded affect hypothesis (H9)	Exposure to like-minded partisan media will decrease viewers' affect for the other party and increase their affect for their own party.	5
Crosscutting affect hypothesis (H10)	Exposure to crosscutting partisan media will decrease viewers' affect for the other party and increase affect for one's own party.	5
Credibility and affect hypothesis (H11)	For viewers that find crosscutting sources to be credible, exposure to crosscutting media will increase their affect for the opposing party and decrease affect for their own party.	5
Trust hypothesis (H12)	Partisan media exposure will make viewers less likely to trust the opposing party.	5
Bipartisanship hypothesis (H13)	Partisan media exposure will make viewers less likely to support bipartisan compromise with the other party.	5
Policy support hypothesis (H14)	Partisan media exposure will make viewers less likely to support policies attributed to the other party.	5
Do partisan media shape viewers' choices in and understanding of elections?		
Vote choice hypothesis (H15)	Exposure to partisan media will increase viewers' support for their party's presidential nominee.	6
Election interpretation hypothesis (H16)	Electoral losers who watch like-minded media will be more likely to attribute their side's loss to delegitimizing factors.	6

CHAPTER FOUR

Can Partisan Media Polarize?

The next few chapters take up the empirical questions I outlined in chapter 1 and offer a framework for understanding the consequences of the growth of partisan media. This chapter begins by tackling the first question I raised in chapter 1: can partisan media polarize their audience? There is certainly evidence that those who prefer partisan media hold more extreme issue positions (Jamieson and Cappella 2008; Stroud 2010; see also table 1.1). But as I explained in chapter 1, actually demonstrating that partisan media can polarize viewers is quite difficult. Does the relationship between preference extremity and partisan media consumption reflect a treatment effect (partisan media polarizing viewers' attitudes), or instead, is it only a selection effect (individuals with more extreme attitudes prefer partisan content)? With observational data, differentiating these two outcomes is extremely difficult.

In this chapter I take up this empirical puzzle and try to determine whether partisan media polarize their audience. To do so, I rely on a series of original experiments. Experiments are well suited to my purposes here because they allow me to separate out treatment effects from selection effects. Because exposure to partisan media is randomly assigned, I know that viewers' characteristics will be uncorrelated with treatment assignment. Given this, I can more accurately estimate the effects of partisan media exposure on viewers' attitudes.

This experimental approach allows me to test the hypotheses discussed in chapter 3 about attitudinal polarization and attitude certainty: specifically, the like-minded, crosscutting, strong attitudes, credibility, differential motivation and ability, duration, repetition, and attitude certainty hypotheses (H1–H8; see table 3.1 for a summary). My tests of these hypotheses yield four important, substantive conclusions about the power of partisan media to shape viewers' attitudes. First, I demonstrate that partisan media do polarize viewers, particularly when subjects watch like-minded media. I also demonstrate that when subjects watch crosscutting media, on average, there is no effect. But this is because crosscutting media polarize some subjects (those with strong prior attitudes), and depolarize others (those who find crosscutting media to be highly credible), highlighting the importance of accounting for moderating variables. Second, I use novel experiment techniques to explore which viewers are most affected by these treatments. I show that the largest effects are concentrated among those who regularly watch partisan media. These viewers come to the experiment somewhat more extreme already, but then watching partisan media makes them *even more* extreme. Thus, partisan media polarize the electorate not by making moderates into extremists but by moving those already somewhat extreme further toward the ideological poles. Third, I show that the polarizing effects of partisan media endure, at least for several days postexposure. While a typical concern with media exposure experiments is that the effects are transitory and ephemeral, my results show that partisan media effects are more stable. Finally, I demonstrate that like-minded media also make subjects more certain that their beliefs are correct, increasing attitudinal certainty. So not only do subjects become more extreme, they become more convinced that their beliefs are the correct ones.

Experimental Design

To test my hypotheses, I conducted a series of original experiments. All of the experiments in this chapter follow one of two basic protocols. In study 1, subjects were recruited to take a study about how individuals learn about politics from the news in the decision-making laboratory of a private urban university. After reading some basic instructions, subjects completed a pretest questionnaire to measure their baseline attitudes and opinions. They then completed a brief distraction task (a series of items from an IQ test), watched the stimulus (see below), and completed the posttest battery of attitudinal items. Experiment 1 therefore allowed me to measure pretest attitudes and attitudinal strength, which is crucial to testing the attitude strength hypothesis in particular. A pre/post design also allowed me to directly measure attitude change in response to the stimulus, so I could know exactly how much more polarized subjects became as a result of watching partisan media.

In the remaining studies, subjects were recruited online to participate in a short, posttest-only design. They began by answering a few background items, then were exposed to the stimulus, and finally complete the posttest attitudinal assessment. While the pre/post design used in experiment 1 has the advantage that one can measure pretest variables and directly measure within-person change, it has the disadvantage that subjects might remember their pretest answers when completing the posttest, even with a distracter task in place. Using both the pre/post and posttest only designs ensures my design does not overly influence my results.

In all experiments, subjects were exposed to the same type of stimulus: a series of video clips from like-minded, crosscutting, or neutral partisan media programs (treatment assignment was held constant for each subject in each experiment). These video clips came from actual news programs and covered issues discussed during the first eighteen months of the Obama presidency. To ensure that the results did not hinge on a particular issue, each experiment used a slightly different mix of issues. I selected the issues by reading program summaries and transcripts from the leading partisan media shows to identify instances where both right-wing and left-wing shows, as well as a more neutral, mainstream source, discussed the same issue.

Within this constraint, I selected moderately salient issues: the Afghanistan surge, whether terrorism suspects should be tried in military or civilian court, the Arizona immigration law, and so forth (see table 4.1 for a list of the issues used in each experiment). These types of moderately salient issues are the types of issues necessary for testing the effects of partisan media outlets on political attitudes (see the discussion in Bartels 1993). Highly salient issues would be less appropriate as experimental stimuli: these topics have been covered so exhaustively in the news media that subjects will have already absorbed any potential effect of partisan media. For example, if I used a stimulus about abortion policy or health care reform or gun control, it is likely that I would have found null effects of partisan media. But is this because the treatment effect is truly zero, or is it because subjects have already absorbed most of the effects of partisan media (i.e., a pretreatment effect, see Druckman and Leeper 2012)? It is not possible to say. On the other hand, if I used obscure issues not connected to any larger debates in American politics, subjects would have likely been pushed around too easily by the stimuli, and hence I would overestimate the effects of partisan media on viewers' attitudes and behaviors. By using middle salience issues connected to larger debates in American politics, I have issues where subjects might be expected to hold some attitudes, but those attitudes are still liable enough to be shaped by a brief video stimulus. In future work, scholars can explore how the salience of the issue shapes the effects of partisan media, but for now, I focus on these middle salience issues as reasonable tests of my underlying theory.

My procedure for selecting issues does impose a constraint on the number and types of issues that can be included in my experiments. As I discussed in chapter 2, these programs typically cover different sets of issues, so there are not many issues where left-wing, right-wing, and mainstream news outlets all discuss the same issue. While true, it is crucial to hold the issues constant to identify the effects of slant itself. If I exposed subjects to stimuli where the two sides talked about different issues, the "treatment" is unclear. While it does narrow the scope of my study, I accept that limitation in order to more precisely estimate the causal quantity of interest: how does the slanted presentation of the news affect subjects' attitudes? Without this type of a design, that question is simply not answerable.

I selected like-minded, crosscutting, and neutral sources using the criteria discussed in chapter 1. I used shows from Fox News and MSNBC as the specific stimuli for right-wing and left-wing shows, respectively. For Democrats shows from MSNBC were the like-minded segments, and shows from Fox News were the crosscutting stimuli; for Republicans, Fox News segments filled the like-minded role, and those from MSNBC were crosscutting.[1] To select a neutral news source, I turned to *PBS News Hour*, which has been shown to be one of the most politically balanced shows on TV (Groseclose and Milyo 2005). The segments used were broadcast; the transcripts are provided in the online appendix.[2]

All experiment subjects heard information about the same issue(s); what differed was the partisan bias of the source. My manipulations, then, estimate the effects exposing subjects to partisan media (with a like-minded or crosscutting message), relative to a control baseline of neutral media (which provides information without any particular partisan bias). An alternative design would use a true apolitical control segment (i.e., a news story about popular movies or some other nonpolitical topic) and then measure effects relative to this baseline. But this design comes at a cost. Here, the difference between treatment and control would contain two differences: the difference in partisan slant as well as the fact that the subjects in the control group would not have learned anything about the issue.[3] This complicates the interpretation of this design, so I opted for the simpler one described above. Happily, however, this choice did not affect my results. In the online appendix, I discuss an additional experiment I conducted where I included an apolitical control condition, and the results replicated my findings below, which should reassure readers that my experimental design did not drive my results.

To ensure that subjects could detect the differences in partisan bias across sources, each experiment included a manipulation check item asking subjects to assess the partisan tilt of the segments they watched. In every experiment, subjects had no difficulty discerning the slant of the sources (see the data appendix), supporting my claim that it is in fact the partisan biases that drive the results below. Given that these were real-world clips (and not manufactured stories), however, there may be some unmeasured difference between the sources that could affect the results in some manner. I used real-world clips to gain greater verisimilitude, even at the expense of having less control over the treatment stimuli. But to ensure that this decision did not bias my results, I conducted an additional experiment where I used manufactured newspaper editorials as the treatment stimuli. Here, I gained greater control over content (and more internal validity) at the expense of realism (and external validity). The results from this follow-up experiment replicated the main findings discussed here, which should bolster the reader's confidence in the results I report below. For the full details of this experiment, see the online appendix.

The subject pools for these experiments came from two sources: some subjects were recruited from the decision-making laboratory of a private urban university (experiment 1); the rest came from an online sample pool (experiments 2–5).[4] To be clear, neither one was a probability sample, so I cannot claim that the results generalize to the broader U.S. population (at least in some facile way). Generalizing to the entire United States population, however, is not the goal in this analysis. To the extent that I am interested in drawing broader inferences, it is drawing inferences about the population of partisan media consumers, rather than the nation as a whole (Druckman and Kam 2011). The general demographics of partisan media consumers can be seen in table 1.1 (see also Stroud

2011; Morris 2005), and the demographic breakdowns of my samples are given in the data appendix. Generally speaking, there are two areas where my samples diverge from the partisan media audience: my samples are decidedly younger and more likely to be Democrats. In other work, I have controlled for age in my analyses, and doing so does not change the substantive findings (see Levendusky 2012a, 2012b). I have also looked for differential partisan effects and generally not found any, though future work with larger samples will be needed to definitively rule out this possibility. That said, however, my results are strikingly consistent across two quite different sample pools. This is confirmation, at a minimum, that my results do not hinge on the use of any particular nonrandom sample. But an important topic for future work will be to replicate these and related findings on broader samples more representative of the entire population of partisan media users.

That still does not necessarily eliminate the broader concerns about external validity, however. No experiment—whether in a lab, embedded in a survey, or in the field—necessarily generalizes to the "real world." But two features of my experimental design (described below) help on this front. First, I conducted a series of experiments that all replicated the same basic findings, suggesting that this is a consistent pattern of media effects (at least in controlled settings). Second, in experiment 3 below, I drew on some novel experimental techniques to directly comment on the generalizability of my findings to real-world settings, at least in one respect (by examining how these effects differ for those who watch partisan media programs in the real world). Further, even if my results did not generalize in any straightforward way, they still speak to the underlying mechanisms through which partisan media change voters' attitudes, and that finding in and of itself is intrinsically valuable (Berkowitz and Donnerstein 1982; Carlsmith, Ellsworth, and Aronson 1989; Anderson and Bushman 1997). Ultimately, however, external validity can only be established by replicating across different settings and environments (McDermott 2011; Mutz 2011), so more work will be needed to see how these results hold up in other contexts. But my results present a crucial baseline for future work.

Plan for the Experiments

To test my hypotheses about the effects of partisan media on attitude polarization and attitude certainty, I conducted five original experiments.

The experiments, the hypotheses they test, the issues they discuss, their subject pools, and the number of waves in each study are given in table 4.1 below.

My analysis begins with experiment 1, which tested my baseline expectations about like-minded and crosscutting media: can either like-minded or crosscutting media polarize viewers? I move on with experiment 2, which tested the credibility hypothesis: when subjects watch crosscutting media, do their beliefs about the credibility of those outlets matter?

Experiment 3 tested the differential motivation and ability hypothesis. Because motivated reasoning drives the effects of partisan media, the most motivated and informed viewers should show the most marked degree of polarization. I explained which viewers should be most strongly affected by these programs (because of their differential motivation and ability), and then designed an experiment to test this effect.

Experiment 4 asked how long these effects endure. Experiments 1–3 followed the typical pattern in political science and related disciplines: they administered the dependent variable immediately after the stimulus. These experiments, therefore, can only show if the treatment has an immediate effect on attitude extremity. But what happens several days

TABLE 4.1. **Description of the experiments used in chapter 4.**

Experiment	Hypotheses being tested	Design	Subject pool	Study waves	Issues discussed
Experiment 1	Like-minded hypothesis Crosscutting hypothesis Attitude strength hypothesis	Pretest and Posttest	On-campus laboratory	1	Prosecuting Bush administration officials for torture; Afghanistan surge; cap and trade policy; trials for terrorism suspects
Experiment 2	Source credibility hypothesis	Posttest	Online panel	1	Trials for terrorism suspects
Experiment 3	Differential motivation and ability hypothesis	Posttest	Online panel	1	Trials for terrorism suspects
Experiment 4	Duration hypothesis	Posttest	Online panel	2	Arizona immigration law
Experiment 5	Repetition hypothesis Attitude certainty hypothesis	Posttest	Online panel	2	Ayotte amendment

later? Can the effects of partisan media still be detected? The duration hypothesis says they can: because of how subjects update their beliefs, these effects should endure several days post exposure. Experiment 4 tested this hypothesis to examine if partisan media shows are simply blips that fade away right after the treatment, or rather if they remain with subjects after they leave the lab.

Finally, experiment 5 examined the effects of repetition. Experiments 1–4 only administered the treatment at one point in time.[5] Yet this is a slightly unrealistic design: few subjects watch partisan media only once; if those choose to watch it, they typically watch it quite regularly (Pew Research Center for the People and the Press 2010). In experiment 5, I examined what happens when subjects receive multiple doses of the experimental stimuli. Does hearing the stimulus multiple times generate a larger treatment effect? And further, does that reinforcement make them more certain of their attitudes? The repetition and certainty hypotheses argue that the answer to both questions is yes: over-time exposure should yield increased extremity, though the marginal impact of each additional exposure should decrease (repetition hypothesis), and repeated stimuli should increase attitude certainty (certainty hypothesis). Together, these experiments allowed me to unpack how partisan media shape respondents' attitudes. For more details on the experiments, the breakdown of their samples, and so forth, see the data appendix.

Data and Analyses

Given my hypotheses, I measured attitude polarization using the magnitude of a respondent's attitude, with larger magnitude indicating greater polarization (i.e., respondents are more polarized when they "strongly agree" with a policy versus when they only "agree" with it). In each posttest, I included items measuring respondents' attitudes on the issues discussed in the stimulus. In all of the experiments below, the results presented are an index of these items; the specific items are given in the data appendix. The index is scaled in these analyses to run from [−1,1]; I do this to make it easier to understand the effect sizes across experiments. In the analyses, I present my findings using simple tables and graphs. This should make the results more comprehensible for readers less familiar with statistical analyses.[6]

There is an important limitation to note about these analyses, however. The items I used tap respondents' attitudes toward the specific issues discussed in the partisan media segments, so the dependent variable measures changes toward the particular issues discussed on the show. So, for example, if the treatment stimulus discussed the Afghanistan surge, then the dependent variable measures attitudes toward the Afghanistan surge. Given the theoretical framework above, this is where I would expect to find any attitudinal changes; I leave it for future work to determine if these sorts of partisan media programs would change global evaluations such as liberal–conservative self-identification.[7]

The results below show my analysis of folded versions of the attitude items, so that higher values indicate stronger agreement with a particular party's position (i.e., Democrats with higher scores take more liberal positions, and Republicans with higher scores take more conservative positions). This folding assumes that the process is equivalent across parties (e.g., that the mechanisms work the same way for Democrats and Republicans). I enforced this constraint here because a more flexible model (where the effect differed by party) found no significant differences by party (see the online appendix for more details and results). I leave it to future work to determine if there are important differences by party, as that will require significantly larger samples than the ones I have here. That said, even if there are party differences, these pooled results still present a theoretically and empirically important baseline.

I begin my analysis here with the data from experiment 1. If the like-minded and crosscutting hypotheses are correct, I should find that subjects exposed to either like-minded or crosscutting partisan media have more extreme attitudes (relative to those in the neutral news condition).

Figure 4.1 shows the change in attitude extremity (posttest minus pretest) for subjects assigned to the control (neutral news), like-minded, and crosscutting conditions. So this graph shows how much more extreme (positive values) or more moderate (negative values) subjects became after watching the treatment. To know if like-minded and crosscutting treatment have significant effects, then, all I have to do is compare the like-minded and crosscutting results to the control condition results.

The figure shows that subjects in the neutral news condition became very slightly more moderate after watching the treatment. But subjects assigned to watch like-minded media became noticeably more extreme: 0.14 units on the [−1,1] scale, a difference that is highly statistically significant (see Levendusky 2012a for the specific statistical results). Substantively, this sized effect translates into moving a subject approxi-

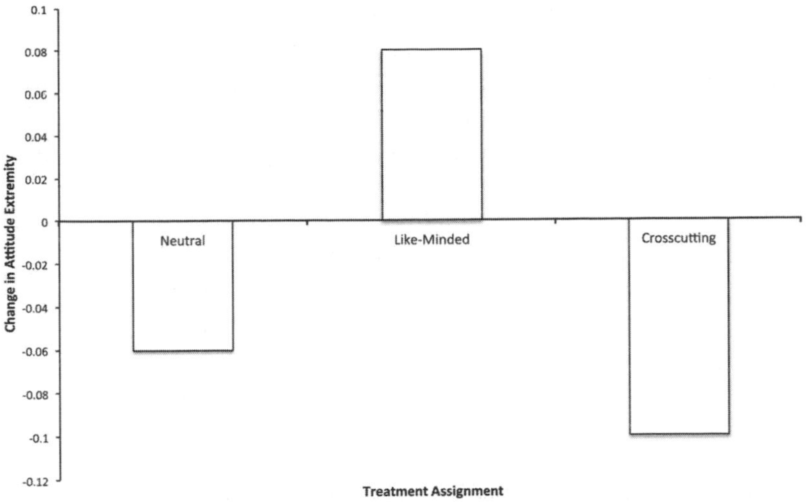

FIGURE 4.1. Effects of partisan media on attitude extremity, experiment 1. The y axis shows pretest or posttest changes in issue position extremity. Values above 0 indicate subjects became more extreme over time; those below 0 indicate becoming less extreme (attitudes are measured on a [−1,1] scale). The three bars show the average effect by treatment condition: subjects in the like-minded condition became more extreme posttreatment; all other subjects became less extreme.

mately half of a scale position on a standard seven-point Likert scale (so moving someone half the distance between "agree" and "strongly agree" with a policy). This might sound like a rather minor change, but it is important to recall that the treatment is only a brief video stimulus, so even a rather modest attitudinal change is an impressive finding. Even a short exposure to partisan media can shape viewers' attitudes.

Because experiment 1 is a pre/post design, I can also examine how many subjects become more extreme pretest to posttest, and how that varies by treatment condition. Subjects in the like-minded condition were 43 percent more likely to hold more extreme attitudes after watching the treatment (33 percent of subjects became more extreme, versus only 23 percent of neutral news subjects and 21 percent of crosscutting subjects). Similarly, subjects in the like-minded condition were 44 percent less likely to moderate their opinions after watching the treatment (9 percent of subjects in the like-minded condition moderate, versus 16 percent of subjects in the neutral news condition and 20 percent in the crosscutting media condition). So subjects in the like-minded condition were more likely to extremify their attitudes and less likely to moderate them, posttreatment, reinforcing the message that like-minded treatment polarizes attitudes. Because subjects assigned to the like-minded condition hear their own beliefs repeated back at them, and they are motivated reasoners, they come to hold more extreme opinions. These results strongly support the like-minded hypothesis: like-minded media makes subjects more extreme.[8]

Figure 4.1 shows, however, that on average, crosscutting media have no effect. There is almost no change in attitudes as a result of the crosscutting stimulus, contrary to the predictions of the crosscutting hypothesis. While crosscutting media may not have an aggregate effect, perhaps it does have an effect for a subset of viewers: those who have strong attitudes. As the strong attitudes hypothesis argues, crosscutting media should only polarize attitudes for subjects who have "strong" attitudes before the stimulus—these are the subjects who can effectively counterargue the stimuli and polarize their attitudes. To test this hypothesis, I broke out the data on crosscutting media from figure 4.1 by attitude strength, and compared two different groups: those with and without strong attitudes.[9]

The results, shown in figure 4.2, support the attitude strength hypothesis. As in figure 4.1, there is a small moderating effect of crosscut-

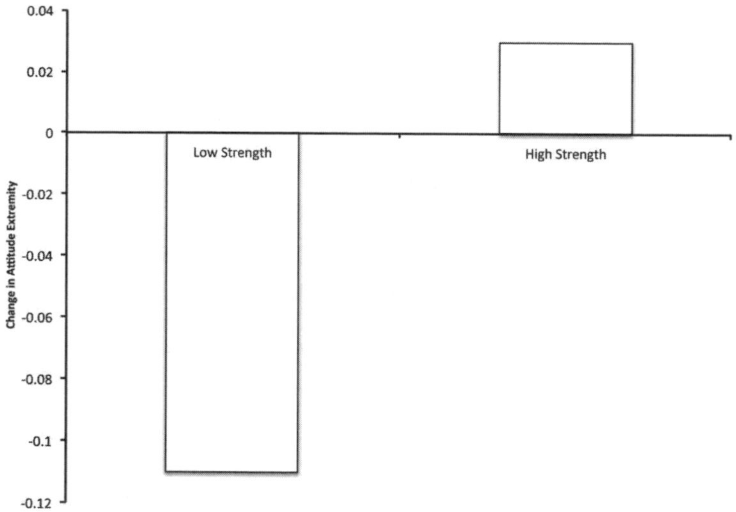

FIGURE 4.2. The moderating role of attitude strength on crosscutting media exposure, experiment 1. Subjects here are subdivided into those who have low or high attitude strength; high-strength subjects become more extreme; low-strength subjects become less extreme.

ting media for those with weak attitudes. But those with strong attitudes become more extreme. For those with strong attitudes—those who can counterargue and rebut the claims made on crosscutting media—polarization ensues, consistent with my theoretical argument in chapter 3 (again, the effect for strong attitudes is statistically significant, while the effect for weak attitudes is not). While the effect is more modest than the effect for like-minded media, this does underline the importance of attitude strength for how subjects process partisan media messages.[10]

This finding also underlines an important point about my underlying theoretical mechanism: motivated reasoning. As I argued in chapter 3, motivated reasoning takes effort, and not all subjects are willing to expend this effort (Taber and Lodge 2006). This is especially true for counterarguing crosscutting messages: only subjects with high levels of motivation and ability—skills generated by holding strong attitudes on a topic—will counterargue against crosscutting messages and polarize. This underlines the importance of accounting for these types of moderating effects to fully understand how partisan media shape viewers' attitudes.

Does Credibility Matter?

Experiment 2 tested the credibility hypothesis: crosscutting media will moderate viewers' attitudes, but only if they perceive them as credible.[11] Figure 4.3 shows the relationships using the data from experiment 2. Experiment 2 (and subsequent experiments in this chapter) were all posttest only designs, so the figures show the posttest attitude extremity (rather than the pretest to posttest change, as in figures 4.1 and 4.2).

When subjects thought media outlets were of low credibility, there was little effect of any type of media. But when sources were seen as highly credible, I found very different effects, particularly for crosscutting media—subjects assigned to the crosscutting media condition who found crosscutting sources to be credible became much more moderate. So crosscutting sources do moderate, but only for those who find them to be credible. As I argued in chapter 3, the messenger—and not just the message—matters.

But the limitation of this finding is that the individuals who want to watch crosscutting media are not a random subset of viewers. The results in figure 4.3 are not simply due to weak partisanship—it is *not* simply the case that those who think crosscutting sources are credible are weak

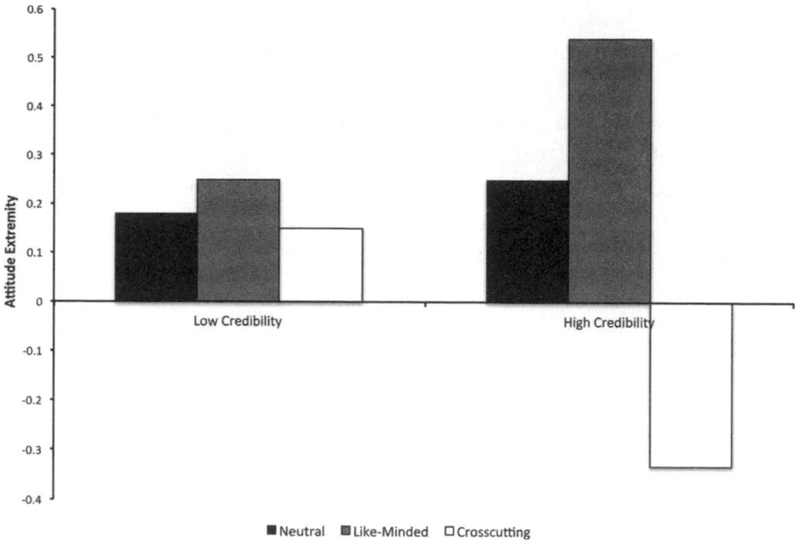

FIGURE 4.3. Source credibility effects for crosscutting media, experiment 2. The *y* axis shows posttest attitude extremity (measured on a [−1,1] scale). Subjects in the left group are assigned to watch programs they perceive to be low credibility; those in the right are assigned shows they perceive to have a high credibility. The shading corresponds to the assigned treatment groups.

partisans. Rather, credibility is a separate factor. It is outside the scope of this project to determine why some viewers see crosscutting sources as credible, but it is an important topic for future research.[12] But for my purposes here, the important finding is that when subjects find crosscutting media to be credible, it moderates their attitudes, moving them away from the poles and toward the center.

Which Viewers Become More Polarized?

Experiments 1 and 2 established some baseline findings about the effects of like-minded and crosscutting partisan media. But one concern with these sorts of experiments is that subjects were assigned to watch stimuli they might never watch in the real world. As I explained in chapter 3, the effects of my experiments might be unevenly distributed throughout the population; some subjects might be more strongly affected by the treatments than others. In particular, I argued that subjects who have higher levels of motivation and cognitive skills would be more likely to polarize in response to partisan media messages (the differential motivation and ability hypothesis).

But which citizens will have this greater motivation and cognitive skills? There are many different ways of operationalizing this hypothesis, but those who regularly watch like-minded partisan media programs certainly have both stronger motivation and more cognitive resources. Like-minded media viewers are more strongly partisan and ideological, and hence have greater incentives to react strongly to the partisan framing of these programs. Further, these subjects also possess more of the cognitive skills needed to process these sorts of messages: they are more politically engaged, better informed, more active in politics, and so forth (Baum and Groeling 2010; Jamieson and Cappella 2008; Stroud 2011). Citizens who choose to watch like-minded programs will therefore be more likely to engage in motivated reasoning, and hence will be more likely to polarize in response to like-minded content. Put slightly differently, like-minded media should primarily polarize those who *want* to watch it.

In contrast, I expect those who prefer crosscutting media to become less polarized in response to crosscutting messages. These individuals are quite out of step with their parties, and are more likely to defect from them and feel psychologically closer to the opposing party—the desire to consume crosscutting media signals that they are "odd" partisans (Holbert, Garrett, and Gleason 2010). They therefore have more motivation to respond to the crosscutting cues. As a result, I expect them to move toward the crosscutting source's position, and thereby hold more moderate (less polarized) attitudes. Subjects' reactions to other types of programs (i.e., how those who prefer like-minded media will respond to crosscutting media) are less clear, and I correspondingly have no ex ante directional expectations in these cases. Here, my test of the differential motivation and ability hypothesis is really a test of viewers' preferences: like-minded media should polarize those who want to watch them, and crosscutting media should moderate those who want to watch those outlets.

I designed experiment 3 to test this expectation. Experiment 3 used a technique from the biomedical literature—the patient preference trial (Torgerson and Sibbald 1998)—to address this issue. In the pretest, I first solicited subjects' preferred treatment. I then randomly assigned subjects to treatment conditions as in the experiments described above. But because I knew subjects' preferred treatment, I could assess whether the treatment was more effective for subjects who preferred to receive that treatment, a "preference effect" in the language of biostatistics (Rucker 1989). This allowed me to isolate the effect on those subjects who would actually watch partisan media, moving me closer to the real-world quantity of interest.

To solicit subjects' preferred treatment, I asked: "In today's media marketplace, there are many different kinds of networks with different kinds of news shows that people might like to watch. For example, some people might like to watch a show from PBS, another might like to watch a show from Fox News. If you had to pick, which of the following types of news show would you most like to watch?" The response options were: "A show from PBS like *The News Hour*"; "A show from Fox News like *The O'Reilly Factor*"; "A show from MSNBC like *Countdown with Keith Olbermann*." Using this item, I could classify subjects into preferring like-minded, crosscutting, or neutral media. Another possibility would be to ask subjects whether they prefer media that reinforces their prior beliefs (like-minded), media that cuts against their prior beliefs (crosscutting), or media without any political bias (neutral media). When the item is phrased this way, however, even many subjects who consume a good deal of like-minded media reported strongly favoring neutral, objective media (Pew Research Center for the People and the Press 2010), suggesting that subjects are signaling something about how they view themselves and what they are "supposed" to prefer, rather than their actual preferences. Asking about their choices over networks and shows was a more direct measure of their underlying preferences that should be less subject to this sort of bias.[13]

There were two important questions remaining about this preference measure, however. First, does it validly measure actual viewing habits? While most respondents preferred to watch neutral news (50 percent), many others preferred more partisan sources: 32 percent wanted to watch like-minded news and 18 percent preferred crosscutting news. To verify that this measure did in fact correspond to actual viewing preferences, I conducted a follow-up survey where I asked subjects about their self-reported TV viewing habits and whether they preferred like-minded, neutral, or crosscutting media content. If these preferences actually validly estimate actual viewing habits, then they should strongly predict actual (self-reported) TV news consumption. And they did: subjects who preferred like-minded media actually watched more like-minded media, and the same relationship held for those who preferred and viewed crosscutting media. For example, 48 percent of those who preferred like-minded media watched it daily, versus only 5 percent for those who preferred another type of media. On average, those who preferred like-minded media watched it at least weekly, versus only a few times of year for those who preferred other types of media; similar patterns hold for crosscutting media.

Second, do those who preferred watching partisan media actually have the differential levels of motivation and ability that I argue they do? Recall that the underlying theoretical mechanism of interest is that subjects who watch like-minded media will be more likely to polarize, because they are more motivated and have the ability to engage in the biased processing of arguments characteristic of motivated reasoners; subjects who watch crosscutting media will be less likely to polarize, being less motivated and lacking the ability to engage. In that same follow-up survey, I asked subjects for the partisanship, as well as their assessments of the political parties, to measure their motivation to engage in motivated reasoning. Those who preferred like-minded media will be stronger partisans and will have more positive assessments of their own party and more negative assessments of the opposite party; subjects who preferred crosscutting media will be weaker partisans with negative assessments of their own party and positive assessments of the opposing party. I also measured ability by examining political activity, given that it is extremely strongly predicted by the components of ability, like interest, engagement, and so forth (Verba, Schlozman, and Brady 1995). Again, I expected those who preferred like-minded media to have higher levels of engagement and those who preferred crosscutting media to have lower levels.

Table 4.2 shows the results; they are exactly what I expected. Those who preferred like-minded partisan media were more likely to be strong partisans, and they had more polarized evaluations of the political parties as well as President Obama; the reverse is true for those who preferred crosscutting media. For example, those who preferred like-minded media were 19 percent more likely to be strong partisans and 16 percent more likely to turn out and vote in a primary election (in both cases, relative to those who did not consume partisan media). This is strong evidence in support of the differential motivation of partisan media consumers. Similarly, those who preferred like-minded media were also differentially politically involved, being more likely to report having voted in a primary election or having engaged in any sort of cam-

TABLE 4.2. **Partisan media, attitude extremity, and participation.**

	Strength of party ID	Same-party feeling thermometer	Other-party feeling thermometer	Obama approval	Primary turnout	Number of campaign activities
Prefer like-minded media	**0.65** **(0.16)**	**6.45** **(3.92)**	2.28 (3.38)	**−0.80** **(0.24)**	**0.68** **(0.39)**	**0.32** **(0.25)**
Prefer crosscutting media	0.31 (0.26)	−2.54 (6.24)	**11.23** **(5.26)**	0.24 (0.46)	0.67 (0.65)	**−0.61** **(0.40)**
Democrat	—	—	—	**1.46** **(0.21)**	—	—
Prefer like-minded media*Democrat	—	—	—	**0.84** **(0.32)**	—	—
Prefer crosscutting media*Democrat	—	—	—	**−1.29** **(0.55)**	—	—
Intercept	**2.62** **(0.10)**	**60.77** **(2.62)**	**19.16** **(2.25)**	**2.26** **(0.16)**	0.14 (0.23)	**1.11** **(0.16)**
N	135	123	117	135	135	136
R^2	0.11	0.08	0.04	0.54	0.02	0.04

Note: Cell entries are ordinary least-squares coefficients with associated standard errors underneath (except for the turnout model, which reports logistic regression coefficients and standard errors). Coefficients that can be statistically distinguished from 0 are given in bold.
Source: Media preferences survey, conducted by the author.

paign activity (and those who preferred crosscutting media were less likely to report performing campaign activities). Further, as I discussed in chapter 1, individuals who consumed partisan media were more politically interested, following elections more closely and discussing politics more frequently (perhaps not surprising from those who voluntarily watch partisan political programming). Combined with previous findings in the literature, this offers support for the differential motivation and ability of those who watch partisan media, especially like-minded media. In short, preferences allow me to tap into the underlying theoretical construct: partisan media consumers have differential motivation and ability that should affect their ability to engage in biased processing (and hence polarize). While there are other ways of operationalizing this hypothesis—and an important topic for future work will be exploring them—my method allows for the testing of the underlying causal logic of this hypothesis.

Figure 4.4 shows how these media preferences condition the effectiveness of the assigned treatment in experiment 3. Relative to neutral media, like-minded and crosscutting media have an effect, but only for subjects who prefer that type of media. Take like-minded media first. For those who preferred like-minded media (the white bar), watching like-minded media made them hold more extreme attitudes—nearly one full scale position more extreme on a seven-point scale, a rather striking effect. But for those who preferred neutral or crosscutting media (the black bar), there was very little effect. The polarizing power of like-minded media (see figure 4.1), then, is the product of subjects who preferred watching like-minded programs.

Likewise, on examination of subjects assigned to watch crosscutting media, I found a similar pattern. Crosscutting media moderate viewers, but only if those viewers want to watch that type of media. Given the somewhat small percentage of viewers who preferred crosscutting media, this likely explains its modest effects in the earlier analyses: because crosscutting media only have an effect for subjects who preferred it, and few subjects preferred it, this helps to explain the earlier null findings for crosscutting media.

These findings are highly consistent with the logic underlying the preference hypothesis. Subjects who preferred like-minded programs had higher motivation and more ability to process like-minded messages, which made them respond more strongly to these partisan media messages, consistent with theories of motivated reasoning (Taber and

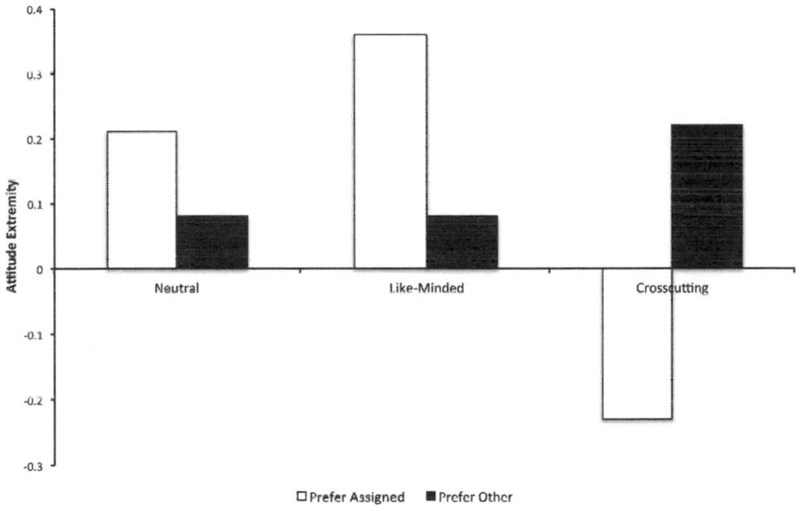

FIGURE 4.4. Media preferences and treatment effects, experiment 3. The *y* axis shows posttest attitude extremity (measured on a [−1,1] scale). Subjects are grouped by their treatment assignment and whether they were assigned to watch their preferred treatment (white bar) or not (black bar).

Lodge 2006). Because they have stronger partisan affiliation, they have more motivation to engage in the biased processing characteristic of motivated reasoners when presented with the partisan media stimuli. Similarly, because they have higher levels of political knowledge and interest, they have a greater ability to process and respond to the messages on these programs. As a result of these two factors, these subjects polarize more sharply after watching these types of segments.

Contrastingly, those who preferred to watch crosscutting had weaker motivation (weaker partisan ties) and less ability (lower knowledge and interest), so they moderated in response to them. Preferences capture important differences in how subjects process these messages, and hence cause subjects to respond differently to them.[14]

These results also have an important implication for how I interpreted the polarizing power of partisan media. Those who preferred like-minded media were already somewhat more extreme than other viewers, as a number of previous authors have demonstrated (Jamieson and Cappella 2008; Morris 2005; Stroud 2010). This implies that like-minded media take people who are already somewhat extreme and make them *even more extreme*. So partisan media increase polarization not by polarizing moderates but by increasing polarization among those already away from the political center. This has particular substantive relevance since these more extreme individuals are likely to make their voices heard in the political process, and are therefore likely to have considerable influence, a point I return to in the conclusion. The effects of partisan media are heterogeneous, and that heterogeneity is politically consequential.

How Long Do These Effects Endure?

Experiments 1–3 show how partisan media shape attitudes and how various moderating variables condition the effectiveness of the treatment. But they all suffer from a common limitation: they all measure respondents' attitudes immediately after administering the treatment. What happens after several days: can the effects of the stimulus still be detected? The duration hypothesis predicts that it can: because subjects adjust their attitudes using online processing, the attitudes updated in response to partisan media messages should endure, at least in the short term. To test this notion, I designed experiment 4. The first wave (time 1) followed the standard posttest-only protocol described earlier. At the close of the experiment, subjects were asked if they would take part in another experiment (time 2) in exchange for an additional cash payment. In the time 2 experiment, subjects were not shown any additional experimental stimuli and were simply asked to complete the posttest portion of the initial study again (the time 1 attitude items were repeated in time 2). Time 2 took place two days after the initial study, so it could only examine whether these effects lasted that long.[15] That said, given that the stimuli were brief video news segments, finding any effect even two days later constitutes important evidence for duration.

Figure 4.5 presents the effects of the treatment on attitudes at time 1 and time 2. Consistent with the results seen above, at time 1, the like-minded treatment polarized attitudes, while the crosscutting treatment had no significant effect on attitudes (relative to the neutral news condition). But more interestingly, the effects at time 2 were basically a mirror of the effects at time 1: there was little difference in effects between time 1 and time 2.[16] Consistent with an account stressing online processing, partisan media engage viewers in a way that has effects postexposure,

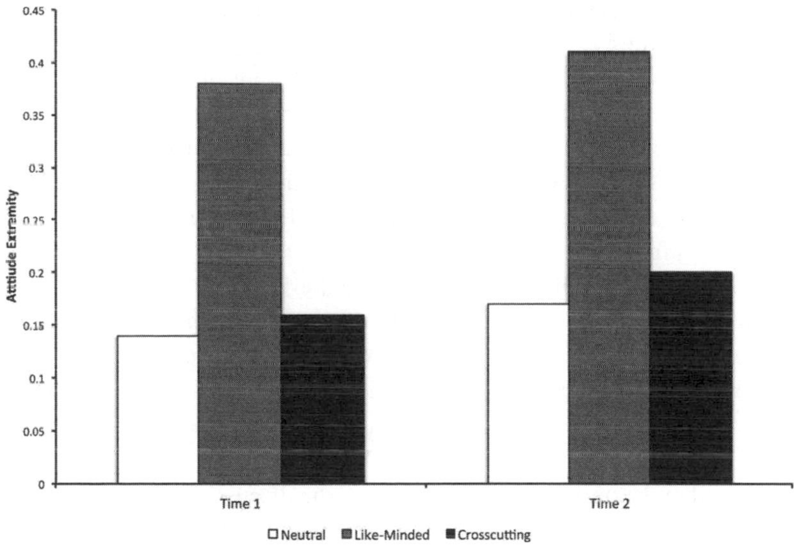

FIGURE 4.5. Duration effects over time, experiment 4. The *y* axis shows posttest attitude extremity (measured on a [−1,1] scale). The left group shows attitudes immediately posttreatment; the right group shows attitudes two days posttreatment.

even several days later. The effects of partisan media are not simply blips that fade away immediately after the treatment; the messages stay with respondents, at least in the short term.[17]

What Are the Effects of Repetition?

Experiments 1–4 showed how a single dose of partisan media can impact viewers' attitudes. While these are important findings, they fail to mimic the real world in a key way: few citizens get just one dose of partisan media. Instead, they get multiple doses across days and weeks. What is the effect of seeing multiple doses of the treatment? The repetition hypothesis predicts that multiple exposures to partisan media messages will continue to impact subjects' attitudes, but at a diminishing rate.

I designed experiment 5, a two-wave design, to test this hypothesis. The first wave proceeded as in experiments 1–4: subjects answered some pretest questions, saw the stimulus, and then answered a posttest attitude battery, and the study closed with a request to recontact them later for a future study.[18] Four days later, subjects were invited to take wave 2 (72 percent of wave 1 subjects returned to take the wave 2 study). Wave 2 mirrored the design of wave 1: subjects were randomly assigned to treatment conditions (independent of their assignment at wave 1) and then answered the same posttest items. The treatment stimuli at time 1 and time 2 are exactly the same (to ensure consistency across waves).[19] Because some subjects were randomly assigned to see partisan media at both time 1 and time 2, I can estimate the effects of repetition on attitude extremity.

There were three differences between experiment 5 and the others used in this chapter. First, given the dearth of statistically significant crosscutting media effects above, subjects here were randomly assigned to receive either the like-minded treatment or the control condition to help maximize statistical power. Second, to gain greater control over the content, I used doctored editorials as the stimulus, as in the editorial experiment discussed in the online appendix (see also the discussion above). Subjects typically processed video-based and text-based stimuli somewhat differently, so I cannot guarantee that the results here would identically replicate if I used a video-based stimulus (though this is an important topic for future research). That said, my results from the editorial experiment described earlier are extremely consistent with the video-based results described elsewhere in the chapter, which suggests that the results are unlikely to diverge too sharply. Third and finally, in the control condition, subjects saw apolitical media rather than the neutral media used in experiments 1–4. Because my focus is on the over-time dynamics, I wanted to ensure that there was a group without any political media exposure (even neutral media exposure) as a control group, since, for example, it may be that partisan and neutral news media's effects decay at different rates. Adding neutral media would make for an interesting future extension, but as a first step, it is important to have an apolitical baseline group.

To analyze the effects of repetition, I looked at the difference between time 2 and time 1 attitudes. Here, the interest centered on whether partisan media have any additional impact on attitudes with repeated exposure. I examined differences in attitudes among four groups of subjects: those who were in the control condition at both times (control/control), those who were in the treatment condition at time 1 and then the control condition in time 2 (treat/control), those who were in the control condition at time 1 and then the treatment condition at time 2 (control/treat), and those who were in the treatment condition at both points in time (treat/treat). In particular, I wanted to know if time 2 attitudes become more extreme than time 1 attitudes, so I examined the difference in attitudes over time: if y_{it} is respondent i's attitude at time t, I examined $(y_{i2} - y_{i1})$. The key question was whether the dual treatment group (treat/treat) became more extreme in time 2 (relative to time 1).

Figure 4.6 shows the results. The largest effect on attitude polarization was for those who were assigned to the control condition at time 1 but were assigned to the treatment condition at time 2; these individuals became markedly more polarized. But this is not terribly surprising: as I showed above in experiments 1–4, the stimulus tended to have a large immediate effect on attitude extremity, and this result simply confirms it. What's more surprising is what happens to those who saw the treatment condition at both points in time. These subjects became somewhat more polarized, relative to their time 1 attitudes. At time 1, the stimulus made these subjects approximately 8 percent more extreme. But at time 2, even conditional on that earlier effect, the stimulus made than even more extreme—about another 4 percent—suggesting the power of partisan media declines by about half with a second exposure. This makes good sense: the initial treatment, when the stimulus is novel, had the largest effect and helped polarize subjects' attitudes. Later hearings had an effect, but it was somewhat smaller, since the initial treatment

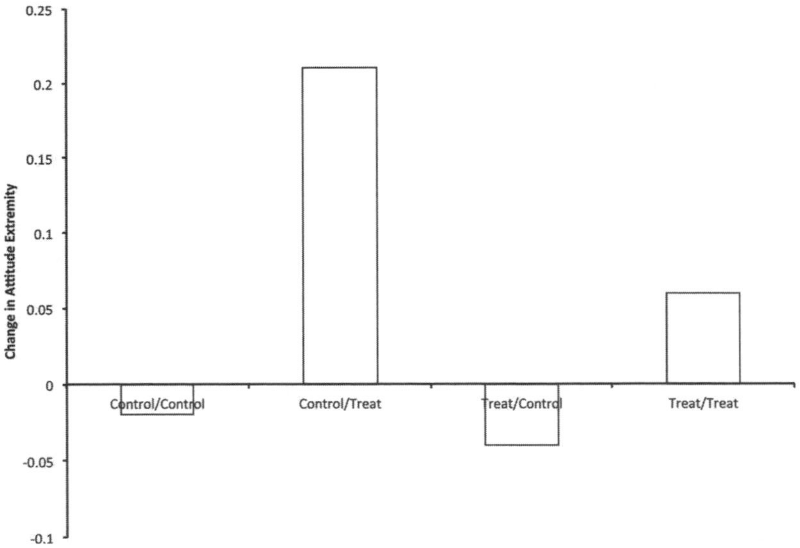

FIGURE 4.6. Repetition effects, experiment 5. The *y* axis shows the change in attitudes between waves 1 and 2. Values above 0 indicate attitudes that become more extreme; values below 0 indicate attitudes that become less extreme. The four bars correspond to the four values of treatment assignment in waves 1 and 2 (wave 1 treatment status is before the slash; wave 2 treatment status is after).

already had such a large effect. Repeated exposure has an effect, but the marginal effect is diminishing over time. Multiple exposures operate like a reinforcement mechanism, reminding subjects of their positions and pushing them toward the extremes.

This also has implications for how I interpret the earlier experiments, especially experiment 3 (the preference trial experiment). These results suggest that (unsurprisingly) the largest effects are for newer and less well-established issues, consistent with a generation of media effects research (Bartels 1993; Druckman and Leeper 2012). For any given issue, the effects will still be larger for those who regularly watch these programs (given that the effects are driven by motivated reasoning), but across issues, the effects will be somewhat larger for novel issues. So partisan media's effects on novel issues may well be to increase polarization, but on more established issues, it likely is an attempt to maintain polarization and emotional activation about the issues. Future studies can more carefully unpack how these effects differ across a variety of different types of issues.

Do Partisan Media Increase Certainty?

The results above show that partisan media increase viewers' attitudinal extremity. But do they also increase their attitudinal certainty? Do they not only make viewers more extreme, but also more convinced that their position is the correct one? The certainty hypothesis argues that like-minded media do have this effect: because like-minded media reinforce viewers existing beliefs, this exposure makes viewers more certain that their positions are the correct ones, and they therefore become more confident and certain in their beliefs. But as I discussed in chapter 2, these effects should be most pronounced when messages are repeated. Perhaps one exposure to partisan media is not enough to engender greater certainty, but repeated message may be. Repeated exposure to information, especially attitude-consistent information, bolsters subjects' confidence in their opinions (Duckman and Bolsen 2011; Visser, Bosner, and Krosnick 2006). Repeated exposure to partisan media—especially like-minded media—should therefore increase attitude certainty.

I tested this with data from experiment 5. In the wave 2 posttest, subjects were asked to rate their attitude certainty (there was no certainty item in the wave 1 instrument). If the certainty hypothesis is correct, I should find that subjects who are assigned to the treatment condition at both wave 1 and wave 2 should have higher levels of attitude certainty.

My results, shown in figure 4.7, support the certainty hypothesis. Subjects who only hear the treatment once were no more certain in their attitudes (relative to those who were in the control condition at both waves). But those who were in the treatment condition in both waves—and hence got multiple doses of the treatment—were significantly more certain, all else equal; seeing the treatment twice made subjects approximately 10 percent more certain of their attitudes. This is approximately 1 point on a seven-point scale, so it is equivalent, say, to taking subjects from "somewhat certain" to "certain," or equivalently, from "certain" to "very certain." Subjects who were in the treatment condition at both points in time were 60 percent more likely to say that they were "very certain" of their attitudes, relative to those in the control condition at both points in time (12.5 percent of subjects in the control condition in both waves were "very certain" of their attitudes, versus 20 percent of subjects in the treatment condition at both points in time). Consistent with my theoretical argument above, it takes repeated exposure to parti-

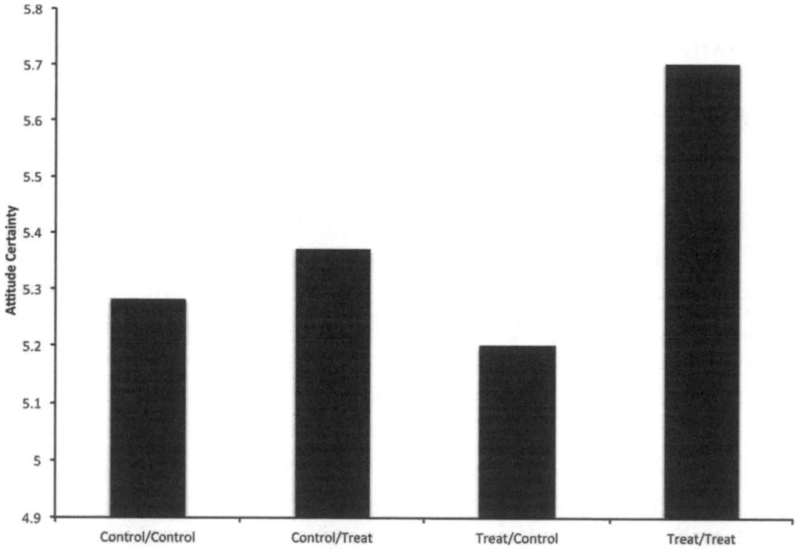

FIGURE 4.7. Repetition and attitude certainty effects, experiment 5. The *y* axis gives attitude certainty on a [1,7] scale (measured in wave 2). The four bars correspond to the four values of treatment assignment in waves 1 and 2 (wave 1 treatment status is before the slash; wave 2 treatment status is after).

san media messages to strengthen the certainty with which subjects hold their attitudes. A one-shot exposure to partisan media does not increase certainty, but repeated exposures do.

This highlights yet another consequence of message repetition. Not only are subjects who hear like-minded messages repeated over time more extreme and polarized, they are also more certain and confident in their opinions. Given that certain attitudes are the types of attitudes that drive behavior, influence vote choice, and so forth (Miller and Peterson 2004), these certain (and extreme) attitudes are consequential, a point I return to in the concluding chapter.

Conclusions

This chapter begins the empirical core of the book by asking whether, and under what conditions, partisan media can polarize viewers. In particular, the chapter focused on the moderators of partisan media's effects on attitudinal polarization. When viewers watch like-minded media that reinforce their attitudes, they become more extreme, and these effects persist for at least several days. On average, crosscutting media have no effect on attitude extremity. But this masks considerable heterogeneity throughout the public. Crosscutting media moderate attitudes for some viewers—those who find crosscutting media to be highly credible and those who want to see crosscutting programs. But for viewers with strong attitudes, crosscutting media increase polarization. I can also show evidence explaining why viewers become more polarized, and show (consistent with my argument) that both motivated reasoning and source credibility factors drive the polarizing power of partisan media. I further demonstrate that like-minded media in particular not only polarize viewers, but also make them more confident that their beliefs are correct.

My results also highlight the key role played by viewer preferences. The effects of like-minded and crosscutting media are concentrated primarily among those who actually watch them in the real world. This has particular importance for like-minded media, since those who watch those programs are already more extreme. Like-minded media takes subjects who are already extreme and makes them *even more* extreme.

Further, the findings here highlight the role played by repeated over-time exposure to partisan media content. Repeated exposure continues to polarize subjects, though at a diminishing rate over time. Equally importantly, multiple exposures also increase subjects' attitude certainty, which makes it more likely their (now more extreme) attitudes will guide them to take action (Gross, Holtz, and Miller 1995; Miller and Peterson 2004). Repeated exposure to partisan media does not take moderates and turn them into extremists, but it does move the engaged and involved further toward the poles and then work to keep them there by reinforcing and strengthening their attitudes. This has important ramifications for how partisan media consumers behave, and for politics more generally.

Appendix

The regression-based analyses for experiments 1, 3, and 4 are given in Levendusky (2012a); I provide the corresponding regression analyses for experiments 2 and 5 below.

TABLE A4.1. **Effect of source credibility on attitude extremity, experiment 2.**

	Estimate
Like-minded treatment	0.10
	(0.12)
Crosscutting treatment	−0.03
	(0.12)
Highly credible source	0.08
	(0.15)
Highly credible source*like-minded treatment	0.18
	(0.23)
Highly credible source*crosscutting treatment	**−0.55**
	(0.40)
Constant	**0.18**
	(0.10)
N	133

Note: Cell entries are ordinary least-squares regression coefficients with associated standard errors underneath. Coefficients that can be distinguished from 0 ($\alpha < 0.10$; one-tailed) are given in bold.

TABLE A4.2. **Repetition and change in attitude extremity, experiment 5.**

Wave 1 treatment, wave 2 control	−0.03
	(0.05)
Wave 1 control, wave 2 treatment	**0.23**
	(0.09)
Wave 1 treatment, wave 2 treatment	**0.08**
	(0.04)
Constant	−0.02
	(0.04)
N	116
R^2	0.15

Note: Cell entries are ordinary least-squares regression coefficients with associated standard errors underneath. Coefficients that can be distinguished from 0 ($\alpha < 0.10$; one-tailed) are given in bold.

TABLE A4.3. **Repetition and attitude certainty effects, experiment 5.**

Wave 1 treatment, wave 2 control	−0.07
	(0.30)
Wave 1 control, wave 2 treatment	0.10
	(0.30)
Wave 1 treatment, wave 2 treatment	**0.43**
	(0.30)
Intercept	**5.27**
	(0.23)
N	116
R^2	0.03

Note: Cell entries are ordinary least-squares regression coefficients with associated standard errors underneath. Coefficients that can be distinguished from 0 ($\alpha < 0.10$; one-tailed) are given in bold.

CHAPTER FIVE

Do Partisan Media Make Viewers Dislike and Distrust the Opposition?

During the health care debate in the summer of 2009, MSNBC host Ed Schultz exclaimed, "The Republicans lie. They want to see you dead. They'd rather make money off your dead corpse. . . . My God, Democrats, what's wrong with you? You can't deal with these people at all" (*The Ed Show*, 23 September 2009). While this particular example is a relatively extreme one, such outbursts of partisan invective are not rare on cable television (Jamieson 2012). Partisan media outlets frequently disparage and discredit the other side, and much as in the example above, argue against bipartisanship and compromise with the other side. The question remains, however: what effect does this have? This is the second question from chapter 1: do partisan media change how viewers perceive the other side, and does it impact their willingness to compromise with them? If it does, it suggests large, direct, and deleterious consequences for American politics given the central place of compromise and consensus in our constitutional system.

The answer to these questions is not clear, however. It is certainly true that those who watch partisan cable outlets have more sharply polarized evaluations of political leaders. For example, in the rolling cross-section component of the 2008 National Annenberg Election Study, 69 percent of Fox News viewers approved of the job President Bush was doing in office, while only 11 percent of MSNBC viewers approved (the figure in the remainder of the sample was 24 percent); evaluations of Obama, McCain, and other political elites followed a similarly polarized pattern. But as I explained in earlier chapters, it is difficult to know whether such findings represent treatment effects or selection effects: does watching

Fox and MSNBC polarize viewers' attitudes about the parties and leaders, or do they tune in to those shows precisely because they are already polarized? In the example above, is Ed Schultz persuading his audience that Republicans are nefarious and unwilling to compromise, or is he just playing to their partisan biases?

As in the previous chapter, I again turn to experiments to try and unpack the answer. I formulated a set of original experiments that allowed me to overcome this selection versus treatment issue so I could more confidently draw inferences about how partisan media influence how viewers perceive the other side. I tested the like-minded affect, crosscutting affect, credibility and affect, trust, bipartisanship, and policy support hypotheses (H9–H14) from chapter 3 to see how partisan media shape the public's attitudes toward the other side, as well as their willingness to compromise with—and more generally trust—them. The answers reinforce the results from chapter 4: partisan media divide and polarize their audience. Viewers who watch like-minded media rate the other party and its leaders less positively, and they also trust them less and are less supportive of bipartisan cooperation. Partisan media help to make gridlock more prevalent, and compromise and consensus more evasive, in American politics.

Research Design

I tested my hypotheses using a series of original experiments. The design and setup of the experiments largely parallel those used in the previous chapter, so I will refer the interested reader to the discussion on pages 67–73 for additional information. The experiments used here differ in one key respect. In chapter 4, I contrasted the like-minded, crosscutting, and neutral news presentation of an issue and estimated the effect of outlet slant on attitudinal polarization. Here, I opted for a slightly different design, and compared like-minded and crosscutting discussion of the same issue to an apolitical control condition. The design differs here because the content of the news segments are different. The stories used in this chapter focused on the parties themselves and their behavior as much as particular issues. As I discussed in chapter 2, this is a frequent topic of conversation on partisan programs, but there is no real analog to these types of stories on neutral news outlets. This largely reflects the different journalistic aims of these shows: partisan media are advancing a particular narrative about the day's events, and a key part of that narrative is why the opposing party is so deeply flawed. In this sort of setup, a story focusing on one party and its flawed policy positions, or its hypocrisy, makes good sense. But such stories would be out of place on a more neutral newscast that reports on the day's news from an objective, balanced point of view. Such a story would deeply violate journalistic norms of balance, so it would not appear on a mainstream news program. Given this, it is not really possible to identify neutral segments that focus on the parties themselves, and even if it were possible, there would be so many differences between the neutral and partisan conditions that the implicit comparison between the two becomes extremely muddled. Given this, I opted for the cleaner comparison of partisan media to apolitical stories.

The implicit comparison between treatment and control condition, then, is between the partisan primes (in the partisan media conditions) and the apolitical control condition. In the control condition, subjects were not given information about the parties, but in the treatment, they were given information about the parties from the particular slant of the program. So the estimated effects are the effects of the information about the parties from this particular slant. This fits both with the hypotheses being tested (see chapter 3), as well as what citizens would encounter in the real world, making it an appropriate design choice.

Plan for the Experiments in this Chapter

The experiments in this chapter aimed to test H9–H14, which focus on the effects of partisan media on attitudes toward the other side, as well as trust in the other party, support for bipartisanship, and support for policies attributed to the other party. I tested these hypotheses using experiments 6, 7, and 8, as I outline in table 5.1.

I began with experiment 6. Subjects were randomly assigned to a treatment condition (like-minded, crosscutting, or apolitical media). Subjects in the like-minded and crosscutting treatment conditions heard about the same issue (in this case, party fundraising efforts in the 2010 elections), albeit from different partisan/ideological slants; subjects in the apolitical media condition watched an apolitical news story. I used this random assignment to treatment conditions to test the effects of partisan media exposure on my key hypotheses. In particular, experiment 6 tested my core hypotheses about partisan media consumption and atti-

TABLE 5.1. **Description of the experiments used in chapter 5.**

Experiment	Hypotheses being tested	Design	Subject pool	Study waves	Issue discussed
Experiment 6	Like-minded affect Crosscutting affect trust Bipartisanship	Posttest	Online panel	1	2010 election fundraising
Experiment 7	Credibility and affect	Posttest	Online panel	1	Obama's foreign policy
Experiment 8	Policy support	Posttest	Online panel	1	Extending the Bush tax cuts

tudes toward one's own party and the other side (the like-minded affect and crosscutting affect hypotheses, H9 and H10; see table 3.1 for a review of all hypotheses). The experiment also allowed me to examine the consequences of these shifts in affect, by testing the effects on trust (the trust hypothesis, H12) and support for bipartisanship (the bipartisanship hypothesis, H13). Experiment 7 then allowed me to test a key moderator: beliefs about the credibility of the outlet, thereby allowing me to test the credibility and affect hypothesis (H11). Finally, experiment 8 tested the policy support hypothesis (H14). As a group, these experiments allowed me to investigate how partisan media shape viewers' attitudes toward the opposition and their willingness to compromise and engage with them.

Do Partisan Media Polarize Affect?

I began by testing my hypotheses about the effects of partisan media on viewers' affect for the parties, using data from experiment 6. In the posttest section, subjects rated both their own party and the opposite party using a standard one-hundred-point feeling thermometer; this same instrument is used in many other surveys, such as the National Election Study. I used the feeling thermometer score as a general measure of affect toward the parties, which is consistent with past work in this vein (Mutz 2007). Here, as in chapter 4, I presented simple visual depictions of the treatment effects. The regression-based analysis of experiments 6 and 7 are given in Levendusky (2012b); the parallel results for experiment 8 are given in the appendix to this chapter.

Figure 5.1 shows strong support for the like-minded affect hypothesis. Like-minded media do decrease viewers' affect for the other party

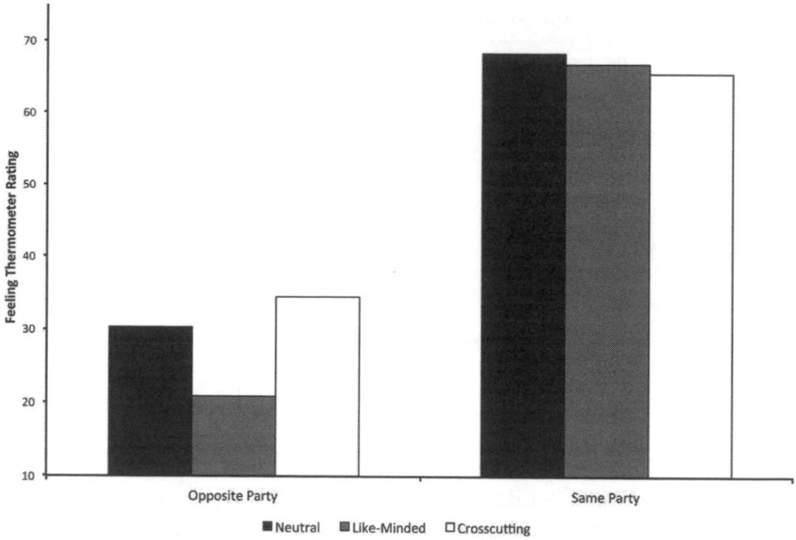

FIGURE 5.1. Effects on party feeling thermometers, experiment 6. The *y* axis gives the (0–100) feeling thermometer scores for the respondents' own party (right group) and the opposite party (left group); the shading of the bars corresponds to treatment assignment.

(relative to the apolitical control condition) by nearly 10 degrees, or approximately 0.5 standard deviations—opposite party feeling thermometer ratings go from 30.4 degrees in the control condition to 20.9 degrees in the like-minded condition. Like-minded media cause viewers to feel less warmly toward the other party.[1]

Note, however, that like-minded media have no significant effect on same-party feeling thermometers. While the like-minded affect hypothesis predicts that subjects will like their own party more in addition to liking the other party less, these results only support the second half of this expectation, and it is unclear why partisan media have no effect on same-party feeling thermometers. I suspect, however, that it stems from two related components. First, as I discussed in the content analyses in chapter 2, these segments typically focus more on the other party's flaws that one's own party's strengths. That is, the segments are more about why the other side is wrong than why "our side" is right (Chalif 2011; Smith and Searles, forthcoming). It may simply be that the message about the other side is a stronger and louder message, and hence the larger effect.[2]

Second, these results are consistent with a theoretical account stressing the centrality of negative information. Negative information is more powerful than positive information (Lau 1985; Baumeister et al. 2001), so it may simply be that the negative information about the other party overwhelms the positive information about one's own party. This parallels Mutz's (2007) findings that incivility decreases the legitimacy of disliked politicians but has no effect on the legitimacy of liked ones. A related study of campaign advertising found that positive ads that praised one's preferred candidate had little effect on reinforcing preferences, but negative ones about the opposing candidate had a much larger effect on attitudes and behavior (Phillips, Urbany, and Reynolds 2008). Interestingly, even when I conducted a follow-up experiment where the partisan media clip contained only positive information about one's own party (e.g., a left-wing segment that praised Democrats without critiquing Republicans), there was still no effect on same-party affect (see the appendix to Levendusky 2012b). Future work to lay out a theoretical argument for this finding will be needed, but the findings from experiment 6 (and the experiments below) show that like-minded media have a much larger effect on attitudes toward the other party than about one's own party.

Crosscutting media, in contrast, have little effect on either same-party or opposite-party feeling thermometers. Viewers simply seem to "tune out" the crosscutting content, leaving their feelings about the parties unchanged. While this is inconsistent with the crosscutting affect hypothesis, it is consistent with the predominantly null findings for crosscutting media seen in chapter 4.

Experiment 6 lacks a measure of outlet credibility, so I could not test the credibility and affect hypothesis. Experiment 7 allowed me to test this hypothesis using a different design than the remaining experiments in this chapter. In experiment 7, subjects were randomly shown either an apolitical control segment or a treatment segment. The treatment segment here came from Fox News and contained a strong critique of President Obama's foreign policy (arguing that the president's foreign policy shows too much weakness). I used only this one treatment clip for both Democratic and Republican subjects, rather than the standard design of paring right-wing and left-wing segments, because I could not locate a suitable corresponding clip from left-wing television discussing the same issue (Obama's foreign policy) in similar terms. Further, even if I could have found a clip from a left-wing media source that praised Obama's foreign policy, it is not clear that it would have a comparable effect, given that subjects process positive and negative information differently (Lau

1985; Baumeister et al. 2001). But I can verify the robustness of the findings from experiment 7 in one key regard. I selected a clip from a left-wing program that criticized Republican foreign policy proposals. The results from that experiment parallel the findings reported below.[3] This should increase the reader's confidence that these findings are more general, and not simply confined to this one segment.

I tested the credibility and affect hypothesis by examining whether beliefs about outlet credibility[4] (here, Fox News) moderate the effectives of the treatment for Democrats. Given that experiment 7 focused specifically on President Obama, and not Democrats more generally, I used the Obama feeling thermometer as my dependent variable.

The results of experiment 7 are given in figure 5.2. Because my interest is in testing the effects of source credibility on the effectiveness of crosscutting media, I focused only on Democrats (the results for Republicans parallel the effects seen above, see Levendusky 2012b for details). There was no treatment effect for Democrats who did not find Fox News to be a credible source. But those who found Fox News to be a credible

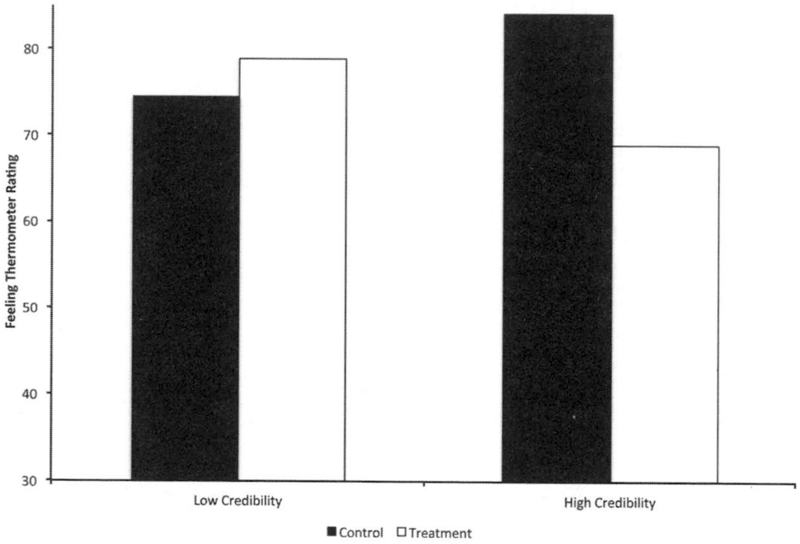

FIGURE 5.2. Source credibility effects, experiment 7. The *y* axis gives the (0–100) feeling thermometer scores for ratings of President Obama. All subjects in this graph are Democrats, and the treatment is watching a Fox News segment criticizing President Obama's foreign policy. Subjects in the left group find Fox to be low in credibility, subjects on the right find it to be high in credibility.

source assigned President Obama much lower feeling thermometer ratings—about 10 degrees lower, which is similarly sized to the treatment effect for like-minded media seen in figure 5.1. Crosscutting media *can* change respondents' affect for the parties and their leaders, but only if subjects think those crosscutting sources are credible.

But this of course raises the question of which subjects find crosscutting media to be credible. Existing research suggests that those who select crosscutting media (or find it to be credible) are less in tune with their own party and more likely to be similar to partisans from the other party. In effect, Democrats who find Fox News credible (or Republicans who find MSNBC credible) are odd, and their selection of this type of media is an indication about their preferences (Holbert, Garrett, and Gleason 2010). Given this, one might worry that the effects about source credibility (shown in figure 5.2) simply reflect partisan strength. Perhaps Democrats who find Fox News credible are disproportionately weak Democrats, and the findings above simply reflect this fact. I tested this possibility in Levendusky (2012b) and found that it could not explain these results. So the effect is not simply due to weak partisan defecting from their party, but seems to be a more general effect of outlet credibility. Though it is beyond the scope of the current book, unpacking the source of these credibility judgments is an important topic for future scholarship.

Effects on Evaluations of Political Leaders, Bipartisanship, and Trust

Figures 5.1 and 5.2 above show that partisan media drive affect toward the parties and their leaders. But as I argued above, theses effects should extend to other evaluations of the leaders. For example, hearing Fox News discuss why President Obama is a flawed leader should make viewers (at least those who are watching like-minded media) more critical of the president and his leadership, consistent with the logic of the like-minded affect hypothesis. I tested this possibility using the data from experiment 7 by asking whether subjects assigned the treatment condition (watching the Fox News clip criticizing the president) were less likely to approve of his handling of national security issues (see figure 5.3). Figure 5.4 shows the parallel results for perceptions of the strength of the president's leadership.

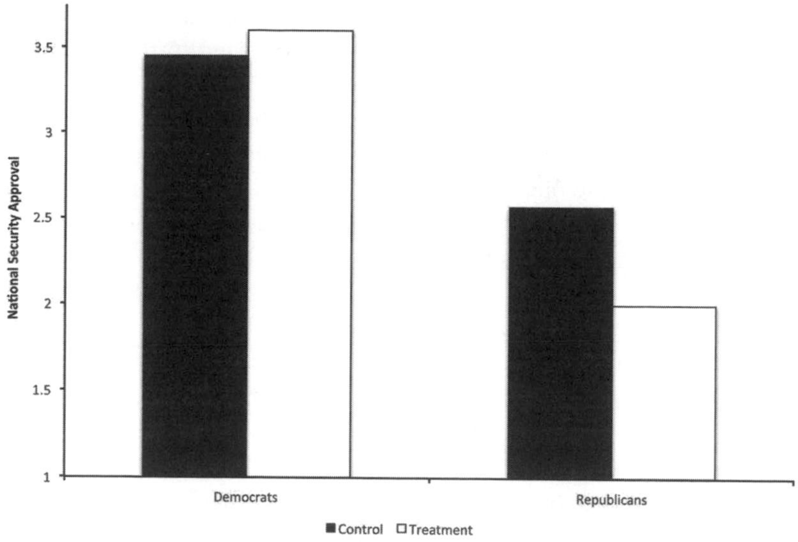

FIGURE 5.3. National security approval, experiment 7. The *y* axis shows approval of President Obama's handling of national security issues (1–5 scale, with higher values indicating greater approval). Democrats are on the left; Republicans are on the right. The treatment is watching a Fox News segment criticizing President Obama's foreign policy.

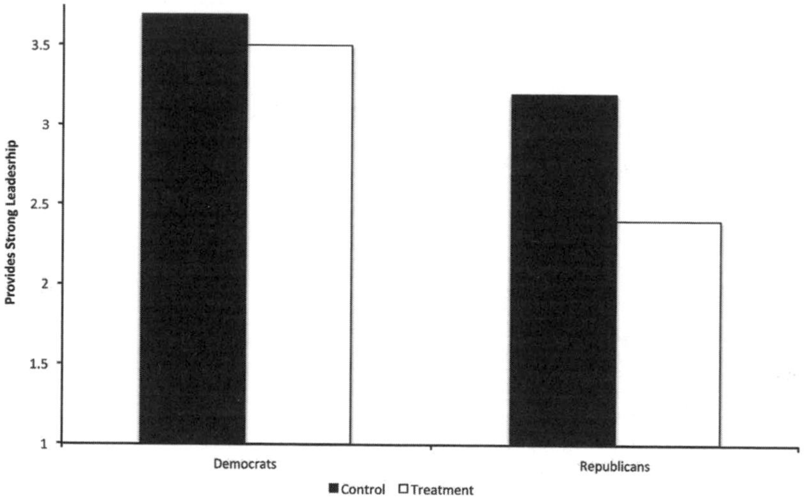

FIGURE 5.4. Perceptions of strong leadership, experiment 7. The *y* axis shows whether subjects regard President Obama as a strong leader (1–5 scale, with higher values indicating stronger leadership). Democrats are on the left; Republicans are on the right. The treatment is watching a Fox News segment criticizing President Obama's foreign policy.

Figures 5.3 and 5.4 show that for Republicans (for whom this constitutes like-minded media), there was an effect for both types of evaluations. Republican subjects not only liked the president less (Levendusky 2012b), but they also viewed him as a weaker leader, and they were less likely to approve of his handling of national security issues (though consistent with the results above, there are no crosscutting effects for Democrats). For example, 43 percent of Republicans in the control condition thought the phrase "provides strong leadership" applied to President Obama "extremely well" or "very well," but that figure dropped to 20 percent in the treatment condition. Likewise, while 15 percent approved of President Obama's handling of national security issues in the control condition, only 10 percent felt the same way in the treatment condition. Like-minded media shape how viewers evaluate political leaders.

Such shifts are not simply psychological ephemera; they have real policy consequences. First, these sorts of perceptions, particularly of being a strong leader, have considerable electoral importance (Druckman, Jacobs, and Ostmeier 2004; Funk 1999). Second, these sorts of perceptions influence leaders' policy positions, particularly in the international arena (Schultz 2005). These types of media segments have real consequences for beyond simply evaluations of leaders, extending to how they conduct themselves on the world stage.

This same type of process should also lead subjects to be less trusting of the other party after watching like-minded media, as I argued in the trust hypothesis. I tested this claim using data from experiment 6 (figure 5.5). Partisan media influence subjects' trust in the other party. Watching like minded media made subjects less trusting that the other party would do what is right for the country (and the difference is statistically significant). On the original five-point Likert scale of the item (with higher values indicating higher levels of trust), trust in the opposite party fell from 2.1 in the control condition to 1.8 in the like-minded treatment condition. In the control condition, 67 percent of subjects trusted the other party to do what is right only "once in a while" or "almost never," but that figure jumped to 84 percent in the like-minded condition. Like-minded media consumption decreases trust in the other party.

Likewise, I also expect a similar effect on support for bipartisanship consistent with the bipartisanship hypothesis. I tested this hypothesis with data from experiment 6 (figure 5.6). Like-minded media made viewers less supportive of bipartisanship and compromise with the other side. On the original five-point Likert scale (with higher values indicating

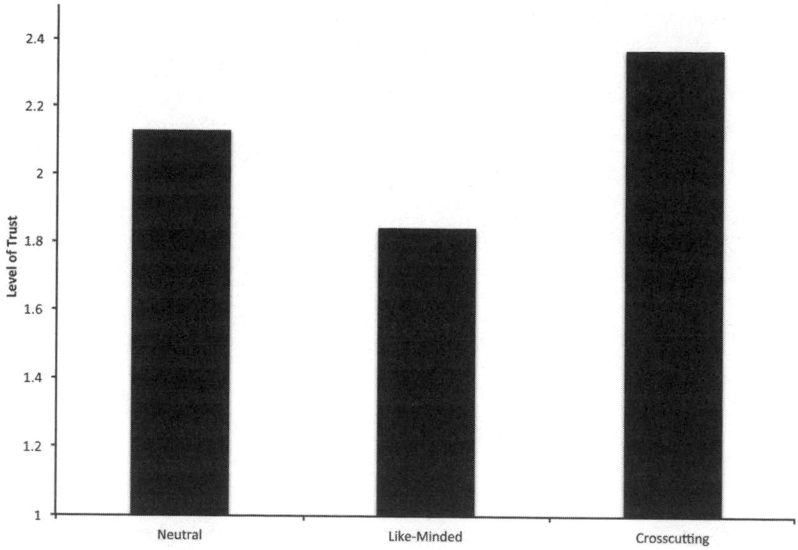

FIGURE 5.5. Trust in the other party, experiment 6. The *y* axis shows respondents' level in trust in the opposing party (1–5 scale, with higher values indicating greater trust). The three bars correspond to treatment conditions.

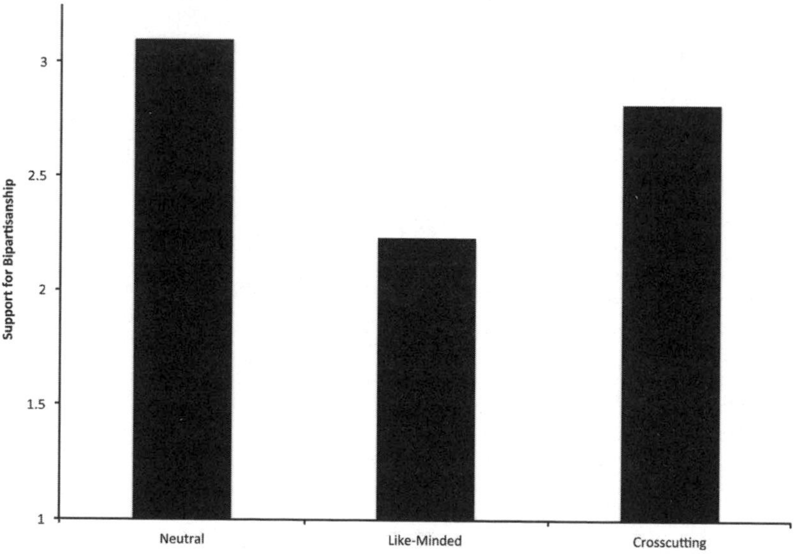

FIGURE 5.6. Support for bipartisanship, experiment 6. The *y* axis shows respondents' level of support for bipartisanship (1–5 scale, with higher values indicating higher support for bipartisanship). The three bars correspond to treatment conditions.

stronger support for bipartisanship), support for bipartisanship fell from 3.1 in the control condition to 2.2 in the like-minded condition; more simply, support for bipartisan cooperation fell from 39 percent in the control condition to 22 percent in the like-minded media condition. Compromise and consensus became less desirable goals when the opposition is portrayed as dishonest and corrupt. It is important to note that while these programs often speak ill of bipartisanship and compromise (see the discussion in chapter 2), these particular segments did not (see the online appendix for the full transcript of the segments used). So these results cannot simply be an artifact of exposing subjects to clips where bipartisanship itself was directly critiqued. Rather, the results stem from hearing negative comments from the other party on like-minded media, which engenders a strong affective reaction in viewers. As a result, viewers would prefer their own party to pursue its own policy goals without reaching out to the other party.

Finally, I can also tested the policy support hypothesis using the data from experiment 8. After watching partisan media, would subjects be less likely to support a policy attributed to the other party? Subjects were asked about a recent policy proposal to reduce the U.S. federal deficit, taken from the Simpson-Bowles deficit reduction plan (the policies were taken from the Simpson-Bowles plan without explicitly naming it; see the data appendix for the exact wording used). Subjects were randomly assigned to hear it described as Democratic or Republican plan; this randomization was separate from and orthogonal to the initial randomization over like-minded, crosscutting, or apolitical media. The Simpson Bowles plan is an especially suitable policy for this manipulation, because it is explicitly bipartisan and was publicly supported by members of both parties, making both versions of the item highly plausible to respondents.

As I explained in chapter 3, the key comparison here holds attribution to the other party constant and compares how subjects respond when they see like-minded versus crosscutting media. This ensures that any effects are not simply the product of the fact that subjects prefer policies attributed to their own party (Cohen 2003; Rahn 1993). Instead, the key comparison is whether watching like-minded media makes subjects less likely to support policies attributed to the other party.

Figure 5.7 presents the results of the experiment. Consistent with the logic underlying the policy support hypothesis, like-minded media

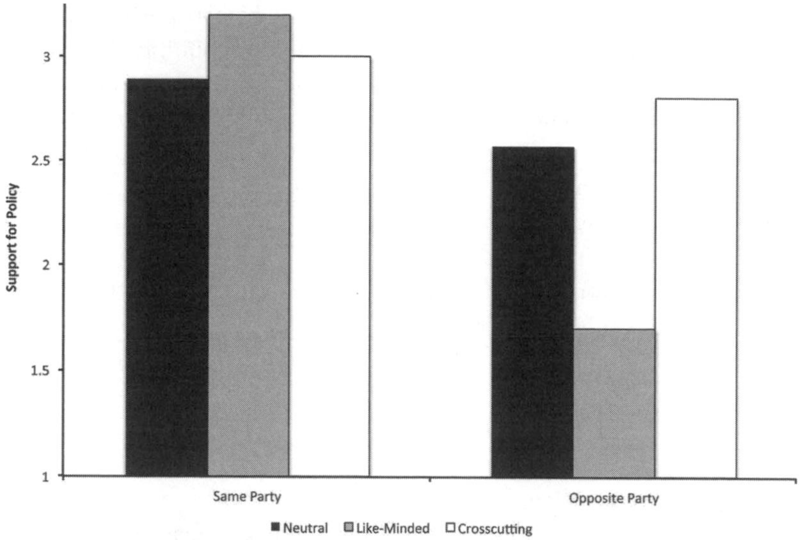

FIGURE 5.7. Support for policy, experiment 8. The *y* axis shows respondents' level of support for a policy (1–5 scale, with higher values indicating greater support). The policy was randomly attributed to the respondent's own party (left side) or the opposite party (right side); the shading of the bars corresponds to treatment assignment to the like-minded, neutral, or crosscutting media conditions.

decreased support for the proposal, but only when it was attributed to the other party (note that there were no effects when the policy is attributed to one's own party). Looking only at subjects where the policy is attributed to the other party, support for the policy (on the five-point Likert scale) went from 2.6 (control) to 1.7 (like-minded); this corresponds to a drop in support from 29 percent in the control condition to 10 percent in the like-minded condition—support fell by nearly two-thirds. Watching like-minded programs has *policy* consequences, not simply affective ones.

As a whole, the findings are clear: partisan media not only make subjects like the other side less, but that negative feeling spills over into other areas, such as evaluations of political trust and bipartisanship. Partisan media have real consequences for subjects' attitudes toward the other party, as well as their willingness to engage with them in the political process.

Addressing Potential Limitations of the Findings

Even if one accepts the validity of the findings above, there are still several potential limitations of these results. First, one might be concerned that my results are real, but they are not due to the partisan slant of the programs, as I argue, but are instead a product of the incivility of these shows. While incivility does have important effects on factors like affect for the opposition (Mutz 2007) and trust in the political system (Mutz and Reeves 2005), my effects cannot be attributed to incivility. Both like-minded and crosscutting television are, to some extent, "uncivil," but as my results demonstrate, they have very different effects on how viewers perceive the opposition. For example, Fox News has a striking effect on the attitudes of Republican viewers, but much less so on Democratic ones, yet it is the same program—and has the same level of civility—in both cases. It is the partisan slant of these shows, rather than the eye rolling or other forms of incivility,[5] which generates my results.[6]

Second, one might be concerned that there are differential motivation and ability effects here, much as there were in chapter 4 (see also the discussion of hypothesis H3 in chapter 3). That is, perhaps the effects of like-minded and crosscutting media are systematically larger for those who are more motivated and capable of engaging in motivated reasoning (see chapter 4 for more discussion of this point). I have tested for these effects, and I did not find them here (see the appendix to Levendusky 2012b). I cannot definitively explain why I found these effects in the experiments discussed in chapter 4 but not here, but I suspect it has to do with the underlying theoretical processes that govern how subjects respond to partisan media. In experiments 1 through 5, to become more polarized, subjects processed the messages, evaluated the arguments (in a biased fashion), and then updated their beliefs. This is a relatively cognitively demanding process—one that would be aided by greater motivation and ability to be a motivated reasoner and engage in biased processing (see the discussion of this point in chapter 4). In contrast, generating affective differences is a simpler process, and one where this type of ability might be less consequential. Because this type of effect is based less on processing messages and evaluating arguments carefully—and more on a straightforward reaction to the other party—having experience with these types of programs will be less helpful. Though motivated reasoning drives both processes, the reaction here is simpler: simply recognizing that the other party is flawed, rather than parsing arguments about policies. For this type of affective effect, all viewers are equally susceptible, though more empirical and theoretical work will be needed in the future to map the boundaries of these types of preference effects more generally.[7]

Third, one could argue that these affective results are not normatively troubling. If, say, Republicans genuinely believe that Obama is making poor foreign policy choices, why shouldn't they be upset when they hear this message on Fox News? If the source of the affective arousal is legitimate (and not based on a distortion of the truth), then why should scholars be concerned by these findings?[8] This is certainly a valid point, but it also misses a more fundamental and troubling ramification of these findings. To the extent that partisan media help paint the opposition in a disparaging light and decrease trust and support for bipartisanship, it has implications for American politics more broadly. Declining trust makes it more difficult for government to solve social problems (Hetherington 2005), and mass support for bipartisanship shapes congresspersons' incentives to support compromise (Harbridge and Malhotra 2011; Wolf, Strachan, and Shea 2012). Whether Republicans *should* be upset with Obama because of his policy decisions is beyond the scope of this work. But the results here demonstrate the significance of these programs for American politics.

A Disliked and Distrusted Opposition

The findings in this chapter demonstrate that like-minded media have a significant effect on how viewers see the opposition: watching like-minded media makes viewers feel less affect for the other party, rate them less positively along a number of dimensions, have less support for bipartisanship, and have less trust in the other side to do what is right for the country. Like-minded media diminish the opposition in the eyes of the audience.

This has deeply troubling consequences on a number of levels. My results show how partisan media reify and harden divisions between the parties in the mass electorate. Watching these sorts of programs make subjects less willing to compromise with the other side, and less trusting of them to do the right thing. Trust is an essential ingredient governments need to solve social problems (Hetherington 2005). For the government to function effectively, citizens need to trust the other party to do what is right, even when they disagree with them (Anderson et al. 2005). By making trust available to only one party or the other, like-minded media contribute to the difficulty government faces in actually solving real-world problems (Fiorina 2006). These shows help polarize viewers into a black-and-white world with good guys and bad guys, with an obvious candidate to blame when things go awry. As I explain in chapter 7, this sort of affective result, especially given the consequences for trust, policy, and bipartisanship, has important ramifications for contemporary American politics.

Appendix

The regression-based analyses of experiments 6 and 7 are given in Levendusky 2012b; I provide the regression-based analysis of experiment 8 below.

TABLE A5.1. **Analysis of policy support item, experiment 8.**

Like-minded treatment	0.31
	(0.55)
Crosscutting treatment	0.11
	(0.67)
Policy attributed to the other party	−0.32
	(0.60)
Like-minded treatment*policy attributed	**−1.18**
to the other party	**(0.81)**
Crosscutting treatment*policy attributed	0.14
to the other party	(0.88)
Intercept	2.89
	(0.40)
N	52
R^2	0.17

Note: Cell entries are ordinary least-squares regression coefficients with associated standard errors in parentheses; coefficients that can be distinguished from 0 are given in bold. The effect of like-minded media (direct and interactive) is statistically significant ($p < .1$; one-tailed).

CHAPTER SIX

Partisan Media's Electoral Effects

The past two empirical chapters have made the case that partisan media can increase viewers' attitudinal polarization, decrease affect for the opposition, and diminish support for bipartisanship and compromise. Those chapters addressed the first two empirical questions raised in chapter 1. I now turn to the third empirical question: can partisan media also shape how citizens behave in elections? The question has relevance not only for the theoretical debates discussed in chapter 3, but also for actual politics and politicians. For example, during the 2008 election, then senator Obama remarked, "I am convinced that if there were no Fox News, I might be two or three points higher in the polls. If I were watching Fox News, I wouldn't vote for me, right? Because the way I'm portrayed 24/7 is as a freak! I am the latte-sipping, *New York Times*–reading, Volvo-driving, no-gun-owning, effete, politically correct, arrogant liberal. Who wants somebody like that?" (Bai 2008).

President Obama's remarks suggest that partisan media consumption can shape vote choice itself, a claim examined by earlier scholars at both the aggregate (Della Vigna and Kaplan 2007) and individual levels (Dilliplane 2010). This chapter builds on these earlier works not only by testing the theoretical linkage between partisan media consumption and vote choice discussed in chapter 3 but also by digging deeper to examine the mediators and moderators of that effect: who responds to partisan media messages, and why do media change how subjects vote? As in previous chapters, I want to know not only whether there is some effect, but who is most strongly affected, and why.

Further, I also investigate how partisan media influence how citizens understand and interpret election outcomes. In the aftermath of elections, media outlets offer various explanations for the results, and these interpretations shape citizens' perceptions of the newly elected leader and his policies (Hershey 1992; Thomas and Bass 1996). These interpretations can range from the conventional (e.g., Obama won in 2008 because of poor economic performance), to the potentially delegitimizing (e.g., Obama won because of media bias or vote fraud). Accepting these sorts of delegitimizing explanations can make citizens view a leader and his policies more unfavorably—if the victory was not legitimate, then neither are the policies (Mutz 2006b). If partisan media can lead citizens to accept these sorts of delegitimizing explanations, then the electoral consequences of partisan media can spill over beyond the ballot box.

The analysis in this chapter points to two important conclusions about partisan media's electoral effects. First, I demonstrate that like-minded media do shape vote choice, though crosscutting media do not. I show that this effect is robust across a variety of different operationalizations and statistical techniques, and is unlikely to be the result of selection effects. I also show that this vote-choice effect is due largely to how voters see the candidates: like-minded media polarizes viewers' affect for the two party's candidates, and it also shapes their perceptions of the candidates' abilities to handle the problems facing the nation. Second, I demonstrate that partisan media's effects extend beyond the ballot box. Voters who support the losing candidate and consume partisan media are more likely to believe delegitimizing explanations for the election outcome. So not only do partisan media shape how viewers behave in the voting booth, they also shape how they understand and interpret the election after the fact. Partisan media's electoral effects extend beyond election day to broader understandings of the legitimacy of the winning candidate and his policies.

Data and Measurement Strategy

To test the vote choice and election interpretation hypotheses (H15–H16; see table 3.1 for a summary), I turned to data from the 2008 National Annenberg Election Study (NAES) panel data set. The 2008 NAES panel interviewed subjects five times between 2007 and the end of 2008. Details on the timing of the waves can be found in the data appendix, but the baseline interview occurred in late 2007 (before the "official" start of the election season), and then the first two waves occurred during the primary season, the third wave occurred during the summer, the fourth wave occurred during the fall campaign, and the fifth wave occurred in the weeks following the 2008 election. Knowledge Networks (now known as GfK/Knowledge Networks) conducted the survey; they administered surveys online, but selected their samples using a random-digit-dialing recruitment method. Data from this study are therefore a high-quality random sample of the American population, comparable to a conventional RDD telephone survey (Chang and Krosnick 2009).[1]

For this analysis, the NAES panel possessed two particularly important features. First, and most importantly, it had excellent measures of partisan media consumption asked at multiple points during the election season. This allowed me to accurately assess which respondents consume partisan media, how that changes over time, and what relationship this has to vote choice. Two key limitations in previous efforts to detect media-based persuasion effects were a lack of quality exposure measures and a lack of panel data to try and disentangle selection effects from exposure effects (Zaller 2002). Happily, the NAES data allowed me to accurately measure media exposure using some novel survey items, and the multiwave design is uniquely rich for political science data, allowing me to partially disentangle selection and treatment effects. Second, it had a large enough sample to allow me to detect even the modest media-based effects that typically exist in real-world data (Zaller 1996). If partisan media shaped vote choice in the 2008 election, this data would allow me to detect those effects.

So note that here, unlike earlier chapters, my analysis does not rely primarily on original experiments. While experiments have a host of advantages (chief among them their ability to isolate causal effects), they are not well suited to answering all questions. First, there are scenarios and outcomes that are difficult to simulate in an experiment, such as the rich information environment of a presidential campaign. While certain kinds of electoral information can be simulated (for example, see the discussion in Lau and Redlawsk 1997), simulating the sort of coverage (especially over-time coverage) provided by partisan media would be far more difficult. This makes the panel-data based approach the more plausible route for this type of analysis.

To measure partisan media exposure, I used a battery of items that ask respondents about their TV news consumption. The NAES data is unique because it measures exposure to television news by asking respondents about particular *programs*, rather than overall aggregate viewing habits (as is typically the case in most election studies). So subjects were asked not to recall their general viewing habits, or how many hours of television per week they watch, or whether they regularly watch the news, all of which has been shown to be problematic measures of media exposure (Price and Zaller 1993; Prior 2009). Instead, they were asked whether they watched individual programs, which should be much easier for respondents to accurately remember. The programs included in the survey were the most popular news and information programs at the time of the study as measured via Nielsen ratings. Previous work using this measure shows that it is highly reliable and valid, especially compared to other media exposure measures (for more details, see Dilliplane, Goldman, and Mutz, forthcoming). Subjects were asked about their TV viewing habits three times during the panel: during the primary campaign (wave 2), during the fall campaign (wave 4), and during the postelection wave (wave 5). Using these data, I accurately tracked not only who watches partisan media, but how their exposure changes over the course of the campaign.

To determine the shows that constitute partisan media exposure, I used the same criteria employed throughout the book. Consistent with my earlier arguments (see chapter 1), shows from Fox News constitute like-minded exposure for Republicans and crosscutting exposure for Democrats; the reverse is true of shows from MSNBC (see the data appendix for the list of programs that constituted partisan media exposure in the NAES data). As a further validity check, in the content analysis described in chapter 2, I examined the content of each network's discussion of the 2008 candidates. The slant on each network was relatively clear, supporting my argument that these programs constitute partisan media exposure.

In the analyses presented below, I measured partisan media consumption as a dichotomy (watched any shows vs. did not watch any), given that the hypothesis of interest is really about the effects of exposure versus nonexposure to these sources. As a robustness check, I also examined various alternative measurement strategies, all of which reach similar substantive conclusions (see the results in tables 6.2 and 6.3). This consistency demonstrates that my results were not simply the product of a particular operationalization of my key independent variable.

Two further notes on the exact construction of the partisan media consumption measure are warranted, however. First, to assess respondent's partisanship (so that I could code like-minded and crosscutting exposure), I used the baseline measure of partisan identity taken in 2007.

This was done to try and remove any election-specific effects on partisanship (Achen 1992), though using the partisanship measure taken early in the campaign would have yielded similar substantive results. This also means that I restricted my analysis to the respondents who joined the panel in wave 1. The 2008 NAES panel design adds a sample of new respondents to the panel at each wave (so while most subjects join at wave 1, a small number are invited to join in wave 2, wave 3, and so forth). Including these new respondents in my sample, however, would have created a significant complication for my study. They completed the baseline study when they joined the panel, and if this occurred during the heat of the campaign, it could have altered their stated partisanship (Achen 1992). Given this complexity, I restricted my analysis to the respondents who join at wave 1. This means that I took as my sample the 10,472 respondents who completed all 5 waves of the panel.

Second, I also homogenized the sample by looking only at those who reported watching at least one news and information program.[2] I did this to make the key analytical comparison clearer. The crux of my argument is that the slanted content presented on partisan media affects vote choice relative to a more neutral news program. That is, if a subject were to substitute partisan media for some neutral media (or add partisan media in addition to neutral media), what would the effect be? If I included those who watched no news or information programming, the comparison would get slightly more muddled: now the comparison was a slanted partisan media source versus no information at all. If I were to find effects in this case, it would be unclear if the effect were due to the biased information, or rather simply the information itself (i.e., is it learning about the candidates from any source causing the change in vote choice, or is it the biased presentation on partisan news?). This is analogous to the discussion in chapter 4 about the experimental design used to test the effects on attitudinal polarization, and I opt for the same choice here as I did there, focusing on the effect of partisan media relative to more neutral information sources. Happily, even if I included individuals who report watching no news and information programs, I would find similar substantive results.

Analytical Strategy

To accurately estimate the electoral effects of partisan media, I had to confront the problem of selection effects. Because the data come from an observational study and not an experiment, subjects chose their treatment. I was not interested in what makes subjects choose to consume partisan media; that process has been ably studied elsewhere (Stroud 2008, 2011). Instead, my interest centered on treatment effects: how does viewing partisan media shape vote choice? Given observational data, there is no perfect way to estimate this quantity, and any estimate I provide below should therefore not be interpreted as causal. I outline methods below that can help to reduce selection effects, but no method of analyzing observational data can ever completely remove them (hence why experiments are so valuable). That said, because experimentation is not feasible here, I proceeded forward using observational data, accepting that this necessarily induces some limitations to the results in this chapter.

In the analyses presented in this chapter, I used two different analytical strategies to estimate the treatment effect of partisan media consumption on vote choice. First, I used matching to try to remove differences between partisan media consumers and nonconsumers (for earlier political science examples of matching, see Barabas 2004; Kam and Palmer 2008; Ladd and Lenz 2009).[3] The logic of matching is straightforward. Suppose I have a respondent who watches some partisan television programs. A matching algorithm then finds the respondent who watches no partisan television but is otherwise identical: they have the same partisanship, age, education, and so forth. So matching finds two individuals who are identical (or as close to identical as possible) on all variables except the treatment (so one consumes partisan TV, and one does not). It does this for the entire data set, and I am left with a control group (non partisan TV consumers) and a treatment group (partisan TV consumers). The only difference between them is whether they consume partisan TV (since I matched them on the other variables), so it is "as if" partisan media consumption were randomly assigned (Ho et al. 2007). While matching cannot solve the problem of nonrandom selection (Arceneaux, Gerber, and Green 2006), it should hopefully reduce the potential for bias (as long as the bias is a function of the observable variables used to generate the matches).

I matched on a variety of baseline attitudinal and demographic factors that should predict whether subjects watch partisan media sources (i.e., partisanship, liberal-conservative self-identification, income, education, general media consumption, etc.; see the online appendix for a full discussion of the matching results and the accompanying balance tests). The treatment group watched partisan media during the fall campaign (wave 4), and the outcome was reporting voting for the respondent's party's candidate in the postelection wave (wave 5).[4] So I matched on variables measured in the baseline study from 2007, or from the first two waves (taken during the primary season), measured the treatment during the fall campaign, and measured the outcome (voting for one's party) in the postelection wave. This temporal separation helped ensure the causal ordering consistent with my theory: it is media exposure that drives vote choice, and not the reverse. Earlier applications of matching recommend this sort of temporal separation (Sekhon 2005), but matching on the post-election wave (wave 5) media exposure gives substantively similar results.

Second, I also exploited the panel nature of the data and use fixed-effects analysis. Here, I estimated $vote_{it} = \beta_0 + \beta_1 LM_{it} + \beta_2 CC_{it} + \alpha_i + u_{it}$ where $vote_{it}$ is respondent i's vote choice at wave t, LM_{it} and CC_{it} are measures of respondent i's consumption of like-minded and crosscutting media, respectively, at wave t, α_i is a respondent-specific fixed effect, and u is a stochastic disturbance term. The α_i term in the equation above is key: it is the individual-level fixed effect. What a fixed effect does is remove the effect of the time-invariant features of each individual on their vote choice. So fixed effects remove the effects of factors like gender, age, race, partisanship, ideology, and so forth (see Allison 2009 for more details). Once these stable factors are removed, the method analyzes how individual-level changes in partisan media consumption predict changes in vote intention. Because a fixed-effects regression is a within-subjects regression, one can interpret the fixed effects estimates as the effect of increasing or decreasing partisan media exposure over the course of the campaign.

Why both matching and fixed effects? I used multiple methods to present more credible inferences to the reader. Both methods try to remove the effect of confounding factors (like age, race, gender, partisanship, interest, etc.), but they do so in different ways. If they arrive at the same substantive answer—which they do—it makes my results more compelling, since they do not depend on the particular assumptions underlying a particular method.

Do Partisan Media Shape Vote Choice?

I begin by considering the role of partisan media on vote choice. The vote choice hypothesis (H15) predicts that both like-minded and crosscutting media will increase the likelihood of a respondent supporting her party's presidential nominee, even above and beyond the baseline tendency for party voting in the contemporary era (Bartels 2000). This follows because of the same motivated reasoning logic that I have used throughout the book. Because these partisan media programs prime viewers' partisan identities and present one-sided arguments (see chapter 2), they motivate subjects to process their messages in light of their prior beliefs. Here, because most subjects favor their party's nominee to begin with, they uncritically accept the messages coming from like-minded media, and they counterargue the critical ones coming from crosscutting media and become more likely to support their party's nominee (see the discussion in chapter 3). So partisan media consumers (relative to nonconsumers) should be more likely to support their party's nominee—partisan media acts like a reinforcement mechanism. This indicates that I should find a positive and significant treatment effect of partisan media consumption on the likelihood of party voting with my matching results.

Table 6.1 gives the results for the matching-based analysis, and tables 6.2 and 6.3 give the corresponding fixed-effects analysis. The findings shown in table 6.1 demonstrate that like-minded media had a significant effect on vote choice, consistent with my theoretical predictions: watching like-minded media made subjects approximately 5 percent more likely to vote for their party's candidate in the 2008 election. Crosscutting media, however, did not have a significant effect, and the point estimate is close to zero. Given the largely null findings for crosscutting media in earlier chapters, this should not be terribly surprising.

The findings using fixed-effects analysis, shown in tables 6.2 and 6.3, reinforce the findings from the matching-based analysis above: like-minded media shape vote choice, but crosscutting media do not. Note that while the fixed-effects results might appear to be smaller than the

TABLE 6.1. **Matching estimates of partisan media.**

	Like-minded media exposure	Crosscutting media exposure
ATT estimate	**0.05**	0.005
	(0.03)	(0.04)
N treated / *N* control	341/397	230/322

Note: Cell entries are ATT (average treatment on the treated) estimates derived using censored exact matching. Coefficients that can be distinguished from 0 ($\alpha = 0.10$; two-tailed) are given in bold.
Source: 2008 National Annenberg Election Study, panel dataset.

TABLE 6.2. **Estimates of the effects of like-minded media.**

	(1)	(2)	(3)	(4)
Any like-minded media exposure	**0.021 (0.006)**	**0.022 (0.006)**	–	–
Number of like-minded media shows	–	–	**0.005 (0.001)**	–
Watch 1 like-minded show	–	–	–	**0.016 (0.006)**
Watch 2 like-minded shows	–	–	–	**0.022 (0.007)**
Watch 3 like-minded shows	–	–	–	**0.028 (0.008)**
Watch 4 like-minded shows	–	–	–	**0.026 (0.01)**
Watch 5 or more like-minded shows	–	–	–	**0.027 (0.01)**
Constant	**0.91 (0.003)**	**0.91 (0.004)**	**0.91 (0.003)**	**0.91 (0.002)**
Includes subject fixed effects	Yes	Yes	Yes	Yes
Includes wave fixed effects	No	Yes	Yes	Yes
N	20040 (8797)	20040 (8797)	20040 (8797)	20040 (8797)
R^2	0.01	0.01	0.01	0.01

Note: Cell entries are ordinary least-squares regression coefficients, with robust standard errors and models include subject-specific fixed effects. Coefficients in bold can be statistically distinguished from 0 at conventional levels.
Source: 2008 National Annenberg Election Study, panel dataset.

matching-based estimates, given the standard errors, the two sets of estimates cannot be differentiated from one another. Further, note that these results are highly consistent across different specifications of partisan media exposure: I can measure partisan media exposure using a dichotomous measure (watched/did not watch), as the number of shows watched, or as a series of dummy variable indicators for the number of shows watched (to control for any nonlinear effects), and I arrive at the same conclusions, suggesting that the results do not hinge on any particular operationalization of this variable.

The crosscutting effects are particularly interesting in this context. In earlier chapters, I found that crosscutting media had an effect for viewers who found these programs to be credible (or who wanted to watch these programs), but here, I found null effects. So once I removed the selection effects, there was no treatment effect. So while crosscutting media seem to have a large effect, it really is just that those who watch crosscutting media are quite different than those who do not. This reinforces a point

TABLE 6.3. **Effects of crosscutting media.**

	(1)	(2)	(3)	(4)
Any crosscutting media exposure	0.006 (0.006)	0.007 (0.005)	—	—
Number of crosscutting Media Shows	—	—	0.004 (0.004)	
Watch 1 crosscutting show	—	—	—	0.004 (0.006)
Watch 2 crosscutting shows	—	—	—	0.001 (0.01)
Watch 3 crosscutting shows	—	—	—	0.01 (0.02)
Watch 4 or more crosscutting shows	—	—	—	0.02 (0.03)
Constant	**0.91 (0.006)**	**0.92 (0.003)**	**0.92 (0.003)**	**0.92 (0.002)**
Includes subject fixed effects	Yes	Yes	Yes	Yes
Includes wave fixed effects	No	Yes	Yes	Yes
N	20040 (8797)	20040 (8797)	20040 (8797)	20040 (8797)
R^2	0.005	0.002	0.001	0.001

Note: Cell entries are ordinary least-squares regression coefficients with robust standard errors and models include subject-specific fixed effects. Coefficients in bold can be statistically distinguished from 0 at conventional level.
Source: 2008 National Annenberg Election Study, panel dataset.

I made earlier: a key next step for future work will be to understand who watches crosscutting media, and why they choose to do so.

While these might seem like modest effects, they need to be put into the proper context. These results do not simply reflect a selection effect: the fixed effects in tables 6.2 and 6.3 remove any stable individual-specific traits that would predict both partisan media viewing and party voting, and matching removes any differences that are function of the matched variables. While partisan media viewers are more partisan, more politically informed, and so forth, the fixed effects remove these between-subject differences. The estimates in the tables above, therefore, do not simply represent baseline differences between partisan media consumers and nonconsumers. Rather, they reflect differences that stem from exposure to partisan media during the election campaign.

Further, because the estimates in tables 6.2 and 6.3 contain respondent-specific fixed effects, the estimates are based on within-subject change. In 2008, few subjects changed their vote intention over the course of the study; once the fall campaign began, 75 percent of subjects reported the same vote intention in all remaining waves, and over

90 percent of subjects eventually reported voting for their party's candidate. Indeed, even among those who reported watching no partisan media, 91 percent supported their party's nominee (see the constant term in table 6.2). On one level, this suggests that the effect of partisan media consumption is to move subjects from supporting their party's nominee with 91 percent probability to supporting him with 93 percent probability, which seems less than impressive. Such an interpretation would be mistaken, however. Because party voting is so ubiquitous here, the seemingly small effects above can indicate a large reinforcing effect of like-minded media. To demonstrate this, I calculated the persuasion rate, the percentage of respondents who, once exposed to like-minded media, were persuaded to support their party's candidate (Della Vigna and Kaplan 2007; Della Vigna and Gentzkow 2010). Here, the persuasion rate was 21 percent, suggesting that partisan media managed to convince approximately one in five respondents who viewed partisan media to support their party's nominee—an impressive media-based effect.[5] Though party voting was quite high among all respondents in 2008, partisan media were still able to persuade many of those exposed to it to support their party's candidate. Considered from this perspective, partisan media had a quite sizable effect on vote choice.

Moderators of the Effects of Partisan Media

If my theoretical account of the effect of partisan media is correct, then the effects of partisan media should be heterogeneous across different groups of voters. Partisan strength is arguably the most obvious source of this heterogeneity. Because strong partisans are so firmly anchored to their party and its nominee, there should be little room for like-minded media to have much of an impact on their behavior; even strong partisans who do not watch like-minded media should vote for their party's candidate, all else being equal. In contrast, like-minded media messages should have a larger effect on weak and leaning partisans who are less strongly tied to the party (Miller and Shanks 1996). I therefore expected to find that like-minded media had a smaller effect for strong partisans (relative to weak/leaning partisans), all else being equal. Given the null findings for crosscutting media above, I restricted my analysis in the remainder of the chapter to like-minded media exposure.

Table 6.4 gives the results. For strong partisans, like-minded media consumption did not have a statistically significant effect on voting be-

TABLE 6.4. **Effects of partisan media, by strength of partisan affiliation**

Consume like-minded media	0.006 (0.005)
Weak/leaning partisan	**−0.05** **(0.008)**
Consume like-minded media*weak/ leaning partisan	**0.03** **(0.001)**
Intercept	**0.93** **(0.004)**
Includes subject-specific fixed effects	Y
N	2040 (8797)
R^2	0.06

Note: Cell entries are ordinary least-squares regression coefficients with robust standard errors and models include subject-specific fixed effects. Coefficients in bold can be statistically distinguished from 0 at conventional levels
Source: 2008 National Annenberg Election Study, panel dataset.

havior. For weak and leaning partisans, however, like-minded media had a much stronger effect (nearly a 4-percentage-point effect; $p < .01$). Strong partisans who were already anchored to the party in a variety of different ways did not need the reinforcement provided by like-minded media to support their party's candidate. Weak and leaning partisans, however, were more strongly affected by the reinforcement provided via like-minded media.

One would also expect that watching like-minded media should increase the probability that inconsistent partisans (those who initially support the other party's candidate) eventually support their party's nominee. Though these voters are initially out of step with their party, seeing the reinforcement provided on like-minded media should increase the probability they ultimately support their party's nominee. The results of this examination (which once again used fixed-effects analysis) are shown in table 6.5. Like-minded media did bring respondents back their party's candidate, at least for those who initially supported another party's candidate. Like-minded media persuaded these voters to eventually return to the party and its nominee.[6] Again, this suggests that like-minded media reinforce and help cement preferences for party voting in the mass electorate.

The Direction of Causality

One concern with the analysis above is that even if there is a relationship between vote choice and partisan media, I have misstated it: the causal

TABLE 6.5. **Effects of partisan media on inconsistent voters.**

Consume like-minded media	**0.18**
	(0.08)
Intercept	**0.34**
	(0.03)
Include subject-specific fixed effects	Yes
N	810
	(698)
R^2	0.001

Note: Cell entries are ordinary least-squares regression coefficients with robust standard errors and models include subject-specific fixed effects. Coefficients in bold can be statistically distinguished from 0 at conventional levels. Inconsistent voters are those who initially say they support the other party's candidate
Source: 2008 National Annenberg Election Study, panel dataset.

arrow runs from vote choice to partisan media consumption, and not the other way around—individuals decide which candidate they will support, and then they seek out media that reflects that preference. With only observational data, this issue can never fully be resolved. That said, however, I can leverage the panel data in several ways to speak to this issue.

First, the matching results above help provide some protection against endogeneity. Here, I matched on baseline variables observed before the election began, measured the treatment during the fall campaign, and then measured vote choice in the postelection wave. Given this, logically it cannot be the case that vote choice (measured in the postelection wave) drives media consumption (measured in the preelection wave).

As a further robustness check, consider the following comparison. Take the universe of voters who were undecided early in the campaign, and then divide it into two groups: those who consumed like-minded media during the campaign and those who did not. Because all voters were initially undecided, it cannot be the case that their vote choice drove the decision to watch partisan media. I can then compare the level of party voting between these two groups in later waves. If it is the case that like-minded media promote party voting, as I argued above, then I should find that the group who watches like-minded media should have higher levels of party voting in later waves of the survey. When I turn to the data, I find support for this argument. Among those who watched partisan media, there is significantly more party voting: 71 percent of nonwatchers voted for their party's nominee, while 77 percent of partisan media consumers did so, a significant difference ($p < .05$). Because all of these voters were initially undecided, this guards against the reverse causal pattern (vote choice driving partisan media consumption), making me more confident in the results above.

Placebo Tests

To further test for the sensitivity to unobserved effects, I conducted a placebo test by examining vote choice questions asked of subjects in 2007 before the election began. In the initial wave of the survey, subjects were asked which candidate they planned to support in the 2008 election. Because the candidates were not known at such an early data, we cannot examine voting for Obama or McCain, but we can look at whether respondents preferred the Democratic or Republican nominee—that is, whether they expressed a preference for their party.[7] Because the treatment here was watching partisan media during the campaign, it cannot be the case that this treatment affected vote preference early in the campaign, since the treatment occurs after vote choice was recorded. If my models properly account for differences between partisan media watchers and nonwatchers, then I should find no effect of fall campaign partisan media exposure on early primary campaign vote choice. Table 6.6 shows the results of testing for this possibility.

The results show that there was no effect: the point estimate (calculated using matching) suggests a less than 1 percent difference in party voting, and it is not statistically significant. This provides additional evidence that my models account for the key differences between partisan media consumers and nonconsumers.

I also conducted a Rosenbaum (2002) sensitivity test as a further check on concerns about unobservable variables. Sensitivity tests ask how large of a hidden bias needs to be present before the results of my analysis would disappear. The idea is that some other variable that causes both the treatment (partisan media consumption) and the outcome (support

TABLE 6.6. **Placebo test.**

	Wave 1 vote choice
ATT estimate	0.004
	(0.02)
N treated/*N* control	335/393

Note: Cell entries contain the ATT (average treatment on the treated) estimates, derived from coarsened exact matching.
Source: 2008 National Annenberg Election Study, panel dataset.

for the party's presidential nominee). The sensitivity analysis asks how big of an effect this other variable would need to have in order for my results to go away. If the other variable only needs to have a small effect, then my results are quite sensitive to this sort of "lurking" variable. But if it would need to have a large effect, then my results are more robust.

Using these methods, I found that for my results to vanish, there would have to be an unobserved variable that predicts consuming partisan media at least as well as political interest or partisan strength.[8] These variables are very strong predictors of partisan media consumption (see Stroud 2011), so this unobserved variable would need to be an excellent predictor of partisan media consumption. Given the robustness across both the fixed effects and matching specifications, a hidden bias this large is unlikely. In short, while I can never definitively rule out some unobserved variable explaining my effects, that is a rather unlikely outcome in this specific case.

Why Does Partisan Media Persuade?

The findings above show that like-minded media persuade viewers, but they do not speak to the underlying mechanism. The theoretical logic from chapter 3 (rooted in motivated reasoning) suggests that treatment effects found above should be the product of shifts in how viewers feel about the candidates. Because the arguments from like-minded media suggest that the party's nominee is "good" and the other nominee is "bad" (on the issues, character, and so forth), I should find affective effects of partisan media consumption. That is, affect should provide a mechanism (at least a partial one) for explaining the reinforcing power of like-minded media. If this is the case, then watching like-minded media should change viewers' feeling thermometer ratings of the presidential and vice presidential candidates; they should like their party's candidates more and the opposing party less. I used matching to estimate the effects of partisan media consumption on feeling thermometer ratings (table 6.7).[9]

There was a large and significant effect on feeling thermometer ratings, somewhere between 2.5 and 7.75 degrees on the one-hundred-point feeling thermometer scale. Put slightly differently, these effects correspond to changing affect by between one-tenth and one-third of a standard deviation, all else being equal. Viewers liked their party's nominee

TABLE 6.7. **Effect of like-minded media on candidate feeling thermometer ratings**

	Same party presidential nominee	Same party vice presidential nominee	Other party presidential nominee	Other party vice presidential nominee
ATT estimate	3.70	7.75	−2.55	−3.51
	(0.92)	(1.05)	(1.01)	(1.04)
N treated/*N* control	1191/1318	1191/1318	1191/1318	1191/1318

Note: Cell entries are ATT (average treatment on the treated) estimates, with associated standard errors in parentheses, of the effect of like-minded media consumption on candidate feeling thermometer ratings. All coefficients can be distinguished from 0 at conventional levels.
Source: 2008 National Annenberg Election Study, panel dataset.

and running mate more and the other party's nominees less, consistent with the one-sided messages propagated on like-minded television. Like-minded media polarize viewers' attitudes toward the nominees and their running mates.

This sort of affective shift should also extend to evaluations of the candidates' qualities. Citizens who watch like-minded media should be more likely to think their party's candidate is more competent, and conversely, that the opposite-party candidate is less competent (Brady and Sniderman 1985). If I find these sorts of effects, they will serve as additional evidence that partisan media changes affect toward the candidates.

I tested this hypothesis using a series of items asked in the Annenberg study in the fall preelection wave. Respondents were asked whether they thought the candidates would do a good job or a bad job handling several valence issues (the economy, homeland security, and health care; see the data appendix for a list of specific question wordings). For simplicity, I combined these issues into an appendix of net competence, where higher scores indicate higher ratings of competence[10] (though I discuss some issue-specific results below). I expected to find that partisan media viewers were more likely to think that their party's candidate would do a good job handling these issues and the opposite-party candidate would do a bad job handling them.

As before, I matched on a series of baseline variables (the same ones used earlier), and used partisan media exposure during the primary season as the treatment variable.[11]

Table 6.8 shows the results. As expected, subjects who consumed partisan media thought their party's candidate was better able to handle these valence issues and the other party's candidate was less able. Take, for example, evaluations of economic competence, which was arguably

TABLE 6.8. **Effects on perceptions of candidate competence.**

	Same party valence evaluation	Other party valence evaluation
ATT estimate	0.18	−0.21
	(0.07)	(0.10)
N treated / *N* control	803 / 864	531 / 614

Note: Cell entries are ATT (average treatment on the treated) estimates, with associated standard errors in parentheses, of the effect of like-minded media consumption on evaluations of candidates' abilities to handle valence issues and issue position agreement. All coefficients can be distinguished from 0 at conventional levels.
Source: 2008 National Annenberg Election Study, panel dataset.

the issue of the 2008 campaign (Kenski, Hardy, and Jamieson 2010). Subjects who watched like-minded partisan media were approximately 5 percent more likely to rate their own candidate as being able to do a good job handling the economy, and were almost 8 percent more likely to rate the other party's candidate as doing a bad job. These may not seem like particularly large effects, but keep in mind that I as matching on a number of factors like partisanship, political interest, and so forth that we would expect to powerfully predict economic evaluations. From this perspective, this is an important—and real—boost to the candidates. Because partisan media changes how viewers see the candidates, it changes how viewers assess their abilities as well.

That said, it is also important to acknowledge a limitation of these effects. Finding mechanism-based effects is extremely difficult in both observational and experimental research (Bullock, Green, and Ha 2010; Imai et al. 2011). I present these results as suggestive that affect at least partially explains why like-minded media reinforce vote choice, but these results do not prove that relationship in any definitive sense, though stronger evidence on this point is an important topic for future work.

Shaping What the Election Means

The material above explains how partisan media shape vote choice by changing how voters feel about the candidates and how they assess the competence of the competing nominees. But partisan media's effect on elections does not stop there—they also influence how citizens *interpret* the election. In the aftermath of the election, both partisan and mainstream outlets offered interpretations of the election's meaning. While most outlets stressed that Obama's victory reflected the poor economy, Bush's unpopularity, and so forth, Fox News emphasized two additional pernicious and delegitimizing explanations for Obama's victory: media bias and vote fraud. To be clear, these were not the only—or even the primary—explanations offered on Fox, but they were offered as rationales more so than on other outlets (see the discussion in chapter 2). The election interpretation hypothesis (H16) predicts that Republicans who watch Fox News will be more likely to accept these delegitimizing explanations for Obama's victory.

I tested this hypothesis using data from the postelection wave of the NAES panel study. In the postelection wave, respondents were asked (in an open-ended item) why they thought Obama had won the election. A full analysis of these items is beyond the scope of this book, but I did test whether Republicans watching Fox News were more likely to attribute Obama's victory to media bias. Using the same matching techniques described above, I found that they did: Republicans watching Fox News were more than twice as likely to blame media bias (relative to Republicans who did not watch Fox) for Obama's victory: 3 percent of non–Fox-viewing Republicans argued that Obama won because of media bias, but 7 percent of Fox-viewing Republicans supported this interpretation ($p < .01$). Partisan media consumers were more likely to believe their party lost for illegitimate reasons.

In addition to media bias, Fox also discussed another potential explanation for Obama's victory: vote fraud and corruption. The coverage of this topic was less extensive than the discussion of media bias, but there were a number of stories on Fox discussing ACORN and its fraudulent efforts at voter registration (see the content analysis discussion in chapter 2). While the story was discussed on the mainstream media as well, the coverage on Fox was notably more extensive (Dreier and Martin 2010). This should also lead to Fox-viewing Republicans being more likely to think there was vote fraud in the election. In the same postelection wave, respondents were asked to assess the degree to which they think the votes were counted accurately—in effect, the likelihood that there was vote fraud (see the appendix for the exact wording). I used this item and the same estimation strategy used earlier to assess beliefs about vote fraud in 2008. When I did so, I found that Republicans watching Fox News were significantly less likely to think the votes were counted fairly and accurately.[12] Republicans who watched Fox were approximately 9 percent less likely to trust that the votes are counted accurately (relative to Republicans who did not watch Fox). This type of belief gives yet another reason to be skeptical of Obama's victory.

To be clear, most Republicans and Fox News viewers did not accept these nefarious explanations. Instead, they thought, like respondents more broadly, that Obama won because of the conventional factors (the economy, Bush's unpopularity, etc.). The effects above are modest ones, affecting some Fox viewers, but hardly all of them. But even a relatively modest increase in support for these sorts of nefarious interpretations has important implications. If individuals believe Obama won because the media was behind him, or because ACORN and affiliated groups committed vote fraud, this has the potential to delegitimize Obama's presidency (Anderson et al. 2005; Mutz 2006b). After all, if McCain lost because the media wanted Obama to win (and not because of unpopular policies, or a poor economy, and so forth), then Obama's victory is illegitimate. It is not a particular stretch to imagine that these voters would then be more likely to oppose Obama and his policies—if the victory is ill-gotten, then the leader is illegitimate. The seeds of discontent are sown in the immediate aftermath of the election. How partisan media sources spin elections has wide-ranging consequences for citizens' attitudes toward the political system and its leaders more generally.

Experimental Evidence of Election Interpretation Effects

Like all observational designs, the analysis above cannot offer a clean test of the causal impact of partisan media consumption on election interpretation. To help supplement this analysis, I conducted an additional original experiment. I wanted to identify a situation where I could isolate the effect of a particular delegitimizing message in the aftermath of an election. Ideally, this would be a competitive national election, much like the 2008 presidential election. Unfortunately, in any national election of any significance, any experimental treatment I could offer would be overwhelmed by the real-world messages being broadcast from media elites.

But I *could* test my logic using a less salient election, such as a state-level ballot initiative campaign. In a less salient election, because the media message will not be so overwhelming, my experimental treatment can actually have some discernible effect on respondents. So I designed experiment 9 to test the election interpretation hypothesis. This experiment focused on the Ohio ballot measure known as Issue 2, which was on the ballot in 2011. The measure would overturn a law passed by the incumbent governor John Kasich that limited the power of public employee unions to engage in collective bargaining. Issue 2 passed, handing Democrats and labor groups a key victory. In the wake of the election, many mainstream sources argued that Republicans overreached and tried to pass a law that was simply too conservative for the median voter in Ohio (Blake and Weiner 2011; Tavernise 2011). In contrast, however, many right-wing blogs and other partisan outlets framed this as a case where Republicans were outmessaged: Republicans had the right policy position (limiting union power is necessary to prevent cuts to important services), but they did not deliver it effectively enough (Holtsberry 2011). Note that this is exactly the sort of explanation that helps to delegitimize the outcome: our side lost not because we had the wrong policy but because our messaging was ineffective. We had the right policy, just the wrong PR team: the outcome reflects style more than substance. If viewers accept these sorts of messages, then policies, elections, and leaders will be delegitimized.

To test this idea, I randomly exposed subjects to one of two print editorials. The treatment editorial explained the outcome by arguing that Republicans were outmessaged, a delegitimizing explanation, while the control editorial presented the more conventional argument that Republicans tried to pass a law that was too conservative for the average Ohioan. If the election interpretation hypothesis is correct, then Republican subjects should accept the delegitimizing explanation when exposed to it, as it constitutes like-minded exposure for them, though there should be no effect for Democratic or Independent subjects.

Figure 6.1 gives the results for this item (a regression-based analysis of the experiment is given in the appendix to this chapter).The results are clear: while the delegitimizing frame had no effect on Democrats or Independent voters (for whom it represented crosscutting exposure), it did have a large effect on Republicans. Republican respondents in the treatment condition were much more likely to accept this explanation for the outcome. Agreement that Republicans were outmessaged increased from 4.33 in the control condition to 5.19 in the treatment condition on the seven-point Likert scale, a difference that is highly statistically significant. Put slightly differently, while 39 percent of Republicans thought they were

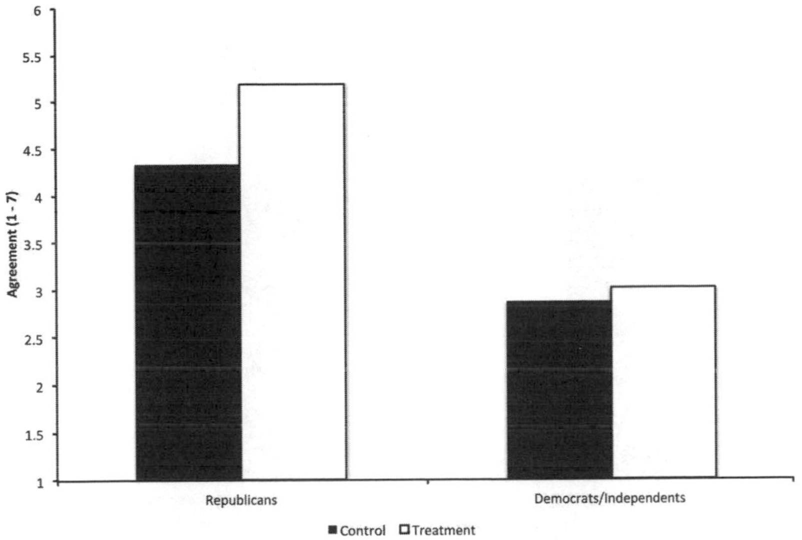

FIGURE 6.1. Belief that Republicans lost due to poor messaging, experiment 9. The *y* axis gives the agreement with the statement, "Republicans in Ohio had the better message, but they lost because they did not deliver it effectively" on a 1–7 scale (with 7 indicating the strongest agreement).

out-messaged in the control condition, 73 percent felt this way in the treatment condition. Consistent with the findings earlier in the book, partisan media can not only shape attitudes and opinions about the other side, they can also shape how subjects interpret election outcomes.

One might also ask whether the treatment also caused Republicans to reject the more mainstream interpretation of Republican ideological overreach. Figure 6.2 presents these results. Fascinatingly, Republican viewers also became less willing to accept this explanation. So after exposure to the like-minded treatment, Republican subjects were more likely to reject the mainstream interpretation and embrace the more partisan but delegitimizing explanation (as before, there is no effect for other subjects). Here, support among Republican respondents for the belief that Republicans overreached fell from 4.17 to 3.43 on the seven-point Likert scale, or in percentage terms, from 42 percent agreement in the control condition to 30 percent agreement in the treatment condition. Partisan media exposure changes how subjects interpret and understand elections.

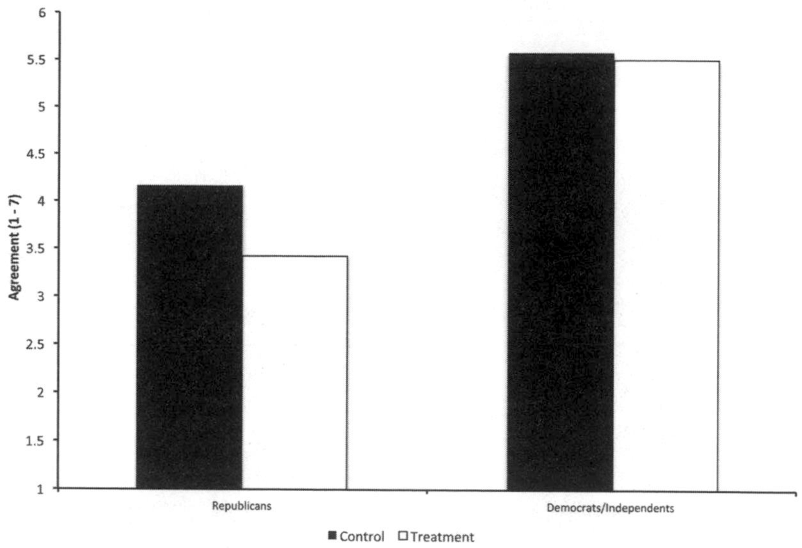

FIGURE 6.2. Belief that Republicans lost because they overreached and passed an overly conservative law, experiment 9. The *y* axis gives the agreement with the statement, "Democrats in Ohio won because Republicans overreached and tried to pass an overly conservative law." on a 1–7 scale (with 7 beings the strongest agreement).

There is an important caveat to these results: I selected an Ohio ballot measure as the subject of a story shown to voters from across the country. For most voters not from Ohio, this was likely their first exposure to this issue. From an experimental design standpoint, this is a good thing: it means that my treatment can actually have some effect. But it also means that these treatment effects in experiment 9 are maximal effects, and in a competitive election, the effects would be much smaller.[13] Indeed, as the analysis from the 2008 NAES study shows, the effects in a competitive election (with many competing messages) are much smaller. But that's fine: the point of experiment 9 was not to try and estimate a particular effect size, it was merely to test the underlying causal logic of the election interpretation hypothesis. From this perspective, it succeeded, as it showed that when exposed to nefarious arguments about why their side lost, viewers embrace them. Partisan media, by offering such delegitimizing explanations, have a powerful ability to shape how viewers come to understand the implications of an election.

Conclusion

This chapter began with a timely question in light of the contemporary media environment: does consuming partisan media, particularly like-minded media, impact individual-level vote choice? Using panel data from the 2008 election, I demonstrated that it does. Like-minded media have a statistically and substantively significant effect on voting—media slant directly shapes vote choice. I further showed that this increase in party voting comes from partisan media's effect on viewers' perceptions of the candidates. The biased presentation on like-minded sources draws viewers toward their party's candidate and away from the opposing one.

That said, these findings also demonstrate how constrained partisan media's direct effect on the vote actually is. Because party voting has become more prevalent in recent elections (Bartels 2000), there simply isn't much room for partisan media to really dramatically change vote choice—after all, even among those who watch no like-minded programs, approximately nine out of ten voters selected their party's candidate. Partisan media have a real effect on vote choice, but because party voting is high due to other factors, this effect is somewhat limited.

Perhaps if this were partisan media's only electoral impact, one might conclude that its effect on elections was relatively muted, especially relative the more pronounced outcomes seen in chapters 4 and 5. But it is not. Partisan media's effect on how citizens understand the election outcomes is more pernicious and troubling. Partisan media also shape how viewers interpret and understand the election. I show that in 2008, Republicans who watched Fox News had a different, and less positive, understanding of why Obama won (compared with Republicans who did not watch Fox). Republicans watching Fox were more likely to attribute his loss to media bias or vote fraud, two topics discussed heavily on Fox as potential factors in Obama's victory. Watching partisan media influences how citizens come to understand the election results. I also verified this relationship using an original experiment conducted after the 2011 elections. Together, these results have troubling implications for citizens' beliefs about leaders' legitimacy, and the legitimacy of the system more broadly (Anderson et al. 2005; Mutz 2006b). Knowing how citizens interpret the election outcomes can be just as important as knowing why they voted the way they did.

Appendix

This appendix reports the regression-based analysis for experiment 9, used in this chapter to understand how voters interpret elections.

TABLE A6.1. **Regression-based analysis, experiment 9.**

	Republicans were out-messaged		Law was too conservative	
	Democrats/ Independents	Republicans	Democrats/ Independents	Republicans
Treatment article	0.15	**0.85**	−0.08	**−0.74**
	(0.31)	**(0.36)**	(0.23)	**(0.40)**
Constant	**2.87**	**4.33**	**5.59**	**4.17**
	(0.21)	**(0.24)**	**(0.14)**	**(0.26)**
N	128	64	129	64
R^2	0.002	0.09	0.001	0.05

Note: Cell entries are ordinary least-squares coefficients with robust standard errors in parentheses; coefficient estimates are reported separately by partisanship. The two left-hand columns report estimates for figure 6.1, the two right-hand columns report estimates for figure 6.2.

CHAPTER SEVEN

How Partisan Media Matter for America

This book began with a broad, overarching question: do partisan media contribute to the gridlock and dissensus that are so frequently at the center of contemporary policymaking? To explore this normative puzzle, I posed four related questions for the book to answer. (1) Do partisan media polarize viewers? (2) Do partisan media decrease support for bipartisanship and compromise? (3) Do partisan media shape how viewers behave in and understand the results of elections? (4) If only a small fraction of Americans watch partisan media, how can these outlets have a large impact on American politics? The previous chapters answered the first three questions, and this chapter steps back to consider the bigger picture and finally answer the fourth question. I argue that partisan media matter for American politics writ large—even for those who never watch partisan media outlets—because of their effects on governance. Because of this, partisan media, despite their relatively limited audience, matter for American politics.

A Brief Synopsis of the Findings

Chapters 4–6 answered the first three questions I raised in chapter 1. First, there is question of whether partisan media polarize their viewers. The answer is that they do, at least when viewers watch like-minded partisan media that reinforce their beliefs, and this effect grows stronger over time with repeated exposures. Further, I also show how—consistent with theoretical model of motivated reasoning laid out in chapter 3—this effect is largest for those who actually watch these programs. But these individuals are already more extreme than the average voter, so like-minded media makes them *even more* extreme. Like-minded media polarize the electorate not by making moderates into extremists but by pushing extremists even further away from the center. They also make subjects more certain that their attitudes are correct, so subjects are both further from the center and more confident in these off-center beliefs.

Second, I asked whether partisan media decrease support for bipartisanship and compromise. As expected, they do just that. This same sort of like-minded, reinforcing content makes viewers dislike and distrust the other party. By calling the other party's motives into question and by painting them in a negative light, like-minded media help discredit the opposition. This, in turn, makes viewers less willing to compromise, less trusting of the other side, and less likely to support policies attributed to the other party. Partisan media decrease viewers' willingness to compromise and increase the difficulty of governance in the contemporary political environment.

Third, I also asked whether partisan media shape how viewers behave during, and understand the causes of, elections. Partisan media increase party voting by changing how voters feel about the candidates and their issue positions. They also impact how viewers, especially those whose party lost the election, construct a narrative to explain the election outcome. In the 2008 election, Republican viewers who watched Fox News were more likely to embrace two particularly delegitimizing explanations for Obama's victory: media bias and vote fraud. Partisan media shape not just vote choice itself but also how viewers understand and interpret the election.

Overall, the answer to all three questions demonstrates that partisan media have a striking, and potentially quite troubling, effect on their audience. After watching partisan outlets (at least like-minded outlets), viewers become more polarized, more certain their beliefs are the correct ones, less willing to compromise and support bipartisanship, and more willing to attribute election victories by the other side to nefarious motives. Partisan media reify and harden divisions within their audiences.

These results show the consistently strong and polarizing effects of like-minded media that reinforce viewers' prior beliefs. But what happens when subjects consume crosscutting sources that cut against, rather than reinforce, their existing beliefs? When, say, a Democrat watches

Bill O'Reilly on Fox News, what happens? Generally speaking, crosscutting media have little effect on attitudes or vote choice. This is perhaps surprising, given the motivated reasoning perspective from chapter 3, which led me to predict that subjects would actively counterargue these crosscutting messages. But time and again, most subjects seemed to reject these crosscutting arguments, and only those with the most motivation and ability—those with strong preexisting attitudes—would counterargue them. Perhaps at some level, this should not be all that surprising: after all, it is much easier to uncritically accept attitudinally consistent information than to counterargue inconsistent information (Ditto et al. 1998; Jerit and Barabas 2012), so I would expect larger like-minded effects. That said, however, these findings reinforce an important point about the underlying theory of motivated reasoning: not everyone is equally equipped to be a motivated reasoner. Only those who deeply care about a topic will engage in this sort of effortful processing (Taber and Lodge 2006). An important topic for future work will be to further unpack and explore the variation in subjects' willingness to effortfully process and counterargue crosscutting information.[1]

But crosscutting media are not impotent for all voters: they move those who perceive crosscutting sources to be particularly credible. This suggests than another important avenue for future research will be to determine the root of these credibility judgments: how do voters form them, what do they reflect, and so forth. What does it mean, for example, for a Democrat to see Fox News as particularly credible? Is this is a signal that this person is just deeply out of step with their party (Holbert, Garrett, and Gleason 2010), or is there a deeper process at work?[2] Unpacking the content and meaning of these types of credibility judgments is an important next step for students of media and politics. Much more information is needed on how, when, and why crosscutting sources affect viewers.

While a deeper understanding of these crosscutting effects is an important topic for future study, the political ramifications of crosscutting media are likely to be much more modest, compared with the effects for like-minded media. Most partisan media consumption is like-minded (Iyengar and Han 2009; Stroud 2011). Further, the audience for like-minded media is more politically engaged, informed, and active than the general public (Stroud 2011), making it the sort of audience that will have it voices heard in the halls of power. In effect, while like-minded partisan media still only represent a relatively narrow segment of the overall media market, it is a market that reaches an important audience, and has a real impact on politics more broadly.

Partisan Media and Self-Selection

Looking at these effects for both crosscutting and like-minded media, however, one still might be skeptical that they represent real effects—after all, most voters do not tune in to watch partisan media. In a series of innovative experiments, Arceneaux and Johnson (2010, forthcoming) allowed voters to change the channel during experiments: subjects were not forced to watch partisan media programs, but rather, could choose whether to watch them (or instead watch something else that's more entertaining). Given the option, most subjects in the experiment simply changed the channel, paralleling real life. After all, most citizens do not watch partisan media. This is undoubtedly true, and an important point to keep in mind when interpreting these results: most people don't want to watch partisan media, and its real-world effect on these nonwatchers is relatively small (though as I explain below, the effect is not zero, even for those who never watch these shows).

But this is really a separate issue from the one I am studying here. A study that allows subjects to change the channel and avoid partisan media is a study in selective exposure: given the choice, do people prefer to watch partisan media? If so, what is the effect? Such selective exposure effects are trying to estimate a particular quantity of interest: the (population) average treatment effect of real-world partisan media exposure. Because people can change the channel—and must therefore choose to watch a partisan program—the estimates correspond to that real-world population average. This is an important quantity of interest and highlights that if we look across the population at large, the direct effects of partisan media are likely to be quite modest.

This might seem, at first blush, to contradict my findings above. But such a reading is ultimately naïve and incorrect. Three key factors explain why. First, I agree completely that the population average effect is likely to be quite small. As I show in chapter 4, the segment of the population who watches partisan media is quite modest. To understand the effects of partisan media, I want to know what these effects are for those who actually watch these programs.[3] Because partisan media consumers are a modest fraction of the electorate, the average effect in the population as a whole will be quite small. But because the partisan media audience is more active and engaged, the overall aggregate effect can be quite consequential.

Second, when considering whether partisan media actually polarize viewers, it is crucial to consider the issues used as the treatment stimulus. As I went to some lengths to explain in chapter 4, selecting appropriate issue-based stimuli is a crucial step in this type of experiment. On an issue like abortion or health care—long-standing controversies in American politics—an additional partisan media segment is unlikely to have much of an impact. The treatment of partisan media has already been received and absorbed (i.e., subjects have already been pretreated), so a brief experimental stimulus appears to have no effect, even for those who should be most responsive to it. For example, some of the issues used by Arceneaux and Johnson (2010) in their study of attitudes—the war in Iraq, Obama's health care reform, and so forth—were well-known issues, so a finding of null results (even for those who like to watch partisan shows) might not be very surprising. Similarly, Arceneaux, Johnson, and Murphy (2012) report that partisan media exposure has no effect on perceptions of mainstream media bias, at least for those who regularly consume these programs. This too could easily be to the result of pretreatment, given the amount of coverage of this topic on partisan outlets (see the discussion in chapter 2). But on more middle-salience issues—like the ones used in chapter 4—the effects are much larger. This highlights an important distinction about the effects of partisan media across different types of issues. On long-standing issues, partisan media primarily serve a reinforcement role (keeping those who are already polarized, well, polarized). But on emerging or less salient issues, partisan media polarize their audience. Given that much of what partisan media discuss are these long-standing issues, much of their role may be to reinforce existing polarization. But as I discussed in chapter 2, they do discuss newer and emerging issues, where they will play a more active polarizing role. This is another example of Bartels's (1993) argument about media effects: the issues we use drive the effects we find (see also Zaller 1996; Druckman and Leeper 2012). An important step for future work will be to explore how partisan media's effects differ depending on the salience and longevity of the issue.

Third, a selective exposure design only considers the direct effects of partisan media (i.e., what is the effect on those who choose to watch?). Again, this is an important question, but it ignores the indirect effects that are an important part of why partisan media matter (see also Arceneaux and Johnson, forthcoming). These indirect effects occur in two ways. First, as I discussed in chapter 2 with the case of Van Jones, partisan media can highlight issues that eventually spread to the mainstream news agenda. So, by shaping the broader mainstream media agenda, partisan media exert an indirect effect on American politics, even for those who would never choose to watch Maddow or O'Reilly. Second, as I discuss below, partisan media also impact politics more broadly because their audience is more politically active and engaged, so that audience will have an outsize effect on the political process. Because their audience impacts the political process more generally, these programs matter for all Americans, not just for their audience. Merely looking at the direct effects alone is not enough if we want to understand the influence of partisan media on contemporary politics.

Again, the point here is not to malign studies of selective exposure: they ask and answer an extremely important question. My argument is simply that both the direct and indirect effects of exposure are worthy of careful study. Even if the direct effect of partisan media averaged over the population is quite small, the effect on American politics need not be.

Partisan Media Beyond Cable TV

The findings throughout the book concern what happens when subjects are exposed to partisan cable television programs, in particular, the most popular prime-time programs on these networks. But these are not the only types of partisan media outlet: there is partisan talk radio (with hosts like Rush Limbaugh or Randi Rhodes), as well as partisan websites (like DailyKos on the Left or TownHall on the Right). Do my findings have anything to say about the effects on these outlets? A definitive answer will (obviously) depend on future studies, but there is good reason to suspect that my findings will generalize to other forms of partisan media. The underlying theoretical mechanisms of motivated reasoning and social identity theory should apply equally well to all forms of partisan media: indeed, there is nothing specific about partisan cable television news in the theory at all. Given this, the causal mechanism (and therefore hopefully the results) should parallel the findings I report here.

One particularly interesting area for future research will be to explore how partisan television news and website consumption reinforce one another. For example, a viewer might hear a story on partisan television and then go to a partisan website—perhaps even one mentioned on the television show—to learn more about the issue. In the post–broadcast media world, with its seemingly endless amount of information, selective exposure on one outlet or medium might prompt additional selective exposure on other outlets. In effect, consuming partisan cable TV news might shape how citizens go online to look for information (or vice versa). How these different types of partisan outlets feed off and reinforce one another will be an important topic for future studies of the partisan media environment.

Partisan Media, Polarization, Attitude Consistency, and Mass Sorting

The discussion in chapter 4 illustrates how partisan media polarize the electorate: not by taking moderates and moving them to the extremes but by taking people who are already more extreme and making them even more extreme. Partisan media do not shift the center of the distribution of mass opinion; rather, they help elongate the tails of the distribution. So partisan media do not "hollow out" the center of the distribution of mass opinion; they still contribute to polarization by modifying the extremes of the distribution.

This polarization also raises the possibility of reinforcing spirals of media consumption (Slater 2007; Jamieson and Cappella 2008; Stroud 2011). Viewers watch partisan media, which polarize them. But as those same viewers become more polarized, they want to consume more partisan media, given that subjects with more extreme attitudes prefer more partisan outlets (Stroud 2008, 2010). Watching additional partisan media in turn makes them even more polarized, which further increases their desire for more partisan programming, and so forth. While previous research theorizes such spirals, there is little empirical evidence either supporting or refuting their existence in the real world, so future work will be needed to unpack these sorts of effects. But this link between partisan media consumption and polarization suggests an exciting possibility for future research.

But these are not the only mechanisms through which partisan media can increase attitudinal polarization in the mass public. Partisan media also generate affective polarization, as I documented in chapter 5—they make viewers dislike the opposition, leading to a greater divergence between feelings for one's own party and the opposite party (and hence affective polarization). At the most obvious level, this sort of affective polarization can generate the mistrust and lack of support for bipartisanship that I document in chapter 5, as well as other negative consequences more generally (Iyengar, Sood, and Lelkes 2012). But this affective polarization might also fuel *attitudinal* polarization as well. If respondents come to distrust and dislike the other side as a result of watching partisan media, then perhaps they will also embrace a more extreme version of their own side's positions (or hold them with more certainty). So, for example, if Democrats listen to Rachel Maddow explain why Republicans are corrupt and hypocritical, they might come to trust Republicans less. But they might also decide that there is no way they could support a Republican policy, so they might move to a more extreme version of the Democratic alternative. This logic parallels Brady and Sniderman's (1985) likability heuristic: if I know I don't like Republicans, and Republicans support tax cuts, then I am even more against tax cuts than I initially suspected. While more work will be needed in the future carefully separate out these sorts of mechanisms and effects, it suggests that the consequences of partisan media might interact in powerful ways.

My results also demonstrate how partisan media can contribute to greater attitudinal consistency in the mass public. Individuals who watch partisan media—especially those who prefer to watch these shows—polarize. So when a Republican Fox News viewer watches Sean Hannity talk about why tax cuts help to stimulate economic growth, he moves to the right on tax cuts. When he hears Hannity discuss why we should take military action against Iran, he moves to the right on that issue. As these programs discuss a host of different issues, subjects move to the poles on these issues. But in the process, their positions become more connected to one another, as they all become (relatively) more extreme and liberal or conservative. After watching these shows, viewers' attitudes should be more tightly connected to one another, and hence, more consistent.[4]

Depending on the rhetoric used on these shows, and the political sophistication of the respondents watching, it might even be possible for these programs to increase subjects' attitudinal *constraint*. Consistency merely requires that subjects hold correlated attitudes: if I know a subject takes a liberal position on abortion, does he also take a liberal position on defense spending? Constraint, by contrast, requires understanding why these positions are related and how they are connected to underlying abstract concepts like liberalism and conservatism (Luskin 1987).[5] If the hosts help viewers to link these sorts of issues together and tie them back to underlying ideological principles, then these shows could potentially increase constraint. Given the centrality of constraint to debates about the competence of the mass public, such a finding would have considerable importance. More detailed content analysis of host rhetoric, and additional experiments will be needed to test this idea; it provides a particularly interesting extension for future research.

Not only can partisan media increase mass polarization, attitude consistency and (possibly) attitude constraint, but they also increase mass sorting—the alignment of party and ideology (Levendusky 2009). They do so in two ways. First, because they can help increase *elite* polarization (see below), partisan media outlets can generate clearer elite cues, which are the crucial piece of evidence voters need to align their partisan and ideological beliefs (Levendusky 2009). Second, many of the active and engaged partisan media viewers are the informal opinion leaders who also act as cue givers for the mass public (Berelson, Lazarsfeld, and McPhee 1954; Carmines and Stimson 1989). So by changing the more informed and engaged segment of the mass public, partisan media can indirectly shape the attitudes of the mass public. They cannot hollow out the mass electorate (given that sorting only very modestly increases polarization, see Levendusky 2009), but they can change the overall composition of the distribution. Indeed, one might argue that the somewhat extensive sorting seen in recently years would not have happened so completely without partisan media (on the media's role in sorting more generally, see Levendusky 2009). By clarifying the party's positions, partisan media can help ordinary voters, even nonwatchers, sort.

This effect has an important ramification even beyond the specific case of sorting itself. So far, I have documented the direct effects of partisan media: what happens to viewers when they are exposed to this sort of content. But this shows that there can be consequences even when people do not watch these shows—the *indirect* effects of partisan media. The consequences of these shows, by changing the broader political environment, extend beyond just the audience for these shows. As I explain in more detail later in the chapter, these shows' impacts extend broadly throughout the political arena.

Different News Agendas, Different Consequences

So far, my results have focused primarily on how left-wing and right-wing media slant the same underlying stories to their advantage. But as I discussed in the content analysis in chapter 2, not only do partisan media slant the news, they also very selectively reports on stories. Fox News does not just give the conservative perspective on the stories it reports; it actively selects stories that fit with a conservative worldview. So viewers who watch Fox and MSNBC see quite a different set of stories on any given day (Baum and Groeling 2008). Given the agenda setting function of the mass media (McCombs and Shaw 1972; Iyengar and Kinder 2009), these different agendas across outlets imply that their audiences will perceive different issues to be important problems that require government attention. Partisan media not only create differences in attitudes in their audience, they also cause them to think government should address different sets of issues.

This type of partisan agenda setting has a perverse consequence relative to the classic agenda setting findings of earlier authors. Because partisan media have more limited audiences, we lose out on one of the most important features of the mass media from the broadcast era: its ability to send one unifying message to all Americans. As audiences splinter, the news they see varies, and hence different audiences will see different issues as more or less important (Mendelsohn and Nadeau 1996; Williams and Delli Carpini 2011). In an update of their classic work, *News that Matters*, Iyengar and Kinder (2009, 141) comment that "the overall consequences of agenda-setting, priming, and framing are likely to be somewhat less sweeping [in the contemporary media environment, relative to that of thirty years ago]. If Americans are being exposed to different agendas, different primes, and different frames, they will be pushed in different directions. The effects of political communication are likely to be more crosscutting." It is not simply that the effect is crosscutting; it is that different people will see different sorts of news, and that news will be correlated with prior beliefs. The unifying function of mass media is not lost completely (because no one only consumes partisan media), but it is certainly diminished by this sort of shift. A heterogeneous media environment means subjects will see different stories as being worthy of the government's attention (see also Stroud 2011). Further, these sorts of issues are likely to be skewed in particular partisan directions, with each side thinking issues their party "owns" (in the sense of Petrocik 1996) being more important.[6] This is deeply related to the idea that there are now important "informational interdependences" between the media and people's opinions (Jacobs and Shapiro 2011, 5): there are many media environments, each with its own outlets and sets of important topics determined by the viewers' partisan predispositions and interests (Bennett and Iyengar 2008). Deciding even on the issues that government should address can become a partisan topic.

Different Facts and Different Interpretations

Not only do these different agendas produce differences in what issues people think matter, but some even argue that they lead individuals to have different factual beliefs about the way the world works. For example, several recent studies have argued that Fox News viewers were more misinformed about a variety of topics, including global warming and the Iraq War (Kull, Ramsay, and Lewis 2003; Krosnick and MacInnis 2010; Voorhees 2011): they were more likely to believe that the United States had found weapons of mass destruction in Iraq, that there was a link between Iraq and al Qaeda, and that a majority of citizens in other nations supported the war effort (Kull, Ramsay, and Lewis 2003). Likewise, they were much more likely to discount the scientific evidence in favor of global warming (Krosnick and MacInnis 2010). Such findings delight liberals and enrage conservatives, but they point to a potentially deeply troubling pattern. If Fox News and other partisan media outlets cause voters to be more misinformed, this has really profound consequences for American politics (Shapiro and Jacobs 2011).

Unfortunately, existing evidence cannot really draw definitive conclusions about this topic. The existing studies linking partisan media consumption to factual misinformation rely on cross-sectional surveys, and hence cannot really differentiate between two possibilities: (1) a selection effect—those who choose to watch partisan media are simply different than those who do not—and (2) a causal effect—watching partisan media causes voters to become more misinformed. Future studies will be needed to disentangle these competing explanations. Additionally, scholars also need to consider the possibility that these sorts of studies may reflect little more than partisan cheerleading: survey respondents may not believe that Obama is a Muslim or that Saddam Hussein caused 9/11, but answering in a particular way is an expressive political act (Moynihan, Langer, and Craighill 2010). More work with careful natural experiments or panel experimental designs will be needed to carefully sort out these possibilities.

But whether partisan media do or do not misinform, my findings point to an even deeper problem. There is an underlying sense that this misinformation is so troubling because with different facts, different citizens will draw different conclusions—Fox and MSNBC viewers live in "different worlds" as a result of their different factual beliefs (Manjoo 2008). But my findings show that even if everyone agreed on the facts (and partisan media had no effect whatsoever on misinformation), this sort of divergence would likely still result. Because citizens are motivated to interpret political evidence in light of their prior beliefs, there will be disagreement about how to interpret even the same pieces of information. When a Democrat and a Republican watched the same partisan media programs, I found vastly different reactions because of how subjects process these sorts of messages. Elites present facts in ways that help them make their arguments, and citizens respond to these messages in ways that are consistent with their beliefs (Gaines et al. 2007). Given this, even factual agreement is no salve for divisions within the electorate (Mutz 2006b). Any partisan bias that may be generated by partisan media exposure will simply compound the problem, but even if it did not exist, there would still be a deep—and troubling—problem.

Political Communication in an Era of Partisan Media

The contemporary resurgence of partisan media also reshapes the relationship between political elites, their campaigns, the press, and the mass public in at least two ways. First, campaigns now produce advertisements that are explicitly aimed at generating discussion on cable news and the Internet (Jamieson 2009). Most advertising money is still spent on segments that are meant to air widely in battleground states. But campaigns are now also beginning to produce "phantom ads" aimed primarily at generating discussion on partisan media, blogs, and so forth. Knowing that partisan cable news outlets need to fill considerable airtime each day, the campaigns produce ads that are only shown a few times for the express purpose of generating discussion on cable news. These ads are designed to reinforce the campaign's talking points, allowing them to build on themes discussed elsewhere by the campaign. For example, when Obama went abroad during the 2008 election to augment his foreign policy credentials, the McCain campaign aired several ads that questioned Obama's lack of foreign policy experience (Harder 2008). Very few voters saw these ads air directly, but they generated additional discussion on cable news of a key McCain talking point, helping to reaffirm for viewers why they should support their candidate. As the media environment changes, so do campaign strategies, and the relationship between the campaigns and the press.

Second, this changes how political elites communicate with the mass public. The demise of the broadcast era of television means that the political elites can no longer easily speak to the whole nation at once. Even a prime-time presidential address now only commands a fraction of the viewers that it did in the 1960s or 1970s (Baum and Kernell 1999). While this creates some difficulties for political elites to convey their message to the American people, it also creates opportunities for them to tailor their political messages to the audience on particular outlets (Cohen 2009; Baum 2011a). During the 2012 primary election season, many of the candidates for the Republican nomination made multiple appearances on Fox News, and during the summer and fall of 2011, Sean Hannity interviewed many of the candidates for the 2012 Republican nomination, calling it the "Hannity Primary." This pattern is not simply confined to *Hannity* but exists on Fox News more generally (Stanley 2011). During the week of 5 December 2011, the candidates vying for the Republican nomination made twenty-one appearances on that channel (Peters 2011). Such appearances have real appeal for a Republican primary candidate: they get a largely sympathetic interviewer and a largely sympathetic audience—one that is more likely to be involved in Republican primary politics. One can interpret this sort of niche television appearance as the TV equivalent of micro-targeting (Hillygus and Shields 2008): giving a specific message to a narrow audience that will be especially likely to be receptive to it. As media outlets diverge ideologically, the strategies elites use to respond to them change as well.[7]

At some level, these sorts of shifts—the different agendas, the different strategies of elites to speak to the mass media, and so forth—need not necessarily be troubling. After all, elites have always conditioned their strategies on the media environment, this is simply the modern continuation of that pattern. But there is a real tension created by these shifts as well. One function of the mass media is to help set a common national agenda and communicate a set of political and cultural norms (Schudson 2008). But this sort of media fragmentation, especially along partisan lines, threatens this in a real way. Prior (2007) points out that there are dangers to having some people watching sports while others watch news. My point is that there are dangers to having some people watch Fox and others watch MSNBC—there are important differences between different types of news outlets. Again, people are exposed to more than just one or the other type of news, and may choose to tune it out. But there are still pressures toward fragmentation and balkanization that are counterproductive given the constraints of the U.S. political system.

Effects Even for Those Who Never Watch

The discussion thus far has centered on the consequences for viewers themselves: how partisan media shape viewers' attitudes, their support for compromise, their view of the nation's important problems (and possibly even political facts), and so forth. But as I argued in chapter 1, this still leaves us with a puzzle: only a small number of Americans—maybe 1–2 percent of the population—actually tune in to any given partisan media program. Even survey data (which typically overreports media exposure; see Prior 2009), shows that only about one-third of the population reports regularly watching Fox or MSNBC (Pew Research Center for the People and the Press 2010). Given this, how can these shows have a large impact on American politics? The answer, I argue, is that these shows shape the broader contours of American politics in ways that do not depend on reaching a large audience. They do so in at least two respects. First, these shows help mold the larger political agenda and political discussion in America. Second, these shows have implications for governance in the contemporary United States. Given this, the effects of partisan media are felt even for those who would never sit down and watch Sean Hannity or Rachel Maddow. Though the partisan media audience is limited, the effects of these shows are not.

Partisan Media and the Mainstream Media Agenda

Earlier, I discussed how partisan media shape the agenda for those who watch these shows. But these shows have an even larger and more profound effect on the nation's agenda. As I discussed in chapter 2 with the Van Jones case study, partisan media outlets can play a key role in promoting stories that eventually spread to the mainstream media. For example, some argue that Fox News played an important role in helping spread the ACORN corruption and prostitution story (Dreier and Martin 2010), and others argue that Fox was instrumental in helping sustain the growth of the Tea Party movement during the 2010 elections (Skocpol and Williamson 2012; Williamson, Skocpol, and Coggin 2011). An even more telling example of this sort of agenda-setting power might be the Swift Boat Veterans for Truth during the 2004 election. When that group initially made their allegations against Senator Kerry, the mainstream media largely ignored them. It was not until cable news, especially partisan media and Fox News, began to discuss the story that it gained widespread attention (Shaw 2006). Partisan outlets can help to set the national agenda.

While this is the more obvious example of the agenda-setting effect of partisan media, there is another, more common, and equally consequential way the partisan press influences the tone of the national debate. Frames from Fox News or MSNBC can also spread to the mainstream media—so even if a partisan outlet is not shaping *which* stories get discussed in the national media, they can influence *how* those stories are discussed by the broader media establishment. This type of frame diffusion is another important mechanism by which partisan media can shape the broader mainstream news agenda, and represents an important topic for future research.

Partisan media's discussion of media bias illustrates how these outlets can both set the agenda and frame the debate surrounding a salient political topic. While most academic studies conclude the mainstream media is typically largely free of overt political biases (D'Alessio and Allen 2000; Watts et al. 1999; for a dissenting view, see Groseclose 2011), such claims are commonplace in more popular discourse (Alterman 2003; Goldberg 2009). Such discussion about media bias is likely due to the frequency of discussion of this topic on partisan media, at least in part. As I detailed in chapter 2, both left-wing and right-wing partisan outlets frequently discuss the extent of bias in the mainstream media. Increased discussion by political and media elites about "media bias" makes the public more likely to believe that the media is, in fact, biased (Ladd 2012; Watts et al. 1999), a claim long recognized by political operatives (Perlstein 2008). Interestingly, many of the allegations of media bias do not reflect actual media bias but instead are strategic efforts to reframe the discussion around certain issues and to get the mainstream press to respond to partisan arguments and outlets (Domke, Watts, Shah, and Fan 1999). By keeping the focus on mainstream media bias, partisan media not only impact how its viewers perceive bias in the mainstream media (following the logic discussed in earlier chapters), but they also shape the broader debate about the extent of media bias, and therefore, the need for other types of outlets (such as partisan media). The partisan media agenda influences the broader mainstream media agenda.

Further, as recent work by Ladd (2012) suggests, these claims of media bias bleed over into broader judgments of media trust. As these outlets, especially right-wing outlets, criticize and critique the news for being biased and unfair, viewers have less faith in the media overall. This in turn has implications for how citizens learn about the issues and how they hold leaders accountable for their performance (see Ladd 2012).

This sort of "agenda bleed," where the partisan media agenda drives the national media agenda, has important implications for theories of media and politics. Scholars traditionally argued that the mainstream media functioned as a key gatekeeper: a relatively small set of media elites decided what was "news" and then reported it as the official record of the day's events. If they covered an event, it was "news," and if they did not, then it was not (White 1950; Gans 1979). As Mark Jurkowitz, associate director of the Pew Project for Excellence in Journalism, argues, this model is journalism is "pretty anachronistic" in the contemporary environment with a greatly decentralized model set of journalistic agents empowered by the Internet and cable TV (Farhi 2011; see also Baum and Groeling 2008). Indeed, as Bill O'Reilly commented on a recent program, Fox News helps "set the daily discussion," something that would have seemed ludicrous even a decade ago (i.e., that a partisan network would help to set the nation's media agenda).[8] With multiple agents who can set the agenda, mainstream media lose the power to shape what is news.

On the one hand, one can imagine that this could be beneficial: after all, one limitation of the gatekeeper model is that it gives a relatively small set of media elites the ability to determine what is news, and, just as importantly, what is not. It is unclear why a small set of media elites *should* have this ability: what makes the Associated Press or the *New York Times* or any other outlet uniquely qualified to codify what "news" means in a diverse and pluralistic society like the United States? Yet on the other hand, without this gatekeeping power, the definition of "news" becomes much more sharply politicized—democratizing the power to shape what news means makes this power much more contested. Partisan outlets do not just randomly sample stories; they deliberately choose stories that fit within a particular partisan narrative (Baum and Groeling 2008). This has troubling implications for what stories get covered, and which ones do not. In effect, partisan media change not only who can set the agenda, but in so doing, what the definition of the "agenda" is and what is and is not worthy of inclusion on it. More stories might be covered, but those need not be the stories that *should* be covered, depending on one's point of view. In this sort of a world, even the agenda itself is up for debate, as is which sources are actually "objective" conveyors of facts.

Ironically, this shift away from the gatekeeper model of mainstream journalism underlies just how important objective news organizations are. Mainstream news outlets are needed to help break and disseminate the facts, especially on these sorts of partisan stories. The fact that stories like the Shirley Sherrod scandal or the Swift Boat Veterans for Truth can spread like they did is as much an indictment of the mainstream press as it is an indictment of the partisan one (Farhi 2011). Fact-checking and ensuring that the whole story is known are still key (Rieder 2004). There is some argument that market pressures will generate truthful news reporting (Gentzkow and Shapiro 2006), but on these sorts of partisan stories, that does not seem to be enough. If anything, in the new world of cable and online news, careful reporting and fact-checking are more important than ever.

Partisan Media, Gridlock, and Contemporary Governance

My findings show that partisan media have a large effect on their audience: polarizing them, making them distrust the opposition, and allowing them to become skeptical of why opposing leaders win elections. But because of these shifts, partisan media have a larger impact on American politics. In particular, they may increase the difficulty of governing in contemporary America. One cannot pin all, or even most, of these problems on partisan media, but partisan media do exacerbate the difficulty of addressing the nation's problems in the current political environment.

First, partisan media can increase elite polarization. As active and engaged voters watch like-minded television, they become more extreme, less willing to compromise, less trusting of the opposition, and so forth. These individuals then put pressure on elected officials to similarly become more extreme and recalcitrant (Layman et al. 2010) and hence more polarized. The system of primary elections only serves to exacerbate this tendency (Brady, Han, and Pope 2007). Though polarized elites preceded the return of partisan media by several decades (McCarty, Poole, and Rosenthal 2006), the shifts in the mass public in recent years driven by partisan media can now constrain elites—even if elites wanted to return to the center, doing so without angering partisan media hosts and their viewers would be quite difficult. For example, when California Republican Darrell Issa argued that Republicans could better advance their agenda by compromising with President Obama on certain issues, Rush Limbaugh forced him to publicly repudiate this claim and promise that he would block efforts to enact Obama's agenda (Zakaria 2011). As the mass public shifts, and media change with it, this can constrain elite behavior (Levendusky 2009; McCarty, Poole, and Rosenthal 2006).

Note that this occurs despite the fact that most ordinary Americans are moderate, and never hear partisan media messages (Fiorina, Abrams, and Pope 2005). But because partisan media's effect is felt more strongly among the more politically engaged, the effects generated there can reverberate throughout the political system. Shifts in the mass public generated by partisan media can have consequences for elites as well. Further, these same processes account for why partisan media can increase pressure to avoid compromises and regard bipartisanship as an anathema. Do partisan media thereby exacerbate and solidify the gridlock many see as endemic to contemporary politics?

I argue that partisan media do increase this gridlock via several related mechanisms. First, their tendency to fuel elite polarization increases the likelihood of gridlock. Members of Congress are punished or rewarded by voters primarily for their position, rather than for the actual policy outcomes (Jones 2011). Particularly in light of the media-induced polarization described above, this sets up a perverse set of incentives. Members can be recalcitrant, taking polarized positions and avoiding compromise with the other side, and not be punished for it. While voters dislike gridlock, they tend to blame the institution writ large rather than individual members for stalemate (Hibbing and Theiss-Morse 1995). Members therefore have much stronger incentives to take extreme positions than they do to compromise and reach across the aisle. After all, primary challengers took down congresspersons who worked across the aisle like Bob Bennett and Michael Castle (Davis 2011), consistent with the general pattern that the most active and partisan members of the electorate (and those most likely to vote in primaries) punish members who are seen as too bipartisan (Harbridge and Malhotra 2011; Wolf, Strachan, and Shea 2012). Congresspersons therefore have more reason to stick to their principles than to compromise.

Second, like-minded media increase attitudinal certainty. Subjects with certain attitudes "know" their position is the correct one and are consequently both more likely to take action based on their attitudes, and be less willing to compromise and find consensus (Gross, Holtz, and Miller 1995). If a viewer is certain that his party's position is the correct one, then why should he compromise with the flawed ideology espoused from the other side? Partisan media act as a reinforcement and reassurance mechanism, helping shore up and reaffirm subjects' beliefs in their side's positions. As a result, they are less supportive of compromise and consensus building.

Third, partisan media's effects might spread more generally throughout the electorate via two-step information flows (Berelson, Lazarsfeld, and McPhee 1954). While the partisan media audience is narrow, it is more politically involved and engaged and hence should be more likely to be the sorts of "opinion leaders" that function in two-step information flows. So partisan media can impact its audience, and then that audience in turn can shape the opinions of their friends and family, even if those individuals themselves never watch partisan cable TV news. So the effects on attitudes and behaviors are not strictly limited to the audience but can spread more broadly throughout the population. This, in turn, can increase the pressures on elites discussed above.

Fourth, partisan media can also contribute to greater activism among its audience. Partisan media outlets, as I demonstrated throughout the book, engender powerful emotional reactions in viewers, in particular, in stimulating negative reactions toward the other party and its leaders. Such negative emotions are highly mobilizing, especially in the political arena (Valentino et al. 2011; MacKuen et al. 2010). Defining a common enemy—the other side, with their devious policies and untrustworthy ways—helps stoke viewers' passions, especially when this is framed in terms of threat (Miller and Krosnick 2004). These shows, especially like-minded shows, offer viewers the types of reinforcement that spur on greater activity and engagement (Mutz 2006a). Indeed, the peak of American political engagement and involvement in the late nineteenth century coincided with the zenith of the partisan press (Schudson 1995). While this is not a causal linkage, per se, other studies show a connection between partisan media consumption and political activity in the contemporary period as well (Dilliplane 2011; Stroud 2010). The emotions aroused by these programs, and their effects on attitudes toward the other party, help to mobilize and engage the mass public.

This might seem like an odd negative consequence: scholars typically assume political activity and political engagement is a normative "good" and a positive consequence: more participation is better. But that is simply not always the case. My results highlight what Fiorina (1999) termed the "dark side" of civic engagement: the most involved also tend to be the most extreme, with unrepresentative preferences, and a stronger preference for gridlock and division (see also Abramowitz 2010). The nation saw this trend play out during the 2009 "town hall" meetings on health care reform (Kraushaar and Lerrer 2009). More participation, if it is by those with extreme and unrepresentative preferences, need not be a normative good, and can contribute to gridlock.

Fifth, partisan media increase the transparency of political horse trading in Congress, which leads to perverse incentives to avoid compromise. When political deal making is played out in public, political elites have an incentive to play the "blame game" and avoid reaching a compromise, blaming the other side for refusing to give in and find a consensus solution (Groseclose and McCarty 2001; Stasavage 2007). This exacerbates the tendency toward position taking over problem solving. By focusing on the details of deal making, and helping to ensure that dealmaking plays out in public, these sorts of programs increase the likelihood that politicians will utilize this sort of strategy. This is especially true given that these programs frequently endorse a message of noncompromise and ideological rigidity. By shining a light on politics, especially one focused so clearly on ideological principles, partisan media contribute to gridlock.

Sixth and finally, partisan media's direct effect on decreasing support for bipartisanship and compromise only exacerbates this tendency. By increasing viewers' dislike for the opposition, these shows make viewers more skeptical of the compromise, bipartisanship, and solutions offered by the other party, in large part because viewers see these elites as untrustworthy and illegitimate. The negative emotions engendered for the opposition decrease subjects' willingness to compromise with the other side (MacKuen et al. 2010). For example, many on the Right have been deeply opposed to President Obama's policies and unwilling to support them under almost any condition. But perhaps this makes sense from the perspective of someone who sees his victory as illegitimate: if Obama's victory is due to media bias or vote fraud or some other illegitimate means, then his policies *should* be opposed. To be clear, other factors—most notably economic performance—largely explain why some Americans disapprove of President Obama's performance in office. But the hearing the idea that Obama came to power via fraudulent means undoubtedly helps to reify and strengthen that opposition.

A recent example illustrates how partisan media exacerbate the tendency toward gridlock and opposition: the debate over President Obama's health care reform.[9] Undoubtedly, much of the Republican opposition stemmed from ideological differences about the best policy to pursue. But some of it also reflected partisan desires to score political points and defeat the president's agenda, regardless of its political merits. At least some of this type of stonewall opposition comes from partisan media hosts and their audiences. For example, a number of partisan media figures, most notably Rush Limbaugh and Glenn Beck, urged members of Congress to resist any effort at compromise on health care (Kurtz 2010; Starr 2010).[10] As David Frum (2010) put it, "Conservative talkers on Fox and talk radio had whipped the Republican voting base into such a frenzy that deal-making [on health care reform, among other issues] was rendered impossible." So even if Republican elites wanted to compromise, the partisan media audience would have rebelled against them had they bargained with the Democrats. Partisan media do not bear all—or even most—of the blame, but they do contribute to the problem (on how partisan media contributed to the health care debate more generally, see Baum 2012).

All of this contributes to what Gutmann and Thompson (2010, 1125) call the uncompromising mind, a set of "attitudes and arguments that encourage standing on principle and mistrusting opponents." This is the mindset that it is better to stand on principle and see nothing done than to compromise and accept a second-best policy. Of course, standing firm has its place, and there are times when compromise may not be the best policy and gridlock may be a good thing. But actors in the political process—ordinary citizens and elites alike—need to be willing to meaningfully engage with each other and leave open the possibility of compromise (Gutmann and Thompson 2010, 2012). As James Madison noted over two centuries ago, democracy does best with a "yielding and accommodating spirit," one that promotes tolerance of opposing points of view and is willing to engage with them.[11] When it is "almost inconceivable" to see how to solve long-term, pressing social problems, that is not a good thing. When conflict extends from large and controversial issues like health care reform and the tax code to seemingly prosaic ones like evaluating the effectiveness of medical treatments (Gerber and Patashnik 2010) or flu vaccines (Baum 2011b), that is not a good thing. When policy becomes about scoring political points rather than trying to make a good-faith effort to solve problems, that is not a good thing (Fiorina 2006).

Of course, these broader conclusions about the significance of partisan media come with two important caveats. First, these points are consistent with my own, and other scholars, findings, and arguments, but I have little direct evidence here. An important task for future work will be to substantiate and flesh out these sorts of downstream consequences of partisan media with actual data and careful experiments. The arguments here are thought-provoking but will need additional empirical work to be fully confirmed. Second, it is important to stress that partisan media does not bear all, or even most, of the blame for these sorts of problems. There are other, far larger structural factors that explain contemporary gridlock and resistance to bipartisan compromise. The argument is simply that partisan media is one of many factors that helps contribute to the problem, especially in light of its more engaged and involved audience. But nevertheless, the findings here will hopefully serve to launch future investigations into more of the broader consequences of the partisan media environment.

Is This Time Really Different?

One potential counterpoint to my argument is that my findings must be hyperbolic: the United States had a partisan press for the first 150 years of our existence, and our democracy survived. Likewise, other nations, like the United Kingdom, have a partisan press alongside a healthy democracy. If the partisan press did not destroy American democracy the first time around and it has not destroyed other nations, why is it so harmful here and now?[12] What makes partisan media pernicious in the contemporary environment?

Take the international comparison first. It is certainly true that other nations have a partisan press and a healthy, vibrant democracy. But the U.S. constitutional system is quite distinct from most of these other nations. Our structure, unlike most parliamentary democracies, is a system of "separated institutions sharing power" in Neustadt's (1960) classic phrasing. The American system is built on the necessity of compromise and consensus to overcome the gridlock built into the system. Comparisons to other political systems are less relevant here, because their constitutional structures give them fundamentally different incentives for compromise and cooperation. So even if other nations thrive with a partisan press, because of our unique system of government, the consequences here are unlike the consequences elsewhere.

Further, the over-time historical comparison is also perhaps less useful than it seems at first glance. While it is true that the United States had a partisan press for much of its existence, the changes in the media environment over the past few decades mean that today's press is unlike that of the eighteenth and nineteenth centuries. Today, in a world of a twenty-four-hour news cycle, stories can reverberate more rapidly through the information environment in a way that was not possible before. In the early years of the republic, people could read a small number of local newspapers (often only published weekly), with few other options for news. These limited outlets meant that news traveled more slowly and there were fewer reverberations between outlets (in part because only a very limited audience has exposure to multiple outlets). That is a fundamentally different environment than the post-broadcast environment of today, where there are dozens of newspapers online, thousands of blogs, and around-the-clock coverage of the issues on cable news. It is hard to imagine stories like Shirley Sherrod or ACORN spreading so rapidly without the constant churning of contemporary media. Likewise, the ability to coordinate messages across so many different information channels and have them reinforce one another makes today's environment quite different. Today's hyper-connected, nonstop news cycle environment makes the consequences of partisan media distinct today from those in previous eras.

All of this suggests that today's partisan media environment has real consequences for American politics, and those consequences are different from other arrangements in the past. What, if anything, can be done remains unclear. Because partisan media's emergence is due to a series of regulatory, technological, and electoral shifts (see the discussion in chapter 1), it would exceedingly difficult to limit the scope of these types of media. Given the current media environment, partisan media are likely to be with us, at least for the near term.

Perhaps a more realistic solution, if there is one at all, is to try and better understand how to reduce the partisan-motivated reasoning that underlies many of the direct effects of partisan media. Past work in social psychology argues that forcing individuals to carefully consider opposing arguments, weigh the competing claims and evidence, and engage in genuine discussions with those from different perspectives helps to minimize partisan motivated reasoning (Druckman 2012; Pettigrew and Tropp 2006). The best way to do this is ultimately unclear, given that most people prefer to avoid these types of situations, precisely because they are uncomfortable (Mutz 2006a). But it poses a fascinating set of challenges for scholars of media and politics moving forward.

Data Appendix

This appendix gives the details for the analysis conducted in the book, beginning with the survey data used in chapter 1, the experiments used in chapters 4, 5, and 6, and the panel data used in chapter 6.

National Annenberg Election Study, Rolling Cross-Section Data

The specific question wording and coding rules for the variables used in the analysis of the National Annenberg Election Study rolling cross-section data used in chapter 1 follows.

WATCH FOX NEWS. Respondents were asked: "In the past week, from what television program did you get most of your information about the 2008 presidential campaign?" Respondents who named a program on Fox News were coded as 1; all others were coded as 0. The Fox News responses are: Fox News Channel (program unspecified), *Fox Report w/ Shepard Smith*, *Glenn Beck*, *Hannity & Colmes*, *The O'Reilly Factor*, *On the Record w/ Greta Van Susteren*, *Special Report w/ Brit Hume*, and *Your World w/ Neil Cavuto*.

WATCH MSNBC. Respondents were asked: "In the past week, from what television program did you get most of your information about the 2008 presidential campaign?" Respondents who named a program on MSNBC were coded as 1, all others were coded as 0. MSNBC responses are: MSNBC (program unspecified), *Countdown with Keith Olbermann*, *Hardball with Chris Matthews*, and *Tucker with Tucker Carlson*.

POLITICAL KNOWLEDGE. Respondents were asked four factual general political knowledge items; the dependent variable used was the number of correct responses. Subjects were asked if they knew (1) which body determines whether a law is constitutional or not,[1] (2) the majority needed to override a presidential veto,[2] (3) the party currently in the majority in the House of Representatives,[3] and (4) the method used to select Supreme Court justices.[4]

FREQUENCY OF POLITICAL DISCUSSION. Respondents were asked: "How many days in the past week did you discuss politics with your family or friends?" Responses were coded 0 to 7.

CAMPAIGN ACTIVITIES. Respondents were asked if they completed any of five campaign activities during the past week: trying to influence someone else's vote,[5] giving money to one of the campaigns,[6] working for a campaign,[7] attending any meetings or rallies,[8] or displaying a sign or button for a candidate.[9]

Pew Media Survey Data

In figure 1.1, I showed over-time trends on partisan media consumption using the biennial Pew Media surveys from 2002 to 2010. The key item was consumption of Fox News, which came from an item asking about how often subjects consume various types of media. The item asks: "Now I'd like to know how often you watch or listen to certain TV and radio programs. For each that I read, tell me if you watch or listen to it regularly, sometimes, hardly ever, or never. First, how often do you [program]: regularly, sometimes, hardly ever, or never?" The list of programs varied from year to year, but for the purposes of this item, the key item was "watch the Fox News Cable Channel." I combined responses for those who said they watched it "regularly" or "sometimes"; just looking at the regular viewers would give a similar answer.

Experiment Details

Experiment 1

Subjects were recruited to take part in a study on how citizens learn about politics from the news in a private urban university's decision-making lab during 9–19 February 2010.[10] Subjects completed this study and 2 others during a one-hour session in exchange for a $10 cash payment (this study, lasting approximately 30 minutes, was administered first). As is typically the case, the subjects were not any sort of a representative sample: 44 percent of the sample was white, 36 percent was male, the average age was 21.5 years, 70 percent were Democrats, and 85 percent were students. While student samples often raise generalizability questions, a number of studies show that students and nonstudents do not typically differ as experimental subjects (Druckman and Kam 2011), a finding that replicates here as well (see the analysis of experiment 1 in the appendix to chapter 3, as well as the results in Levendusky 2012a).

When subjects arrived at the lab, they were initially given a pretest instrument to gather their baseline political attitudes and opinions and were then given a brief distracter task (a battery of items from an IQ test). Subjects were then exposed to the treatment, a series of short video clips, one clip per issue, where the difference across conditions was the partisan/ideological slant of the source for the clips. The sources were left-wing partisan media sources (*Countdown with Keith Olbermann*), right-wing partisan media sources (*Hannity* and *The O'Reilly Factor*), or neutral sources with no overt partisan slant (*The News Hour with Jim Lehrer*), with treatment assignment held constant for each subject (so all subjects saw clips from only one type of media; see the discussion in chapter 4 for a detailed discussion of why these sources were chosen). Finally, subjects were given a posttest questionnaire to record their attitudes and opinions. The key question was whether the ideological tenor of the news source (i.e., left-wing, right-wing, or neutral) affected viewers' attitudes.

The experimental stimulus consisted of clips about four issues discussed in the news during the first year of the Obama presidency: whether George W. Bush administration officials should be prosecuted for torture, whether the U.S. should pass "cap-and-trade" legislation to control greenhouse gas emissions, whether Americans should support the Afghanistan surge, and whether Khalid Sheikh Mohammed (the alleged 9/11 mastermind) should be tried in military or civilian court. These issues were all significant policy debates during the first year of the Obama presidency, and all were discussed on all three types of media.

To ensure that subjects actually perceived the partisan slant of the clips, the posttest instrument included a manipulation check asking whether the segments they saw on balance supported the Democratic or Republican parties. Subjects had no difficulty differentiating the partisan tilt of the shows, with subjects seeing the left-wing shows as most supportive of Democrats, right-wing shows as most supportive of Republicans, and the neutral shows as most balanced (a one-way ANOVA yields $F(2,174) = 275.1$; $p < .01$). For example, only 2 percent of subjects assigned to the left-wing condition saw the treatment as strongly supporting the Republican Party, whereas 83 percent of subjects assigned to the right-wing condition felt this way.[11] This manipulation check demonstrates (unsurprisingly) that subjects could correctly identify the partisan slant of the sources, and so the differences below are a function of that slant. In all experiments all subjects were included in the analysis, even those that incorrectly identified the slant of the programs. Restricting the analysis to those that correctly identified it would not substantively alter the results.

Experiment 2

Experiment 2 tested whether source credibility moderates the effects of crosscutting media on attitude polarization. The remaining experiments all follow the same design: subjects were recruited online using Amazon's Mechanical Turk web service and were offered a small cash payment for completing the study (this study took approximately 8 minutes; subjects were paid $1.50). Before beginning the actual study, all online subjects passed a small screening test to ensure that they could actually watch Flash videos on their computers (the treatment clips were shown to respondents in Flash); only those who successfully completed the screener actually completed the study.[12] Study 2 was completed during 17–19 September 2010.

All online experiments followed the same basic protocol: they began with some background items, exposure to the stimulus, and then participants answered the posttest attitude extremity items. The subjects were still a nonrandom sample but were somewhat more heterogeneous (especially in terms of age) than the typical laboratory experiment. Of the sample, 58 percent were Democrats (including Democratic leaners), 68 percent were female, 72 percent were under 40 years of age, 56 percent had at least a college degree (19 percent had a graduate degree), and 85 percent were Caucasian. Subjects again could detect the partisan bias across sources. Using the manipulation check item repeated from experiment 1 yielded $F(2,146) = 1.65, p < .1$ (one-tailed).

Online subjects pools like Mechanical Turk are relatively new to political science, so some readers may be skeptical of them. Work examining the quality of Mechanical Turk subjects, however, suggests that these individuals are at least as attentive as convenience laboratory samples and are more representative of the general population (Berinsky, Huber, and Lenz 2012; Paolacci, Chandler, and Ipeirotis 2010). Work using Mechanical Turk subjects has now been published in several psychology journals (e.g., Alter, Oppenheimer, and Zemla 2010; Eriksson and Simpson 2010). Further, note that my laboratory-based sample (composed of students, university staff, and community members) generates results that look like the ones from my Mechanical Turk samples, consistent with the claim that these individuals offer the ability to validly conduct experiments online (see also Horowitz and Levendusky 2011 for a similar finding). While more work will be needed to see how Mechanical Turk subjects perform at different kinds of tasks, the results here suggest they offer exciting possibilities for experimentation beyond the traditional laboratory setting.[13]

Experiment 3

Experiment 3 carried out the patient preference trial; subjects were again recruited online and paid $1.25 for taking an 8–9 minute experiment. The study was fielded 1–2 June 2010. Of subjects 61 were percent female, 46 percent had a college degree, 80 percent were Caucasian, and 47 percent were 18–29 years of age. Subjects watched treatment clips about trying terrorism suspects in civilian versus military courts, and also detected the partisan bias of the sources (one-way ANOVA, $F(2,166) = 20.15; p < .01$).

Experiment 4

Experiment 4 was designed to test the duration of the effects of partisan media. Subjects were recruited via Mechanical Turk and offered $2 for completing an approximately 8-minute study. Subjects who completed the first wave were then asked if they wanted to be enrolled in a follow-up study in exchange for an additional $1 payment; those who agreed were invited to take wave 2 (see the discussion in chapter 4 for the details on sample sizes and retention). Wave 1 was administered on 14 June 2010; wave 2 was administered on 16–17 June 2010. Subjects saw clips in wave 1 about the Arizona immigration law; subjects in wave 2 saw no clips. Of the sample (that completed both waves), 68 percent were female, 88 percent were Caucasian, 46 percent were ages 18–29, and 54 percent had a college degree. Again, the manipulation check revealed that subjects could differentiate the partisan bias of the sources (one-way ANOVA, $F(2,77) = 4.5$; $p = .01$).

Experiment 5

Experiment 5 was the over-time repetition study from chapter 4. Subjects were recruited online and received $1.25 per wave for participating. Wave 1 of the study was fielded on 11 November 2011, and wave 2 was conducted on 15 November 2011 (wave 2 invitations were sent via e-mail). Seventy-three percent of the wave 1 respondents returned and completed wave 2. Of subjects who completed both waves, 56 percent were female, 36 percent were ages 18–29, 63 percent had a college degree, and 89 percent were Caucasian. Subjects read doctored newspaper editorials about the Ayotte amendment that would force the U.S. government to try all foreign terrorism suspects in military tribunals rather than civilian courts.

Experiment 6

Experiment 6 followed the design described in chapter 5 and asked how partisan media changes their affect for the opposing party. Subjects were recruited online and paid $1.50 for completing an 8–9 minute task. The experiment was completed 20–21 October 2010. Subjects watched news segments about the funding of the U.S. Chamber of Commerce's electioneering efforts. Of the sample, 57 percent were Democratics (including Democratic leaners), 68 percent were female, 44 percent were ages 18–29, 45 percent had at least a college degree, and 82 percent were Caucasian. The posttest manipulation check was accidentally left off this experiment, but given the strong and consistent results found in earlier studies, there is no reason to suspect that subjects failed to detect the slant in the stories.

Experiment 7

Experiment 7 was used to assess the role of (perceived) outlet credibility on the ability of partisan media to change attitudes toward the other party. Subjects watched a news segment discussing President Obama's foreign policy. Subjects were recruited online and paid $1.75 for completing an 8–9 minute task, which took place on 30–31 October 2010. Fifty-nine percent of the sample were female, 47 percent were ages 18–29, 77 percent were Caucasian, and 40 percent had at least a college degree. Because there was only one partisan media segment used in this experiment (see the discussion in chapter 5), there was no perceived slant item.

Experiment 8

Experiment 8 followed the same protocol as experiment 6 in terms of subject recruitment and basic design. The experiment was conducted on 1–2 December 2010, and subjects watched segments about whether to extend the Bush tax cuts. Of the sample, 52 percent were Democratics (including leaners), 63 percent were female, 58 percent were ages 18–29, 46 percent were college graduates, and 83 percent were Caucasian. Subjects had no difficulty detecting the slant of sources ($F(2,64) = 37.10$; $p < .01$).

Experiment 9

Experiment 9 was designed to test arguments about how individuals interpret election outcomes. Subjects were recruited online and paid $0.50 for participating in a 5-minute study, which took place on 9 November 2011 (the day after the 2011 midterm elections). The design otherwise followed the other studies given above. Fifty-five percent of the sample were female, 35 percent were under the age of 30, and 47 percent had have at least a bachelor's degree.

Question Wording, by Experiment

Before each set of attitudinal items, subjects were told: "In this next section, we will ask you to give your opinion about a set of political issues. The most important thing is for you to relax and take your time. For these items, there are no right or wrong items, only opinions, and it is your opinion we want you to share."

Comments on response scales and so forth are given in brackets. For all branched items, subjects were only asked the branched item if appropriate. Subjects who skipped the item were not branched (they were simply treated as missing data, though very few subjects skipped the dependent variable items). The party ID item was asked in every experiment in the same fashion. Responses can be combined into the standard NES 7-point party ID scale.

Experiment 1

Generally speaking, do you think of yourself as a Democrat, a Republican, or an Independent?

A. Democrat
B. Republican
C. Independent

[If Democrat/Republican:] Would you call yourself a strong [Democrat/Republican], or a not very strong [Democrat/Republican]?

A. Strong
B. Not very strong

[If Independent:] Do you think of yourself as closer to the Democratic Party or the Republican Party?

A. Closer to the Democratic Party
B. Closer to the Republican Party
C. Closer to neither party

ATTITUDE ITEMS. Note that subjects completed the same attitude items in both the pretest and posttest waves of the experiment. Here, there is no measure of Cronbach's alpha, because the items were analyzed as a panel.

Recently, the United States announced that we will send 30,000 additional troops to Afghanistan. Do you think that this is too many additional troops, about the right number of additional troops, or too few additional troops?

A. Far too many additional troops
B. Somewhat too many additional troops
C. About the right number of additional troops
D. Somewhat too few additional troops
E. Far too few additional troops

Under a proposal called "cap and trade," the federal government would limit the amount of greenhouse gases that companies could produce in their factories or power plants. If companies exceeded those limits, they would either pay a fine or pay money to other companies that produced smaller amounts of greenhouse gases. Would you favor or oppose this proposal?

A. Strongly oppose a cap and trade system
B. Somewhat oppose a cap and trade system
C. Neither support nor oppose a cap and trade system
D. Somewhat support a cap and trade system
E. Strongly support a cap and trade system

Recently, the United States announced that we would begin to withdraw our forces from Afghanistan in 2011. Which comes closest to your view about setting a timetable for beginning to withdraw U.S. troops from Afghanistan in 2011—you agree with that timetable, you think the U.S. should start withdrawing troops sooner than that, or you think it is too soon to set a timetable for withdrawing troops from Afghanistan?

A. Begin withdrawing troops before 2011
B. Agree with the timetable as is
C. Too soon to set a timetable for withdrawing troops

[If A or C is selected:] Do you hold this position strongly, or not so strongly?

A. Strongly
B. Not so strongly

A recent report details the harsh interrogation techniques used on terrorism suspects during the Bush administration. Some argue that a criminal investigation is needed to determine if these techniques broke laws and constituted torture. Would you support such an investigation?

A. Strongly support a criminal investigation
B. Somewhat support a criminal investigation
C. Neither support nor oppose a criminal investigation
D. Somewhat oppose a criminal investigation
E. Strongly oppose a criminal investigation

The man allegedly responsible for planning the 9/11 attacks, Khalid Sheikh Mohammed, is due to stand trial. Would you rather see him brought to trial in a criminal court run by the civilian judicial system, or would you rather see him tried by a military court run by the U.S. armed forces?

A. Prefer a trial in a military court
B. No preference
C. Prefer a trial in a civilian court

[If A or C is selected:] Do you prefer a [military/civilian] trial strongly, or only somewhat prefer it?

A. Strongly prefer a [military/civilian] trial
B. Somewhat prefer a [military/civilian] trial

ATTITUDE STRENGTH ITEMS. Attitude strength is a combined scale of items measuring attitude certainty, (self-perceived) attitude knowledge, and attitude importance; see the discussion in chapter 4 for more details. [For all attitude strength items, subjects were asked separately about each of the following issues:

- Creating a cap-and-trade system to regulate greenhouse gases
- Sending additional troops to Afghanistan
- Creating a timetable for withdrawing troops from Afghanistan
- Launching a criminal investigation into interrogation techniques
- Trying Khalid Sheikh Mohammed in civilian vs. military court

ATTITUDE CERTAINTY, MEASURE #1: Please use the scale below to indicate how sure you are that your position on that issue is the correct one. [Respondents were shown a four-point Likert scale: "very sure," "pretty sure," "not very sure," and "not at all sure."]

(SELF-PERCEIVED) ATTITUDE KNOWLEDGE: Please use the scale below to indicate how knowledgeable you are the issue. [Respondents were shown a five-point Likert scale: "extremely knowledgeable," "very knowledgeable," "somewhat knowledgeable," "not too knowledgeable," and "not at all knowledgeable."]

ATTITUDE IMPORTANCE, MEASURE #1: Please use the scale below to indicate how important it is to you that the federal government do what you think is best. [Subjects were shown a five-point Likert scale: "extremely important," "very important," "somewhat important," "not too important," and "not at all important."]

ATTITUDE IMPORTANCE, MEASURE #2: Please use the scale to tell us how important it is to you personally. [Respondents were shown a five-point Likert scale: "extremely important," "very important," "somewhat important," "not too important," and "not at all important."]

ATTITUDE CERTAINTY, MEASURE #2: Please use the scale below to indicate how likely you are to change your position on the issue. [Respondents were shown a five-point Likert scale: "very likely," "somewhat likely," "neither likely nor unlikely," "somewhat unlikely," and "very unlikely."]

These attitude strength items were combined into an index ($\alpha = 0.63$). Those with strong attitudes (see figure 3.2) were the top decile of that scale (other breakpoints gave similar results). I also reanalyzed the data without the self-perceived knowledge item, and the ensuing index has $\alpha = 0.76$, but the substantive results are the same.

[The manipulation check item was asked in each experiment.]

In the news footage you saw earlier, would you say that the newscasters were more supportive of either the Democrats or the Republicans?

A. Much more supportive of Democrats
B. Somewhat more supportive of Democrats

C. Equally supportive of both Democrats and Republicans
D. Somewhat more supportive of Republicans
E. Much more supportive of Republicans

Experiment 2

SOURCE CREDIBILITY. In general, how much do you trust and confidence do you have in [outlet] when it comes to reporting the news fully, accurately, and fairly: a great deal, a fair amount, not very much, or none at all?

Respondents were asked separately about Fox News, MSNBC, and PBS. In the analysis in figure 4.3, respondents considered a source to be highly credible if they have "a great deal" of trust in the outlet.

ATTITUDE EXTREMITY ITEMS ($\alpha = 0.89$). The following set of items all share a nine-point Likert scale, running from "very strongly agree" to "very strongly disagree":

- Trying terrorists in civilian courts gives them constitutional rights and protections they do not deserve.
- Trying terrorists in civilian court demonstrates the strength of the rule of law: our laws beat their terror.
- Civilian courts have successfully tried and convicted terrorism suspects in the past, and they can do so again in the future.
- Terrorists are war criminals, and war criminals should be tried by military tribunals.

If forced to choose, would you prefer that terrorism suspects be tried in civilian or military courts?

A. Civilian court
B. Military courts
C. No preference

[If prefer civilian or military court:] Do you strongly prefer civilian/military trials, or only somewhat prefer it?

A. Strongly prefer
B. Somewhat prefer

[The following demographic items were asked in all future experiments.]
I am:

A. Male
B. Female

My age is:

A. 18–29
B. 30–40
C. 41–64
D. 65 or older

My highest level of schooling is:

A. Did not finish high school
B. High school graduate, no further schooling
C. Some college, but no degree
D. Community college/associates degree
E. Bachelor's degree or equivalent
F. Graduate or professional degree

I consider myself to be:

A. Caucasian (white)
B. African American
C. American Indian or Native American
D. Asian American

Experiment 3

In today's media marketplace, there are many different kinds of networks with different kinds of news shows that people might like to watch. For example, some people might like to watch a show from PBS, and others might like to watch a show from Fox News. If you had to pick which of the following types of news should would you most like to watch?

A. A show from PBS like *The News Hour*
B. A show from Fox News like *The O'Reilly Factor*
C. A show from MSNBC like *Countdown with Keith Olbermann*

ATTITUDE EXTREMITY ITEMS ($\alpha = .089$). [Items share a common response set: a nine-point Likert scale ranging from "very strongly agree" to "very strongly disagree."]

- Trying terrorists in civilian courts gives them constitutional rights and protections they do not deserve.
- Civilian courts have successfully tried and convicted terrorism suspects in the past, and they can do so again in the future.
- Trying terrorists in civilian courts demonstrates the strength of the rule of law: our law beats their terrors.
- Terrorists are war criminals, and war criminals should be tried by military courts, not civilian ones.

If forced to choose, would you prefer that terrorism suspects be tried in civilian or military courts?

A. Military courts
B. Civilian courts
C. No preference

[If prefer military or civilian court:] Do you strongly prefer a [military/civilian] trial, or only somewhat prefer it?

A. Strongly prefer a [military/civilian] trial
B. Somewhat prefer a [military/civilian] trial

Media Preferences Survey

How often do you watch [media outlet]: daily, weekly, monthly, a few times a year, or never?

A. Daily
B. Weekly
C. Monthly
D. A few times a year
E. Never

Subjects were asked separately about Fox News, MSNBC, local news, nightly broadcast news, and PBS. The results reported in chapter 4 report only on the Fox News and MSNBC items.

Do you approve or disapprove of the way Barrack Obama is handling his job as President?

A. Strongly approve
B. Approve
C. Neither approve nor disapprove
D. Disapprove
E. Strongly disapprove

One of the things we need to know is whether or not people really did go to vote in presidential elections. Thinking back to the November 2008 presidential election, did you go and vote for president?

A. Yes, I did vote
B. No, I did not vote

In the past two years, have you [performed activity]?

A. Yes
B. No

Respondents were asked separately about whether they gave money to a political party or candidate, attended a meeting or rally, volunteered for a campaign, talked to others to convince them to vote for or against a candidate or party, displayed a campaign button or sign for a candidate/party, and voted in a primary election.

Experiment 4

[The following set of items all share a seven-point Likert scale, running from "strongly agree" to "strongly disagree."]

- The U.S. should build a fence along the U.S.–Mexico border to keep out illegal immigrants.
- Laws like the one recently passed in Arizona unfairly discriminate against all Latinos.
- Illegal immigrants take away jobs from ordinary Americans.
- Most illegal immigrants obey the laws and only want a better life for their families.

- Laws like the one recently passed in Arizona increase crime by making immigrants afraid to talk to the police.

Cronbach's alpha, wave 1: 0.84
Cronbach's alpha, wave 2: 0.81

Experiment 5

The attitude extremity items from experiment 3 were used in this study as well.

ATTITUDE CERTAINTY ITEMS ($\alpha = 0.78$). How likely is it that you will change your position on the issue of civilian vs. military trials for terrorism suspects?

A. Very unlikely
B. Unlikely
C. Somewhat unlikely
D. Neither likely or nor unlikely
E. Somewhat likely
F. Likely
G. Very likely

How certain are you about your opinion about civilian vs. military trials for terrorism suspects?

A. Very uncertain
B. Uncertain
C. Somewhat uncertain
D. Neither certain nor uncertain
E. Somewhat certain
F. Certain
G. Very certain

Experiment 6

MEASURE OF PARTISAN TRUST. How much of the time do you think you can trust [Republicans/Democrats] in Congress to do what is right for the country?

A. Almost always
B. Most of the time
C. About half the time
D. Once in a while
E. Almost Never

PARTY FEELING THERMOMETERS. We would like to get your feelings toward some of our political leaders and other people who are in the news these days. We would like you to rate that person using something we call the feeling thermometer. Ratings between 50 degrees and 100 degrees mean that you feel favorable and warm toward the person. Ratings between 0 degrees and 50 degrees mean that you don't feel favorable toward the person and that you don't care too much for that person. You would rate the person at the 50 degree mark if you don't feel particularly warm or cold toward the person. Please use the feeling thermometers below to rate each of the following individuals. [Subjects were shown a 0–100 feeling thermometer and asked to rank the Democratic and Republican parties.]

SUPPORT FOR BIPARTISANSHIP. Subjects were only asked about their party in the item below (e.g., Democrats only see the version about Democrats, and Republicans only see the version about Republicans).

Which do you think should be a higher priority for [President Obama and congressional Democrats/congressional Republicans]—working in a bipartisan way with [Republicans/Democrats] in Congress, or sticking up for [Democratic/Republican] policies?

A. Work in a bipartisan fashion with Republicans/Democrats
B. Do both equally
C. Stick to Democratic/Republican policies

Subjects who said they support working in a bipartisan fashion or sticking with policies were asked if they hold that position strongly or not strongly, to make a five-point scale of bipartisanship.

Experiment 7

OBAMA FEELING THERMOMETER. Respondents saw the same instructions and task as in experiment 8, but here rated President Obama.

APPROVE OF NATIONAL SECURITY. Do you approve or disapprove of the job President Obama is doing in handling foreign policy and national security?

A. Strongly approve
B. Approve
C. Neither approve nor disapprove
D. Disapprove
E. Strongly disapprove

STRONG LEADERSHIP. How well does the phrase "provides strong leadership" describe President Obama?

A. Extremely well
B. Very well
C. Somewhat well
D. Not too well
E. Not well at all

SOURCE CREDIBILITY. See the source credibility section from experiment 2.

Experiment 8

Subjects were randomly assigned to see either the Republican or the Democratic version of the following item. This randomization was separate from the initial randomization into like-minded, crosscutting, or apolitical media.

Recently, there has been a great deal of attention to the federal budget. A recent [Democrat/Republican] proposal suggest gradually increasing the age when workers can claim full Social Security benefits, instituting a new national sales tax, and cutting both defense and domestic spending. Would you approve or disapprove of this type of plan to reduce the deficit?

A. Strongly approve
B. Approve
C. Neither approve nor disapprove

D. Disapprove
E. Strongly disapprove

Experiment 9

Both items used here had the standard introduction (see experiment 2), and respondents answered on a seven-point Likert scale, running from "strongly agree" to "strongly disagree."

- Republicans in Ohio had the right message, but they lost because it did not deliver it effectively.
- Democrats in Ohio won because Republicans over-reached and tried to pass an overly conservative law.

Analysis Details, 2008 National Annenberg Election Study Panel Data

This section gives the details for the analysis of the 2008 National Annenberg Election Study panel data used in chapter 5. The NAES data is a five-wave panel spanning from late 2007, before the official start of the primary season, to early 2009, after Obama's victory. Wave 1 occurred from 2 October 2007 to 31 December 2007; wave 2 occurred from 1 January 2008 to 31 March 2008; wave 3 occurred from 2 April 2008 to 28 August 2008; wave 4 occurred from 29 August 2008 to 4 November 2008; and wave 5 occurred from 5 November 2008 to 20 January 2009. For more details on the sampling and so forth, see Johnston 2009.

Measure of Partisan Media Exposure

As I explained in chapter 6, the 2008 NAES panel data used a unique item to gauge media exposure. In lieu of asking about general media exposure, the NAES asked about exposure to a list of specific programs. Respondents were asked: "Which of the following programs do you watch regularly on television? Please check any that you watch at least once per month." Subjects were then shown a series of options (see Dilliplane, Goldman, and Mutz, forthcoming, for a complete list).

For my purposes, right-wing programs come from Fox News, and left-wing programs come from MSNBC. The Annenberg study asked respondents if they watch 11 Fox News programs: *The Beltway Boys, Fox & Friends, Fox News, The Fox Report w/ Shepard Smith, Geraldo at Large, Hannity & Colmes, Hannity's America, The O'Reilly Factor, Special Report with Brit Hume, Studio B with Shepard Smith*, and *Your World with Neil Cavuto*. They also asked subjects about three programs from MSNBC, coded here as left-wing shows: *Countdown with Keith Olbermann, Hardball with Chris Matthews*, and *MSNBC Live*.

Measure of Dependent Variables

VOTE CHOICE. In the 2008 presidential election, who did you vote for? Options given were: "John McCain and Sarah Palin, the Republicans"; "Barack Obama and Joe Biden, the Democrats"; "Ralph Nader and Matt Gonzalez, the Independents"; "Bob Barr and Wayne Allyn Root, the Libertarians"; and "Other, please specify." In the analysis reported in chapter 6, those voting for third-party candidates (a small fraction of the sample) are treated as missing data.

CANDIDATE FEELING THERMOMETERS. Please rate the following person on a thermometer that runs from 0 to 100 degrees: [candidate]. Rating above 50 means that you feel favorable and warm toward the person. Rating below 50 means that you feel unfavorable and cool toward the person. Respondents rated the major-party presidential and vice presidential nominees.

POSITIVE OR NEGATIVE VALENCE EVALUATIONS. Are there any candidates who you think would do a particularly good (bad) job of handling [issue]? The issues used were "the nation's economy," "the health care situation," and "homeland security."

Notes

Chapter One

1. Eventually the Obama administration reversed this decision and decided that Mohammed (and other high-profile suspects) would be tried in military tribunals in Guantanamo Bay (Serrano 2011).

2. For example, Bill O'Reilly debated Democratic congressmen Joe Sestak and Anthony Weiner about Mohammed's trial on his show (*The O'Reilly Factor*, 13 November 2009).

3. Note that gridlock and drift can be pernicious for both liberals and conservatives. While liberals typically want government to do more (and so should be more frustrated by gridlock), conservatives can also have something to fear from gridlock when the status quo is too liberal (hence, they would prefer a change to a more conservative policy).

4. As John Stewart remarked on *The Daily Show* regarding partisan media, "You pick your narrative and you stick with it. And if you news doesn't fit your narrative, change your [expletive] news" (Stewart 2010).

5. Note that this logic also implicates elite polarization for the rise of these outlets as well, both for its role in generating mass electoral shifts and for generating the content and issues that sustain these programs (see also Berry and Sobieraj 2008).

6. Further, studies of the effects of partisan websites have to confront a series of practical challenges, for example, how to measure how many viewers actually visit each website and are exposed to it (since measuring unique visits is extremely challenging; see Hindman 2008), how individuals respond to user-generated versus site-generated content, and how to deal with cross-posting (i.e., when websites post stories or links created by others).

7. While MSNBC was initially more neutral in tone, after the 2004 election, it tilted to the Left (Steinberg 2007; Pew Project for Excellence in Journalism 2009). Some scholars also code CNN as a more liberal/Democratic outlet (e.g.,

Turner 2007; Stroud 2011). This is a slightly more controversial choice, given that others argue CNN is a more neutral outlet (Pew Project for Excellence in Journalism 2009). Because of this, I avoid labeling CNN as a partisan outlet, but doing so would not fundamentally change my analysis.

8. Throughout the book, I focus on these types of more explicitly partisan media, avoiding the debates about whether the mainstream media is biased toward one party or the other, a charge hurled from both the Left (Alterman 2003) and the Right (Goldberg 2003). Numerous detailed content analyses suggest that the mainstream media avoids taking positions that favor one side or the other (D'Alessio and Allen 2000; Watts et al. 1999; though for a dissenting view, see Groseclose 2011). Though interesting, debates about bias in the mainstream media would take us far away from the topic of interest here.

9. While I simply compare various descriptive statistics here, a regression-based analysis would yield very similar conclusions (for example, see Morris 2005).

10. While other studies show that selective exposure exists at a given point in time (e.g., Ieyngar and Han 2009), they do not assess the over-time patterns.

11. If I did look at the years since MSNBC moved more to the Left, I would find that in both 2008 and 2010, approximately 50 percent of Democrats reported watching the network.

12. If I looked at conservatives instead of Republicans, I would find nearly identical patterns.

13. *The O'Reilly Factor*, 23 July 2010.

14. The idea that partisan media (with its stronger biases and one-sided information flows) would generate larger media effects than more mainstream sources is highly consistent with Zaller's (1996) theory of media effects (see chapter 3 for more on this point).

15. While the Della Vigna and Kaplan (2007) study is arguably the closest of these to the current study (as they examine how Fox News availability in a county impacts county-level vote share for Republicans), the analysis takes place at the aggregate level, making it inappropriate to test individual-level theories of persuasion and reinforcement developed in later chapters.

16. In the social psychology literature, such signals are known as "disconfirming cues" (Eagly, Wood, and Chaiken 1978).

Chapter Two

1. "Climategate" refers to the release of a series of e-mails from climate research scientists at the University of East Anglia in the United Kingdom by an anonymous source. Some initially claimed that these e-mails discredited the sci-

entific evidence supporting man-made global warming, though several detailed investigations showed this claim to be false (Gillis 2010; Milbourn 2010; Sheppard 2010).

2. Story counts retrieved by searching LexisNexis for "Solyndra" in that three-month period from both networks.

3. One might wonder if these shows ever criticize members of their own party (e.g., if a left-wing show ever criticizes Democrats). This is relatively rare, but it does happen, mostly when those figures are not ideological or partisan enough. So, for example, Rachel Maddow criticizes conservative Democrats such as Nebraska senator Ben Nelson for working too much with Republicans and going against Democratic and liberal policies (*The Rachel Maddow Show*, 19 October 2011). This fits with the one-sided presentation of the news seen on these programs.

4. While my electoral content analysis focused only on the 2008 election, the discussion of the 2012 election on both Fox and MSNBC showed the same patterns of biased coverage (Pew Project for Excellence in Journalism 2012; Peters 2012).

5. Doing a LexisNexis search on the program transcripts, I found thirty-two transcripts referencing the phrase "media bias" between 1 September and 1 December 2008 on Fox News. A parallel search on MSNBC gave three transcripts, and three transcripts for ABC and CBS News combined (NBC News is not available on LexisNexis during this time frame).

6. Results from another LexisNexis transcript search showed that Fox News used the phrase "ACORN" 153 times and the phrase "vote fraud" or "voter fraud" 96 times between 1 August and 31 December 2008. The parallel figures for MSNBC were 29 and 15, and for ABC and CBS News combined, 16 and 8.

7. This background on the federal debt ceiling comes from the summary provided by Robert Smith (2011). For more in-depth details of the history of the debt ceiling, see Austin and Levit 2012.

8. To ensure that I did not miss any relevant coverage, I started by analysis one week before the Treasury notice and ended one week after President Obama signed the bill into law; the time frame for the analysis was 9 May–9 August 2011.

9. Here, I identified the relevant stories by searching for the term "debt ceiling" in the relevant date period. I then selected the fifteen stories that were examined using a random number generator.

10. Those same deals, such as the Gang of Six proposal, were criticized on MSNBC for being too conservative (*The Rachel Maddow Show*, 19 July 2011).

11. MSNBC was arguably somewhat more nuanced in its treatment of bipartisanship, except on the issue of entitlement reform, where its hosts and guests drew a harsh line (*The Ed Show*, 7 July 2011).

12. Here, because there were far fewer stories than in the debt ceiling debate, it was possible to examine the population of stories rather than merely a sample of them.

13. As I explain later in the chapter, I began my analysis with the first discussion of Jones on Fox News and ended the story several weeks after Jones's resignation, when his story faded. The time period of the study was 15 July 2009–26 September 2009.

14. While I focused here on the coverage on Fox News (given my attention to Fox and other partisan TV outlets), Jones was also being discussed at the same time on right-wing websites (for example, see Klein 2009). An interesting extension for future work would be to consider how the Fox coverage helped feed into website discussion, and vice versa.

15. For figure 2.1, stories appearing on Fox News, MSNBC, and the *Washington Times* count as "partisan" stories; stories in all other outlets appearing in the "Major U.S. and World Publications" and "TV and Radio Broadcasts" categories in LexisNexis are labeled as mainstream news stories. Counting only Fox and MSNBC stories as partisan (that is, dropping the *Washington Times*) would not change the substantive implication of the results shown in the figure.

16. For example, Fox News (in particular, Sean Hannity) spent a great deal of time urging the removal of Kevin Jennings, but that story never spread beyond that channel (Farhi 2011).

Chapter Three

1. Note, however, that having strong attitudes should not predict greater polarization in response to like-minded media. Polarization in response to like-minded media only involves uncritically accepting congenial arguments, not counterarguing hostile ones. Given this, strong attitudes will more strongly polarize viewers after crosscutting, but not like-minded, exposure.

2. Note that this also gives an additional reason why like-minded media will polarize viewers: these messages come from credible sources (given the credibility comes from perceived common interest, such as a shared partisan or ideological label).

3. Note that while attitude extremity and attitude certainty are often strongly correlated, they are theoretically and empirically distinct (Gross, Holtz, and Miller 1995). One can be certain of a moderate position or uncertain of an extreme one.

4. Further, the types of negative emotions generated about the other side by these processes will heighten motivated reasoning processes (Biek, Wood, and Chaiken 1996; Ditto and Lopez 1992), which will intensify the types of effects described here.

5. This persuasion can occur via two distinct mechanisms. First, in-group messages are seen as especially persuasive, so these messages persuade viewers to adopt the host's view (Mackie 1986). Second, viewers might also come to believe that a trait of, say, Democratic identification is disliking Republicans (as the out-group), so they adopt that attitude as their own (Turner 1991). Note that this same logic also applies to the case of attitude polarization, discussed earlier in this chapter.

6. Note, however, that there should not be any effects here for crosscutting media for electoral losers: because crosscutting media will focus on why the winning candidate won, it will tend to emphasize the winning candidate's skill, strategy, and so forth, rather than the delegitimzing explanations offered by like-minded media.

Chapter Four

1. Partisan leaners were treated as partisans (Keith et al. 1992); pure Independents (those who do not lean toward either party) were dropped from the analysis. Including them did not change the substantive results; see the online appendix for more details.

2. The online appendix can be found at http://www.press.uchicago.edu/books/levendusky/.

3. Further, note that adding a fourth group (the apolitical control) also would diminish the statistical power of the experiments, which is always a concern, especially with only a modest number of subjects.

4. The online subjects came from Amazon's Mechanical Turk, an increasingly popular choice for experimental research (Berinsky, Huber, and Lenz 2012). I discuss the strengths and weaknesses of Mechanical Turk in the data appendix at the end of the book.

5. In experiment 4, while I measured subjects' attitudes at two points in time, they only received the treatment stimulus once (in the initial session of the experiment).

6. Readers interested in additional regression-based analyses of these data are also referred to Levendusky 2012a for the analyses of experiments 1, 3, and 4; I provide the regression-based analyses of experiments 2 and 5 in the appendix to this chapter.

7. To be clear, my experiments tested for issue polarization (i.e., changes in attitude extremity on particular issues) rather than a more general ideological polarization.

8. Given the coding of the dependent variable here, however, the results could be equally consistent with a sorting story, rather than a polarization one. Maybe partisan media reminds "out of step" Democrats that they should take more lib-

eral positions (i.e., partisan media drives sorting), rather than causing liberal Democrats to embrace more extremely liberal positions (i.e., partisan media drives polarization; I thank a reader for making this suggestion to me). I can estimate these models separately and find support for both; see the online appendix for details.

9. Here, attitude strength was measured as an additive index of attitude certainty, importance, and (self-perceived) knowledge about the issue (see the data appendix for the specific items). Those in the top decile of attitude strength have "strong" attitudes, while others have weak attitudes. If I code strong attitudes as those above the mean, I get substantively similar, albeit weaker, results, suggesting that much of the effect of attitude strength is concentrated among those with the very strongest attitudes.

10. One concern with these sorts of moderator effects, however, is that they might be picking up other differences between subjects. For example, maybe those with stronger attitudes are simply more interested in politics, and hence pay closer attention to the stimuli and the resulting questions, generating the effects seen in the text (I thank a reader for pointing this out to me). I can never completely rule out this possibility, but I can offer a test of the underlying idea. I can interact the treatment with both attitude strength and a measure of political interest/attentiveness. If attitude strength is just a proxy for general interest/engagement, then the attitude strength results should go away once I include the interaction with the interest/engagement measure. When I do this, my results survive, suggesting that strength (and not just interest/engagement or some other factor) drives these results. See the online appendix for more details.

11. The measure of credibility was asked in the pretest instrument: "In general, how much trust and confidence do you have in [media outlet] when it comes to reporting the news fully, accurately, and fairly: a great deal, a fair amount, not very much, or none at all?" To help avoid cueing subjects as to the treatments being used here, they were asked to rate a variety of different news organizations.

12. This is discussed further in Levendusky 2012b.

13. One limitation of this item is that I did not include a nonpolitical media option (i.e., what if subjects do not prefer any type of news, but instead prefer to watch sports or entertainment TV?). While my focus is on political media, an important topic for future work is to examine the consequences of including nonpolitical media (see Arceneaux and Johnson 2010, forthcoming).

14. I cannot, however, *prove* these moderating effects by definitively showing that, say, preferences polarize because of differences in motivation/ability. In general, it is not possible with a standard experimental design to credibly demonstrate mediation effects (Bullock, Green, and Ha 2010; Imai et al. 2011). While my evidence is highly consistent with this account, an important topic for future work (as with all mediator-based analysis) will be to try and design stud-

ies to more fully trace out these effects and test the underlying hypothesis in different ways.

15. Subjects were sent two requests for participation via e-mail. All subjects who completed the study did so within two days of the request, with the majority (83 percent) doing so on the first day (i.e., two days after the original study).

16. One concern was that subjects might simply remember the items from t1 to t2, making the effects here more about memory than duration. I designed another experiment to rule out this possibility by only asking the attitude items at t2. Even here, I found duration effects (see the online appendix).

17. In future research, it would fruitful to explore how processing style impacts these effects (Chong and Druckman 2010) and how these effects decay over longer periods of time (Gerber et al. 2011).

18. Subjects were not told that this recontact was for a follow-up study to avoid priming them to remember their attitudes.

19. An interesting extension for future research would be to consider the effects of varying stimuli over time, to capture the fact that partisan media's treatment of an issue evolves over time (see the discussion in chapter 2).

Chapter Five

1. Note, however, that with my experiments, I cannot differentiate between the two potential mechanisms outlined in the theoretical discussion in chapter 3 (identity priming and in-group persuasion). Future work will be needed to differentiate these competing pathways; I thank a reader for making this point to me.

2. This also parallels the findings in Smith and Searles (forthcoming): partisan media exposure shapes attitudes toward and perceptions of the opposing party candidate but has remarkably little effect on views of the same party candidate.

3. See the appendix to Levendusky 2012b for more details.

4. The measure of credibility is the same one used in experiment 2; see the discussion of that experiment in chapter 4 for additional details.

5. For a discussion of the types of incivility on these shows, see Sobieraj and Berry 2011.

6. An interesting possibility for future research is that responses to incivility may be asymmetric: a Republican may respond quite differently to the incivility on Fox News (where it does not affect them) than on MSNBC (where it may have a larger effect). This would be consistent with the motivated reasoning account in chapter 3, though more work will be needed to unpack and test it.

7. Indeed, there are reasons to suspect that viewers who prefer like-minded

media might be more susceptible to certain effects on partisan media and less susceptible to others (due to, say, pretreatment effects). It will be important to explore how these moderators shape the effects of partisan media more generally moving forward.

8. I thank a reader for making this point to me.

Chapter Six

1. For more details on the NAES panel survey, sampling procedures, and so forth, see Johnston 2009.

2. The list of news and information shows is quite large, and consists of many mainstream and partisan choices (for the full list, see Dilliplane, Goldman, and Mutz, forthcoming). Subjects who do not watch any of these shows are likely quite different from those who watch at least one (Prior 2007).

3. I did so using the coarsened exact matching algorithm (Iacus, King, and Porro 2009, 2011). See the online appendix for more details on the matching process.

4. As is standard in models of U.S. vote choice, I omitted the small percentage of respondents who support third-party candidates. As in earlier chapters, I omitted pure Independents from my analysis and treated Independent leaners as partisans.

5. Della Vigna and Gentzkow (2010) give the formula as $100 * \frac{y_T - y_C}{e_T - e_C} \frac{1}{1 - y_C}$, where y_T is the proportion of those watching partisan television who vote for their party's nominee, and y_C is the proportion who do not watch partisan television who vote for their party's nominee. e_T and e_C are the rates of exposure to partisan television for the groups (here, 1 for those who watch and 0 for those who do not). Here, $y_T - y_C$ is the estimate from table 6.2 (2.1 percent), and y_C is the rate of party voting among those with no like-minded media exposure, which is the intercept from the fixed effects model (0.9; see table 6.2). I assume that exposure is recorded perfectly (i.e., all subjects who say they watch partisan media do watch partisan media, while those claim to not watch do in fact not watch). If I use the true-score reliability to correct for measurement error in exposure, the persuasion rate rises to 24 percent.

6. Another possible source of heterogeneity would be over-time effects, with potentially larger effects coming late in the campaign, as both more viewers tune in to these shows and these shows devote more attention to the presidential race. I tested for such effects, but found only minor ones here, with slightly larger effects of media found during the fall campaign. The limitation here, of course, is that all viewers increase their media consumption over the course of the campaign, making it difficult to detect a distinct partisan media effect.

7. Subjects who did not have a preference or indicated that it depends on the candidate were excluded from the analysis.

8. Calculations come from Keele's (2010) rbounds program.

9. I used matching here because the feeling thermometers for the vice presidential nominees were only asked in wave 4 (during the fall campaign). Because the outcome was measured in wave 4, I measured the treatment wave 2 (during the primary campaign).

10. That is, the measure is the number of issues (out of three) where the respondent thinks the candidate will do a good job minus the number of issues where they think the candidate will do a bad job. Analyzing the data splitting out good and bad evaluations separately gave substantively similar answers, as did combining both candidates' evaluations into a single aggregate rating.

11. Here, because these valence items were asked repeatedly, I also matched on the earlier iteration of these same valence items administered in wave 1. To preserve sample size, I matched on subjects having a positive, negative, or neutral overall judgment of the candidate's competence. Omitting matching on these lagged evaluations gave the same substantive results.

12. Here, the treatment effect was −0.17 (with a standard error of 0.05); $p<.01$ (with the dependent variable measured on a 1–4 scale).

13. One test of this would be to look at respondents from Ohio (who presumably had some pretreatment exposure to this issue). Unfortunately, I have no way of knowing subjects' state of residence, since it was not asked in the experiment.

Chapter Seven

1. This is not to say that subjects did not engage in any sort of motivated reasoning when processing crosscutting information. Motivated reasoning can also predict that subjects would just ignore the crosscutting arguments (or process them but not be moved by them; I thank a reader for making this point to me). But more generally, this still leaves a puzzle: why is this so much variation in the willingness to counterargue these positions? In general, a richer theory of crosscutting media needed.

2. One possibility, for example, is that some viewers simply find all media outlets, including partisan media ones, to be credible news sources (and hence see them as a valid source of information).

3. This underlines another important point for future research: it will be important to try and further unpack exactly why those who prefer to watch these shows differ and explore how other moderators (like information, political expertise, and so forth) shape these effects.

4. Another interesting area for future study would be to examine treatment

spillover: does hearing about one issue on partisan media impact your attitude on a related topic? For example, if you watch Bill O'Reilly discuss health care reform, does this shape your attitude on, say, taxes as well? There is some evidence of spillover for highly related areas (Druckman, Fein, and Leeper 2012), but more work will be needed to document these consequences for partisan outlets.

5. Converse (1975) explains how consistency can increase without a parallel increase in constraint (see also Levendusky 2010).

6. A related point is that these different agendas might change the issues subjects use when evaluating leaders (priming). This is another important topic for future research (though for difficulties in assessing priming, see Lenz 2009).

7. A related concern is that this gives elites further incentives to engage in the sort of "crafted talk" discussed by Jacobs and Shapiro (2000), especially given that the goal on partisan media is more to mobilize sympathetic partisans than to convert the undecided.

8. O'Reilly's remarks come from the 23 July 2010 episode of his show *The O'Reilly Factor.*

9. For another example of how partisan media contributes to gridlock, see the discussion of partisan media's role in the 2011 debt ceiling debate in chapter 2.

10. The same dynamic played out during the "super committee" deliberations: one of the major stumbling blocks was the inability of activists on either side to accept a compromise solution (Faler and Sloan 2011).

11. The phrase comes from Madison's discussion of the Constitutional Convention in "Jared Sparks: Journal," .http://www.consource.org/document/jared-sparks-journal/.

12. I thank a reader for making this point to me.

Data Appendix

1. The item asks: "Who has the final responsibility to determine if a law is constitutional or not? Is it the president, the Congress, or the Supreme Court?"

2. The item asks: "How much of a majority is required for the U.S. Senate and House to override a presidential veto?"

3. The item asks: "Do you happen to know which party has the most members in the United States House of Representatives?"

4. The item asks: "To the best of your knowledge, do you happen to know how Supreme Court justices are chosen? Are they nominated by a nonpartisan congressional committee, elected by the American people, nominated by the president and then confirmed by the Senate, or appointed if they receive a two-thirds majority vote of the justices already on the court?"

5. The item asks: "In the past week, have you talked to any people and

tried to show them why they should vote for or against one of the presidential candidates?"

6. The item asks: "In the past week, did you give money to any of the presidential candidates?"

7. The item asks: "In the past week, did you do any work for one of the presidential candidates?"

8. The item asks: "In the past week, have you gone to any political meetings, rallies, speeches, dinners, or things like that in support of a particular presidential candidate?"

9. The item asks: "In the past week, did you wear a presidential campaign button, put a campaign sticker on your car, or place a sign in your window or in front of your house?"

10. Transcripts of the stimuli used in the experiments are given in the online appendix (see also the appendices of Levendusky 2012a and 2012b).

11. Indeed, no subjects who watched the right-wing treatment viewed the segments as even somewhat supportive of the Democratic Party.

12. The screening test has subjects watch a short video clip (approximately 30 seconds) from a popular television show and then complete a brief quiz about said clip. In order to successfully complete the quiz, subjects must be able to both see and hear the video clip.

13. For more detailed descriptions of the demographics and motivations of Mechanical Turk subjects, see Paolacci, Chandler and Iperotis 2010.

References

Abrams, Dominic, Margaret Wetherell, Sandra Cochrane, Michael Hogg, and John Turner. 1990. "Knowing What to Think By Knowing Who You Are: Self-Categorization and the Nature of Group Formation, Conformity, and Group Polarization." *British Journal of Social Psychology* 29 (2): 97–119.

Abramowitz, Alan. 2010. *The Disappearing Center.* New Haven, CT: Yale University Press.

Achen, Christopher. 1992. "Social Psychology, Demographic Variables, and Linear Regression: Breaking the Iron Triangle in Voting Research." *Political Behavior* 14 (3): 195–211.

Allison, Paul. 2009. *Fixed Effects Regression Models.* Los Angeles: Sage.

Alter, Adam, Daniel Oppenheimer, and Jeffrey Zemla. 2010. "Missing the Trees for the Forest: A Construal Level Account of the Illusion of Explanatory Depth." *Journal of Personality and Social Psychology* 99 (3): 436–51.

Alterman, Eric. 2003. *What Liberal Media? The Truth About Bias and the News.* New York: Basic Books.

Alvarez, R. Michael. 1997. *Information and Elections.* Ann Arbor: University of Michigan Press.

Anderson, Christopher, Andre Blais, Shaun Bowler, Todd Donovan, and Ola Listhaug. 2005. *Losers' Consent: Elections and Democratic Legitimacy.* New York: Oxford University Press.

Anderson, Craig, and Brad Bushman. 1997. "External Validity of 'Trivial' Experiments: The Case of Laboratory Aggression." *Review of General Psychology* 1 (1): 19–41.

Arceneaux, Kevin, Alan Gerber, and Donald Green. 2006. "Comparing Experimental and Matching Methods Using a Large-Scale Field Experiment on Voter Mobilization." *Political Analysis* 14 (1): 37–62.

Arceneaux, Kevin, and Gregory Huber. 2007. "Uncovering the Persuasive Effects of Presidential Advertising." *American Journal of Political Science* 51 (4): 961–81.

Arceneaux, Kevin and Martin Johnson. 2010. "Does Media Fragmentation Produce Mass Polarization? Selective Exposure and a New Era of Minimal Effects." Paper presented at the Annual Meeting of the American Political Science Association, Washington DC.

———. Forthcoming. *Changing Minds or Changing Channels? Partisan News in an Age of Choice*. Chicago: University of Chicago Press.

Arceneaux, Kevin, Martin Johnson, and Chad Murphy. 2012. "Polarized Political Communication, Oppositional Media Hostility, and Selective Exposure." *Journal of Politics* 74 (1): 174–86.

Austin, D. Andrew, and Mindy Levit. 2012. "The Debt Limit: History and Recent Increases." *Congressional Research Service Report*, RL31967.

Bai, Matt. 2008. "Working for the Working Class Vote." *New York Times*, 15 October.

———. 2009. "Cable Guise." *New York Times*, 6 December.

Barabas, Jason. 2004. "How Deliberation Affects Policy Opinions." *American Political Science Review* 98 (4): 687–701.

Barker, David, and Kathleen Knight. 2000. "Political Talk Radio and Public Opinion." *Public Opinion Quarterly* 64 (2): 149–70.

Bartels, Larry. 1993. "Messages Received: The Political Impact of Media Exposure." *American Political Science Review* 87 (2): 267–85.

———. 2000. "Partisanship and Voting Behavior, 1952–1996." *American Journal of Political Science* 44 (1): 35–50.

Baum, Matthew. 2011a. "Preaching to the Choir or Converting the Flock: Presidential Communication Strategies in the Age of Three Medias." In *iPolitics: Citizens, Elections, and Governing in the New Media Age*, edited by Richard Fox and Jennifer Ramos. New York: Cambridge University Press.

———. 2011b. "Red State, Blue State, Flu State: Media Self-Selection and Partisan Gaps in Swine Flu Vaccinations." *Journal of Health Politics, Policy, and Law* 36 (6): 1021–59.

———. 2012. "Partisan Media and Attitude Polarization: The Case of Health Care Reform." In *Regulatory Breakdown: The Crisis of Confidence in U.S. Regulation*, edited by Cary Coglianese. Philadelphia: University of Pennsylvania Press.

Baum, Matthew, and Tim Groeling. 2008. "New Media and the Polarization of American Political Discourse." *Political Communication* 25 (4): 345–65.

———. 2009. "Shot by the Messenger: Partisan Cues and Public Opinion Regarding National Security and War." *Political Behavior* 31 (2): 157–86.

———. 2010. *War Stories: The Causes and Consequences of Public Views on War*. Princeton, NJ: Princeton University Press.

Baum, Matthew, and Phil Gussin. 2008. "In the Eye of the Beholder: How Information Shortcuts Shape Individual Perceptions of Bias in the Media." *Quarterly Journal of Political Science* 3 (1): 1–31.

Baum, Matthew, and Samuel Kernell. 1999. "Has Cable Ended the Golden Age of Presidential Television?" *American Political Science Review* 93 (1): 99–114.

Baumeister, Roy, Ellen Bratslavsky, Catrin Finkenauer, and Kathleen Vohs. 2001. "Bad Is Stronger than Good." *Review of General Psychology* 5 (4): 323–70.

Bennett, W. Lance, and Shanto Iyengar. 2008. "A New Era of Minimal Effects? The Changing Foundations of Political Communication." *Journal of Communication* 58 (4): 707–31.

Berelson, Bernard, Paul Lazarsfeld, and WIlliam McPhee. 1954. *Voting: A Study of Opinion Formation in a Presidential Campaign*. Chicago: University of Chicago Press.

Berinsky, Adam, Gregory Huber, and Gabriel Lenz. 2012. "Evaluating Online Labor Markets for Experimental Research: Amazon.com's Mechanical Turk." *Political Analysis* 20 (3): 351–68.

Berkowitz, Leonard, and Edward Donnerstein. 1982. "External Validity Is More than Skin Deep." *American Psychologist* 37 (3): 245–57.

Berry, Jeffrey, and Sarah Sobieraj. 2008. "The Outrage Industry." Paper presented at the Conference on Going to Extremes, Dartmouth College, Hanover, NH.

———. 2011. "Understanding the Rise of Talk Radio." *PS: Political Science and Politics* 44 (4): 762–67.

Biek, Michael, Wendy Wood, and Shelly Chaiken. 1996. "Working Knowledge, Cognitive Processing, and Attitudes: On the Determinants of Bias." *Personality and Social Psychology Bulletin* 22 (6): 547–56.

Blake, Aaron, and Rachel Weiner. 2011. "Ohio Repeals Law Restricting Unions; Mississippi Blocks 'Personhood' Amendment." *Washington Post*, 8 November.

Brady, David, Hahrie Han, and Jeremy Pope. 2007. "Primary Elections and Candidate Ideology: Out of Step with the Primary Electorate?" *Legislative Studies Quarterly* 32 (1): 79–105.

Brady, Henry, and Paul Sniderman. 1985. "Attitude Attribution: A Group Basis for Political Reasoning." *American Political Science Review* 79 (4): 1061–78.

Brewer, Marilyn. 1991. "The Social Self: On Being the Same and Different at the Same Time." *Personality and Social Psychology Bulletin* 17 (5): 475–82.

Broder, John. 2009. "White House Official Resigns After GOP Criticism." *New York Times*, 6 September.

Bullock, John, Donald Green, and Shang Ha. 2010. "Yes, But What's the Mechanism? (Don't Expect an Easy Answer)." *Journal of Personality and Social Psychology* 98 (4): 547–57.

Cacioppo, Jon, and Richard Petty. 1989. "Effects of Message Repetition on Argument Processing, Recall, and Persuasion." *Basic and Applied Social Psychology* 10 (1): 3–12.

Carlsmith, J. Merrill, Phoebe Ellsworth, and Elliot Aronson. 1989. *Methods of Research in Social Psychology.* Reading, MA: Addison-Wesley.

Carmines, Edward, and James Stimson. 1989. *Issue Evolution: Race and the Transformation of American Politics.* Princeton, NJ: Princeton University Press.

Chalif, Rebecca. 2011. "Bias on MSNBC and Fox News: An Empirical Analysis of the Content Found on Cable News." *Electronic Media and Politics,* 30 June. http://www.emandp.com/post/single/bias_on_msnbc_fox_news.

Chang, Linchiat, and Jon Krosnick. 2009. "National Surveys via RDD Telephone Interviewing Versus the Internet: Comparing Sample Representativeness and Response Quality." *Public Opinion Quarterly* 73 (4): 641–78.

Chiang, Chun Fang, and Brian Knight. 2011. "Media Bias and Influence: Evidence From Newspaper Endorsements." *Review of Economic Studies* 78 (3): 795–820.

Chong, Dennis, and James Druckman. 2010. "Dynamic Public Opinion: Framing Effects Over Time." *American Political Science Review* 104 (4): 663–80.

Cillizza, Chris, and Aaron Blake. 2011. "The Tea Party, The Debt Ceiling, and John Boehner's Conundrum." *Washington Post,* 12 July.

Cohen, Geoffrey. 2003. "Party Over Policy: The Dominating Impact of Group Influence on Political Beliefs." *Journal of Personality and Social Psychology* 85 (5): 808–22.

Cohen, Jeffrey. 2009. *Going Local: Presidential Leadership in the Post-Broadcast Age.* New York: Cambridge University Press.

Converse, Philip. 1975. "Public Opinion and Voting Behavior." In *Handbook of Political Science,* edited by Fred Greenstein and Nelson Polsby. Reading, MA: Addison-Wesley.

D'Alessio, Dave, and Mike Allen. 2000. "Media Bias in Presidential Elections: A Meta-Analysis." *Journal of Communication* 50 (4): 133–56.

Dalton, Russell, Paul Beck, and Robert Huckfeldt. 1998. "Partisan Cues and the Media: Information Flows in the 1992 Presidential Election." *American Political Science Review* 92 (1): 111–26.

Davis, Tom. 2011. "Time to Tear Down Ideological Walls." *Politico.com,* 11 September. http://dyn.politico.com/printstory.cfm?uuid=96345564-B3A8-4E73-8303-B9BEE93E3D51.

Della Vigna, Stefano, and Matthew Gentzkow. 2010. "Persuasion: Empirical Evidence." *Annual Review of Economics* 2 (1): 643–69.

Della Vigna, Stefano, and Ethan Kaplan. 2007. "The Fox News Effect: Media Bias and Voting." *The Quarterly Journal of Economics* 122 (3): 1187–234.

De Waal, Ester, Klaus Schonbach, and Edmund Lauf. 2005. "Online Newspapers: A Substitute or Complement for Print Newspapers and Other Information Channels." *Communications: The European Journal of Communication Research* 30 (1): 55–72.

Dickinson, Tim. 2011. "The Fox News Fear Factory." *Rolling Stone*, 9 June 54–84.

Dilliplane, Susanna. 2010. "More than Minimal Effects." Manuscript. University of Pennsylvania, Annenberg School for Communication.

———. 2011. "All the News You Want to Hear: The Impact of Partisan News Exposure on Political Participation." *Public Opinion Quarterly* 75 (2): 287–316.

Dilliplane, Sussana, Seth Goldman, and Diana Mutz. Forthcoming. "Televised Exposure to Politics: New Measures for a Fragmented Media Environment." *American Journal of Political Science*.

Ditto, Peter, and David Lopez. 1992. "Motivated Skepticism: Use of Differential Decision Criteria for Preferred and Non-preferred Conclusions." *Journal of Personality and Social Psychology* 63 (4): 568–84.

Ditto, Peter, James Scepansky, Geoffrey Munro, Anne Marie Apanovitch, and Lisa Lockhart. 1998. "Motivated Sensitivity to Preference Inconsistent Information." *Journal of Personality and Social Psychology* 75 (1): 53–69.

Domke, David, Mark Watts, Dhavan Shah, and David Fan. 1999. "The Politics of Conservative Elites and the 'Liberal Media' Argument." *Journal of Communication* 49 (4): 35–58.

Dreier, Peter, and Christopher Martin. 2010. "How ACORN Was Framed: Political Controversy and Media Agenda Setting." *Perspectives on Politics* 8 (3): 761–92.

Druckman, James. 2001a. "On the Limits of Framing Effects: Who Can Frame?" *Journal of Politics* 63 (4): 1041–66.

———. 2001b. "Using Credible Advice to Overcome Framing Effects." *Journal of Law, Economics, and Organization* 17 (1): 62–82.

———. 2012. "The Politics of Motivation." *Critical Review* 24 (2): 199–216.

Druckman, James, and Toby Bolsen. 2011. "Framing, Motivated Reasoning, and Opinions about Emergent Technologies." *Journal of Communication* 61 (4): 659–88.

Druckman, James, Jordan Fein, and Thomas Leeper. 2012. "A Source of Bias in Public Opinion Stability." *American Political Science Review* 106 (2): 430–54.

Druckman, James, Lawrence Jacobs, and Eric Ostermeier. 2004. "Candidate Strategies to Prime Issues and Image." *Journal of Politics* 66 (4): 1180–202.

Druckman, James, and Cindy Kam. 2011. "Students as Experimental Participants: A Defense of the 'Narrow Data Base.'" In *Handbook of Experimental Political Science*, edited by James Druckman, Donald Green, and James Kuklinski. New York: Oxford University Press.

Druckman, James, and Thomas Leeper. 2012. "Learning More from Political

Communication Experiments: Pretreatment and Its Effects." *American Journal of Political Science* 56 (4):875–96.

Druckman, James, and Kjersten Nelson. 2003. "Framing and Deliberation: How Citizens' Conversations Limit Elite Influence." *American Journal of Political Science* 47 (4): 729–45.

Druckman, James, and Michael Parkin. 2005. "The Impact of Media Bias: How Editorial Slant Affects Voters." *Journal of Politics* 67 (4): 1030–49.

Eagly, Alice, Wendy Wood, and Shelly Chaiken. 1978. "Causal Inferences about Communicators, and Their Effect on Opinion Change." *Journal of Personality and Social Psychology* 36 (4): 424–35.

Eriksson, Kimmo, and Brent Simpson. 2010. "Reactions to Losing Explain Gender Differences in Entering a Risky Lottery." *Judgment and Decision Making* 5 (3): 159–63.

Faler, Brian, and Steven Sloan. 2011. "Supercommittee Unlikely to Reach Deficit Deal" *Bloomberg Businessweek*, 20 November. http://www.bloomberg.com/news/2011–11-19/debt-supercommittee-moves-further-apart-as-negotiations-enter-homestretch.html.

Farhi, Paul. 2011. "From the Fringe to the Mainstream." *American Journalism Review*, December/January. http://www.ajr.org/article.asp?id=4979.

Feldman, Lauren, Edward Maibach, Connie Roser-Renouf, and Andy Leiserowitz. 2012. "Climate on Cable: The Nature and Impact of Global Warming Coverage on Fox News, CNN, and MSNBC." *International Journal of Press/Politics* 17 (1): 3–31.

Finn, Peter, and Carrie Johnson. 2009. "Alleged Sept. 11 Planner Will be Tried in New York." *Washington Post*, 14 November.

Fiorina, Morris. 1999. "A Dark Side of Civic Engagement." In *Civic Engagement and American Democracy*, edited by Theda Skocpol and Morris Fiorina. Washington DC: Brookings Institution Press.

———. 2006. "Parties as Problem Solvers." In *Promoting the General Welfare*, edited by Alan Gerber and Eric Patashnik. Washington DC: Brookings Institution Press.

Fiorina, Morris, Samuel Abrams, and Jeremy Pope. 2005. *Culture War? The Myth of a Polarized America*. New York: Pearson Longman.

Fischer, Peter, Eva Jonas, Dieter Frey, and Stefan Schulz-Hardt. 2005. "Selective Exposure to Information: The Impact of Information Limits." *European Journal of Social Psychology* 35 (4): 469–92.

Franke-Ruta, Garance, and Anne Kornblut. 2009. "White House Says Little about Embattled Jones." *Washington Post*, 5 September.

Frey, Dieter. 1986. "Recent Research on Selective Exposure to Information." In *Advances in Experimental Social Psychology, Volume 19*, edited by Leonard Berkowitz. Orlando, FL: Academic Press.

Frum, David. 2010. "Waterloo." *FrumForum*, 21 March. http://www.frumforum.com/waterloo/.

Funk, Carolyn. 1999. "Brining the Candidate into Models of Candidate Evaluation." *Journal of Politics* 61 (3): 700–20.

Gaines, Brian, James Kuklinski, Paul Quirk, Buddy Peyton, and Jay Verkuilen. 2007. "Same Facts, Different Interpretations: Partisan Motivation and Opinion on Iraq." *Journal of Politics* 69 (4): 957–74.

Gans, Herbert. 1979. *Deciding What's News: A Study of* CBS Evening News, NBC Nightly News, Newsweek, *and* Time. New York: Vintage Books.

Garrett, R. Kelly. 2009. "Politically Motivate Reinforcement Seeking: Reframing the Selective Exposure Debate." *Journal of Communication* 59 (4): 676–99.

Gentzkow, Matthew, and Jesse Shapiro. 2006. "Media Bias and Reputation." *Journal of Political Economy* 114 (2): 280–316.

———. 2010. "What Drives Media Slant? Evidence From U.S. Daily Newspapers." *Econometrica* 78 (1): 35–71.

Gentzkow, Matthew, Jesse Shapiro, and Michael Sinkinson. 2012. "The Effect of Newspaper Entry and Exit on Electoral Politics." *American Economic Review* 101 (7): 2980–3018.

Gerber, Alan, James Gimpel, Donald Green, and Daron Shaw. 2011. "How Large and Long-Lasting Are the Persuasive Effects of Televised Campaign Ads? Results From a Randomized Field Experiment." *American Political Science Review* 105 (1): 135–50.

Gerber, Alan, Dean Karlan, and Daniel Bergan. 2009. "Does the Media Matter? A Field Experiment Measuring the Effect of Newspapers on Voting Behavior and Political Opinions." *American Economic Journal: Applied Economics* 1 (2): 35–52.

Gerber, Alan, and Eric Patashnik. 2010. "Problem Solving in a Polarized Age: Comparative Effectiveness Research and Politicization of Evidence-Based Medicine." *The Forum* 8 (1). DOI: http://dx.doi.org/10.2202/1540-8884.1353.

Gillis, Justin. 2010. "British Panel Clears Scientists." *New York Times*, 7 July.

Goldberg, Bernard. 2003. *Bias: A CBS Insider Exposes How the Media Distort the News*. New York: Harper.

———. 2009. *A Slobbering Love Affair: The True (and Pathetic) Story of the Torrid Romance between Barack Obama and the Mainstream Media*. New York: Regency Press.

Goren, Paul, Christopher Federico, and Miki Caul Kittilson. 2009. "Source Cues, Partisan Identities, and Political Value Expression." *American Journal of Political Science* 53 (4): 805–20.

Green, Donald, Bradley Palmquist, and Eric Schickler. 2002. *Partisan Hearts and Minds: Political Parties and the Social Identities of Voters*. New Haven, CT: Yale University Press.

Greene, Steven. 1999. "Understanding Party Identification: A Social Identity Approach." *Political Psychology* 20 (2): 393–403.

Groeling, Tim. 2010. *When Politicians Attack: Party Cohesion in the Media*. New York: Cambridge University Press.

Groseclose, Tim. 2011. *Left Turn: How Liberal Media Bias Distorts the American Mind*. New York: St. Martin's Press.

Groseclose, Timothy, and Nolan McCarty. 2001. "The Politics of Blame: Bargaining Before an Audience." *American Journal of Political Science* 45 (1): 100–19.

Groseclose, Tim, and Jeffrey Milyo. 2005. "A Measure of Media Bias." *Quarterly Journal of Economics* 120 (4):1191–237.

Gross, Sharon, Rolf Holtz, and Norman Miller. 1995. "Attitude Certainty." In *Attitude Strength: Antecedents and Consequences*, edited by Richard Petty and Jon Krosnick. Mahwah, NJ: Lawrence Erlbaum Associates.

Grossback, Lawrence, David Peterson, and James Stimson. 2006. *Mandate Politics*. New York: Cambridge University Press.

Gutmann, Amy, and Dennis Thompson. 2010. "The Mindsets of Political Compromise." *Perspectives on Politics* 8 (4): 1135–43.

———. 2012. *The Spirit of Compromise: Why Governing Demands It and Campaigning Undermines It*. Princeton, NJ: Princeton University Press.

Harbridge, Laurel and Neil Malhotra. 2011. "Electoral Incentives and Partisan Conflict in Congress: Evidence from Survey Experiments." *American Journal of Political Science* 55 (3): 494–510.

Harder, Amy. 2008. "Q & A: Campaigns Capitalize on 24/7 News Cycle with 'Phony' Ads." *National Journal.Com*, 18 September. http://adspotlight.nationaljournal.com/2008/09/qa-campaigns-capitalize-on-247.php.

Heilemann, John, and Mark Halperin. 2010. *Game Change: Obama and the Clintons, McCain and Palin, and the Race of a Lifetime*. New York: HarperCollins.

Hershey, Marjorie. 1992. "The Constructed Explanation: Interpreting Election Results in the 1984 Presidential Race." *Journal of Politics* 54 (4): 943–76.

Hetherington, Marc. 2005. *Why Trust Matters*. Princeton, NJ: Princeton University Press.

———. 2009. "Putting Polarization in Perspective." *British Journal of Political Science* 39 (2): 413–48.

Hibbing, John, and Elizabeth Theiss-Morse. 1995. *Congress as Public Enemy: Public Attitudes toward Political Institutions*. New York: Cambridge University Press.

Hillygus, D. Sunshine, and Todd Shields. 2008. *The Persuadable Voter: Strate-*

gic Candidates and Wedge Issues in Presidential Campaigns. Princeton, NJ: Princeton University Press.

Hindman, Matthew. 2008. *The Myth of Digital Democracy*. Princeton, NJ: Princeton University Press.

Ho, Daniel, Kosuke Imai, Gary King, and Elisabeth Stuart. 2007. "Matching as Nonparametric Preprocessing for Reducing Model Dependence in Parametric Causal Inference." *Political Analysis* 15 (3): 199–236.

Holbert, R. Lance, R. Kelly Garrett, and Laurel Gleason. 2010. "A New Era of Minimal Effects? A Response to Bennett and Iyengar." *Journal of Communication* 60 (1): 15–34.

Holbrook, Thomas, Clayton Clouse, and Aaron Weinschenk. 2012. "Bringing the President Back In: The Collapse of Lehman Brothers and the Evolution of Retrospective Voting in the 2008 Presidential Election." *Political Research Quarterly* 65 (2): 263–74.

Holtsberry, Kevin. 2011. "Ohio Issue 2: Let's Not Over-React or Fall for Media Templates." *RedState.com*, 8 November. http://www.redstate.com/kevin_holtsberry/2011/11/08/ohio-issue-2-lets-not-over-react-or-fall-for-media-templates/.

Horowitz, Michael, and Matthew Levendusky. 2011. "Drafting Support for War: Conscription and Mass Support for Warfare." *Journal of Politics* 73 (2): 524–34.

Hovland, Carl, and Walter Weiss. 1951. "The Influence of Source Credibility on Communication Effectiveness." *Public Opinion Quarterly* 15 (4): 635–50.

Huddy, Leonie. 2001. "From Social to Political Identity: A Critical Examination of Social Identity Theory." *Political Psychology* 22 (1): 127–56.

Iacus, Stefano, Gary King, and Giuseppe Porro. 2009. "CEM: Software for Coarsened Exact Matching." *Journal of Statistical Software* 30 (9):1–27.

———. 2011. "Multivariate Matching Methods that Are Monotonic Imbalance Bounding." *Journal of the American Statistical Association* 106 (493): 345–61.

Imai, Kosuke, Luke Keele, Dustin Tingley, and Teppei Yamamoto. 2011. "Unpacking the Black Box of Causality: Learning about Causal Mechanisms from Experimental and Observational Studies." *American Political Science Review* 10 5(4): 765–89.

Iyengar, Shanto, and Kyu Han. 2009. "Red Media, Blue Media: Evidence of Ideological Selectivity in Media Use." *Journal of Communication* 59(1): 19–39.

Iyengar, Shanto, and Donald Kinder. 2009. *News That Matters*. Updated edition. Chicago: University of Chicago Press.

Iyengar, Shanto, Gaurav Sood, and Yphtach Lelkes. 2012. "Affect, Not Ideology: A Social Identity Perspective on Polarization." *Public Opinion Quarterly* 76 (3): 405–31.

Jacobs, Lawrence, and Robert Shapiro. 2000. *Politicians Don't Pander: Political Manipulation and the Loss of Democratic Responsiveness*. Chicago: University of Chicago Press.

——. 2011. "The Democratic Paradox: The Waning of Popular Sovereignty and Pathologies of American Politics." In *The Oxford Handbook of American Public Opinion and the Media*, edited by Robert Shapiro and Lawrence Jacobs. New York: Oxford University Press.

Jamieson, Kathleen Hall. 2005. *Electing the President, 2004: The Insider's View*. Philadelphia: University of Pennsylvania Press.

——. 2009. *Electing the President 2008: The Insider's View*. Philadelphia: University of Pennsylvania Press.

——. 2012. "Cable News Networks Increase Amount and Public Accessibility of Incivility." Annenberg Public Policy Center press release, 27 March. http://www.annenbergpublicpolicycenter.org/NewsDetails.aspx?myId=482.

Jamieson, Kathleen Hall, and Joseph Cappella. 2008. *Echo Chamber: Rush Limbaugh and the Conservative Media Establishment*. New York: Oxford University Press.

Jamieson, Kathleen Hall, and Bruce Hardy. 2013. "What Is Civil Engaged Argument and Why Does Aspiring to It Matter?" In *Can We Talk? The Rise of Rude, Nasty, Stubborn Politics*, edited by Daniel Shea and Morris Fiorina. New York: Pearson.

Jamieson, Kathleen Hall, Bruce Hardy, and Daniel Romer. 2007. "The Effectiveness of the Press in Serving the Needs of American Democracy." In *A Republic Divided: The Annenberg Democracy Project*, edited by Kathleen Hall Jamieson. New York: Oxford University Press.

Jerit, Jennifer, and Jason Barabas. 2012. "Partisan Perceptual Cues and the Information Environment." *Journal of Politics* 74 (3): 672–84.

Johnston, Richard. 2009. "Modeling Campaign Dynamics on the Web in the 2008 National Annenberg Election Survey." *Journal of Elections, Parties, and Public Opinion* 18 (4): 401–12.

Jones, David. 2002. "The Polarizing Effect of New Media Messages." *International Journal of Public Opinion Research* 14 (2): 158–74.

Jones, Philip. 2011. "Which Buck Stops Here? Accountability for Policy Positions and Policy Outcomes in Congress." *Journal of Politics* 73 (3): 764–82.

Kahan, Dan, Hank Jenkins-Smith, and Donald Braman. 2011. "Cultural Cognition of Scientific Consensus." *Journal of Risk Research* 14 (2): 147–74.

Kam, Cindy, and Carl Palmer. 2008. "Reconsidering the Effects of Education on Political Participation." *Journal of Politics* 70 (3): 612–31.

Keele, Luke. 2005. "The Authorities Really Do Matter." *Journal of Politics* 67 (3): 432–51.

——. 2010. *Rbounds: An R Package for Sensitivity Analysis with Matched Data*. http://www.personal.psu.edu/ljk20/rbounds.html.

Keith, Bruce, David Magleby, Candice Nelson, Elizabeth Orr, Mark Westlye, and Raymond Wolfinger. 1992. *The Myth of the Independent Voter*. Berkeley: University of California Press.

Kenski, Kate, Bruce Hardy, and Kathleen Hall Jamieson. 2010. *The Obama Victory: How Media, Money, and Message Shaped the 2008 Election*. New York: Oxford University Press.

Klapper, Joseph. 1960. *The Effects of Mass Communication*. Glencoe, IL: Free Press.

Klayman, Joseph, and Young-Won Ha. 1987. "Confirmation, Disconfirmation, and Information in Hypothesis Testing." *Psychological Review* 94 (2): 211–28.

Klein, Aaron. 2009. "Will a 'Red' Help Blacks Go Green?" *WorldNetDaily.Com*, 12 April. http://www.wnd.com/2009/04/94771/.

Klein, Jill, and Rohini Ahluwalia. 2005. "Negativity in the Evaluation of Political Candidates." *Journal of Marketing* 69 (1): 131–42.

Knowlton, Brian, and Michael Barbaro. 2012. "Biden 'Comfortable' with Gay Marriage." *The Caucus: The Politics and Government Blog of the Times*, 6 May. http://thecaucus.blogs.nytimes.com/2012/05/06/biden-comfortable-with-gay-marriage/.

Kraushaar, Josh, and Lisa Lerer. 2009. "Health Care Town Hall Anger Rages On." *Politico.com*, 14 August. http://www.politico.com/news/stories/0809/26049.html.

Krosnick, Jon, and Bo MacInnis. 2010. "Frequent Viewers of Fox News Are Less Likely to Accept Scientists' Views of Global Warming." Manuscript. Stanford University.

Kuklinski, James, and Norman Hurley. 1994. "On Hearing and Interpreting Political Messages: A Cautionary Tale of Citizen Cue-Taking." *Journal of Politics* 56 (3): 729–51.

Kull, Steven, Clay Ramsay, and Evan Lewis. 2003. "Misperceptions, the Media and the Iraq War." *Political Science Quarterly* 118 (4): 569–98.

Kunda, Ziva. 1990. "The Case for Motivated Reasoning." *Psychological Bulletin* 108 (3): 480–98.

Kurtz, Howard. 2010. "Conservative David Frum Loses Think-Tank Job after Criticizing GOP." *Washington Post*, 26 March.

Ladd, Jonathan. 2012. *Why Americans Hate the Media and Why It Matters*. Princeton, NJ: Princeton University Press.

Ladd, Jonathan, and Gabriel Lenz. 2009. "Exploiting a Rare Communication Shift to Document the Persuasive Power of the News Media." *American Journal of Political Science* 53 (2): 394–410.

Langer, Gary, and Jon Cohen. 2005. "Voters and Values in the 2004 Election." *Public Opinion Quarterly* 69 (5): 744–59.

Lau, Richard. 1985. "Two Explanations for Negativity Effects in Political Behavior." *American Journal of Political Science* 29 (1): 119–38.

Lau, Richard, and David Redlawsk. 1997. "Voting Correctly." *American Political Science Review* 91 (3): 595–98.

Layman, Geoffrey, Thomas Carsey, John Green, Richard Herrera, and Rosalyn Cooperman. 2010. "Activists and Conflict Extension in American Party Politics." *American Political Science Review* 104 (2): 324–46.

Lee, Eun-Ju. 2007. "Deindividualization Effects on Group Polarization in Computer-Mediated Communication: The Role of Group Identification, Public-Self-Awareness, and Perceived Argument Quality." *Journal of Communication* 57 (2): 385–403.

Lenz, Gabriel. 2009. "Learning and Opinion Change, Not Priming: Reconsidering the Priming Hypothesis." *American Journal of Political Science* 53 (4): 821–37.

Levendusky, Matthew. 2009. *The Partisan Sort*. Chicago: University of Chicago Press.

———. 2010. "Clearer Cues, More Consistent Voters: A Benefit of Elite Polarization." *Political Behavior* 32 (1): 111–31.

———. 2012a. "Why Do Partisan Media Polarize?" Manuscript. University of Pennsylvania.

———. 2012b. "Partisan Media Exposure and Attitudes toward the Opposition." Manuscript. University of Pennsylvania.

Levi, Margaret, and Laura Stoker. 2000. "Political Trust and Trustworthiness." *Annual Review of Political Science* 3 (1): 475–507.

Lodge, Milton, Kathleen McGraw, and Patrick Stroh. 1991. "An Impression-Driven Model of Candidate Evaluation." *American Political Science Review* 83 (2): 399–419.

Lodge, Milton, Marco Steenbergen, and Shawn Brau. 1994. "The Responsive Voter: Campaign Information and the Dynamics of Candidate Evaluation." *American Political Science Review* 89 (2): 309–26.

Lodge, Milton, and Charles Taber. 2001. "Three Steps toward a Theory of Motivated Reasoning." In *Elements of Reason*, edited by Arthur Lupia, Mathew McCubbins, and Samuel Popkin. New York: Cambridge University Press.

———. 2005. "The Automaticity of Affect for Political Leaders, Groups, and Issues: An Experimental Test of the Hot Cognition Hypothesis." *Political Psychology* 26 (3): 455–82.

Lupia, Arthur, and Mathew McCubbins. 1998. *The Democratic Dilemma: Can Citizens Learn What They Need to Know?* New York: Cambridge University Press.

Luskin, Robert. 1987. "Measuring Political Sophistication." *American Journal of Political Science* 31 (4): 856–99.

Mackie, Diane. 1986. "Social Identification Effects in Group Polarization." *Journal of Personality and Social Psychology* 50 (4): 720–28.

Mackie, Diane, Leila Worth, and Arlene Asuncion. 1990. "Processing of Persuasive in-Group Messages." *Journal of Personality and Social Psychology* 58 (5): 812–22.

MacKuen, Michael, Jennifer Wolak, Luke Keele, and George Marcus. 2010. "Civic Engagements: Resolute Partisanship Or Reflective Deliberation." *American Journal of Political Science* 54 (2): 440–58.

Manjoo, Farhad. 2008. *True Enough: Learning to Live in a Post-Fact Society.* New York: John Wiley and Sons.

McCarty, Nolan, Keith Poole, and Howard Rosenthal. 2006. *Polarized America: The Dance of Ideology and Unequal Riches.* Cambridge, MA: MIT Press.

McCombs, Maxwell, and Donald Shaw. 1972. "The Agenda-Setting Function of Mass Media." *Public Opinion Quarterly* 36 (2): 176–87.

McDermott, Rose. 2011. "Internal and External Validity." In *Cambridge Handbook of Experimental Political Science*, edited by James Druckman, Donald Green, James Kuklinski, and Arthur Lupia. New York: Cambridge University Press.

Meffert, Michael, Sungeun Chung, Amber Joiner, Leah Waks, and Jennifer Garst. 2006. "The Effects of Negativity and Motivated Information Processing During a Political Campaign." *Journal of Communication* 56 (1): 27–51.

Memoli, Michael, and Kathleen Hennessey. 2012. "Obama Declares Support for Same-Sex Marriage." *Los Angeles Times*, 9 May.

Mendelsohn, Matthew, and Richard Nadeau. 1996. "The Magnification and Minimization of Social Cleavages by the Broadcast and Narrowcast News Media." *International Journal of Public Opinion Research* 8 (4): 347–89.

Milbourn, Cathy. 2010. "EPA Rejects Claims of Flawed Climate Science." U.S. Environmental Protection Agency press release, 29 July. http://yosemite.epa.gov/opa/admpress.nsf/0/56EB0D86757CB7568525776F0063D82F.

Miller, Joanne, and Jon Krosnick. 2004. "Threat as a Motivator of Political Activism: A Field Experiment." *Political Psychology* 25 (4): 507–24.

Miller, Joanne, and David Peterson. 2004. "Theoretical and Empirical Implications of Attitude Strength." *Journal of Politics* 66 (3): 847–67.

Miller, Warren, and Ola Listhaug. 1990. "Political Parties and Confidence in Government: A Comparison of Norway, Sweden, and the United States." *British Journal of Political Science* 20 (3): 357–86.

Miller, Warren, and J. Merrill Shanks. 1996. *The New American Voter.* Cambridge, MA: Harvard University Press.

Mindich, David. 1998. *Just the Facts: How "Objectivity" Came to Dominate American Journalism.* New York: New York University Press.

Mirkinson, Jack. 2010. "Fox News Boss Ordered Staffers to Cast Doubt on Climate Change Science." *Huffington Post*, 15 December. http://www.huffingtonpost.com/2010/12/15/fox-news-climate-change-email_n_796963.html.

Morris, James, Nancy Squires, Charles Taber, and Milton Lodge. 2003. "Activation of Political Attitudes: A Psychophysiological Examination of the Hot Cognition Hypothesis." *Political Psychology* 24 (4): 727–45.

Morris, Jonathan. 2005. "The Fox News Factor." *Harvard International Journal of Press/Politics* 10 (3): 56–79.

Moscovici, Segre, and Marisa Zavalloni. 1969. "The Group as Polarizer of Attitudes." *Journal of Personality and Social Psychology* 12 (2): 125–35.

Moynihan, Patrick, Gary Langer, and Peyton Craighill. 2010. "An End to a Means: Partisanship, Policy Preferences, and Global Warming." Paper presented at the Annual Meeting of the American Association for Public Opinion Research, Chicago, IL.

Mullen, Brian, Rupert Brown, and Colleen Smith. 1992. "Intergroup Bias as a Function of Salience, Relevance, and Status: An Integration." *European Journal of Social Psychology* 22 (2): 103–22.

Mullainathan, Sendhil, and Andrei Shleifer. 2005. "The Market for News." *American Economic Review* 95 (4): 1031–53.

Mutz, Diana. 2006a. *Hearing the Other Side*. New York: Cambridge University Press.

———. 2006b. "How the Mass Media Divide Us." In *Red and Blue Nation?*, edited by Pietro Nivola and Brady David. Washington DC: Brookings Institution Press.

———. 2007. "Effects of 'In-Your-Face' Television Discourse on Perceptions of a Legitimate Opposition." *American Political Science Review* 101 (4): 621–35.

———. 2011. *Population-Based Survey Experiments*. Princeton, NJ: Princeton University Press.

Mutz, Diana, and Byron Reeves. 2005. "The New Videomalaise: Effects of Televised Incivility on Political Trust." *American Political Science Review* 99 (1): 1–15.

Neustadt, Richard. 1960. *Presidential Power, the Politics of Leadership*. New York: John Wiley and Sons.

O'Keefe, Daniel. 2002. *Persuasion: Theory and Research*. Thousand Oaks, CA: Sage.

Paolacci, Gabriele, Jesse Chandler, and Panagiotis Iperotis. 2010. "Running Experiments on Amazon Mechanical Turk." *Judgment and Decision Making* 5 (5): 411–19.

Perlstein, Rick. 2008. *Nixonland: The Rise of a President and the Fracturing of America*. New York: Scribner.

Peters, Jeremy. 2011. "Campaigns Take Ad War to TV after Months of Holding Fire." *New York Times*, 5 December.

———. 2012. "Dueling Bitterness of Cable News." *New York Times*, 5 November.

Petrocik, John. 1996. "Issue Ownership in Presidential Elections, with a 1980 Case Study." *American Journal of Political Science* 40 (3): 825–50.

Pettigrew, Thomas, and Linda Tropp. 2006. "A Meta-Analytic Test of Inter-

Group Contact Theory." *Journal of Personality and Social Psychology* 90 (5): 715–83.

Petty, Richard, and Jon Krosnick. 1995. *Attitude Strength: Antecedents and Consequences*. Mahwah, NJ: Lawrence Erlbaum Associates.

Pew Research Center for the People and the Press. 2010. "Americans Spending More Time Following the News." http://people-press.org/report/652/.

———. 2012. "Cable Leads the Pack as Campaign News Source." http://www.people-press.org/2012/02/07/cable-leads-the-pack-as-campaign-news-source/?src=prc-headline.

Pew Project for Excellence in Journalism. Various Years. "State of the News Media." http://www.stateofthemedia.org/.

Pew Project for Excellence in Journalism. 2012. "The Final Days of the Media Campaign 2012." 19 November. http://www.journalism.org/analysis_report/final_days_media_campaign_2012.

Phillips, Joan, Joel Urbany, and Thomas Reynolds. 2008. "Confirmation and the Effects of Valenced Political Advertising: A Field Experiment." *Journal of Consumer Research* 34 (6): 794–806.

Polborn, Mattias, Stefan Krasa, and Dan Bernhardt. 2008. "Political Polarization and the Electoral Effects of Media Bias." *Journal of Public Economics* 92 (5–6): 1092–104.

Pomerantz, Eva, Shelly Chaiken, and Rosalind Tordesaillas. 1995. "Attitude Strength and Resistance Processes." *Journal of Personality and Social Psychology* 69 (3): 408–19.

Price, David. 2010. "After the 'Housequake': Leadership and Partisanship in the Post-2006 House." *The Forum* 8 (1). DOI: http://dx.doi.org/10.2202/1540–8884.1361.

Price, Vincent. 1989. "Social Identification and Public Opinion: Effects of Communicating Group Conflict." *Public Opinion Quarterly* 53 (2): 197–224.

Price, Vincent, and John Zaller. 1993. "Who Gets the News? Alternative Measures of News Reception and Their Implications for Research." *Public Opinion Quarterly* 57 (2): 137–45.

Prior, Markus. 2007. *Post-Broadcast Democracy: How Media Choice Increases Inequality in Political Involvement and Polarizes Elections*. New York: Cambridge University Press.

———. 2009. "Improving Media Effects Research Through Better Measurement of News Exposure." *Journal of Politics* 73 (1): 130–43.

Pronin, Emily, Carolyn Puccio, and Lee Ross. 2002. "Understanding Misunderstanding: Social Psychological Perspectives." In *Heuristics and Biases: The Psychology of Intuitive Judgment*, edited by Thomas Gilovich, Dale Griffin, and Daniel Kahneman. New York: Cambridge University Press.

Puglisi, Ricardo, and James Snyder. 2011. "The Balanced U.S. Press." NBER Working Paper 17263

Ray, Devin, Diane Mackie, Robert Rydell, and Eliot Smith. 2008. "Changing Categorization of Self Can Change Emotions about Outgroups." *Journal of Experimental Social Psychology* 44 (4): 1210–13.

Rahn, Wendy. 1993. "The Role of Partisan Stereotypes in Information Processing about Political Candidates." *American Journal of Political Science* 37 (2): 472–96.

Redlawsk, David. 2001. "You Must Remember This: A Test of the Online Model of Voting." *Journal of Politics* 63 (1): 29–58.

———. 2002. "Hot Cognition or Cool Consideration: Testing the Effects of Motivated Reasoning on Political Decision-Making." *Journal of Politics* 64 (4): 1021–44.

Rieder, Rem. 2004. "The Swift Boat Conundrum: How Should the Mainstream Media Deal With Such Stories?" *American Journalism Review*, October/November. http://www.ajr.org/article.asp?id=3771.

Robinson, Michael. 1981. "Reflections on the Nightly News." In *Understanding Television: Essays on Television as a Social and Cultural Force*, edited by Richard Adler. New York: Praeger.

Rosenbaum, Paul. 2002. *Observational Studies*. New York: Springer-Verlag.

Rosensteil, Thomas. 2006. "How the Mass Media Divide Us—Two Alternative Perspectives." In *Red and Blue Nation?*, edited by Pietro Nivola and David Brady. Washington DC: Brookings Institution Press.

Rucker, Gerta. 1989. "A Two-Stage Trial Design for Testing Treatment, Self-Selection, and Treatment Preference Effects." *Statistics in Medicine* 8 (4): 477–85.

Sabato, Larry. 2009. *The Year of Obama: How Barack Obama Won the White House*. New York: Longman.

Schroeck, Eric. 2010. "Garrett Confirms What We Already Know: Fox 'Wants to Keep' the Media Polarized." *Media Matters for America*, 25 October. http://mediamatters.org/blog/201010250009.

Schudson, Michael. 1995. *The Power of News*. Cambridge, MA: Harvard University Press.

———. 2001. "The Objectivity Norm in American Journalism." *Journalism* 2 (2): 149–70.

———. 2008. *Why Democracies Need an Unlovable Press*. Malden, MA: Polity Press.

Schultz, Kenneth. 2005. "The Politics of Risking Peace: Do Hawks Or Doves Deliver the Olive Branch?" *International Organization* 59 (1): 1–38.

Sears, David, and Jonathan Freedman. 1967. "Selective Exposure to Information: A Critical Review." *Public Opinion Quarterly* 31 (2): 194–213.

Sekhon, Jasjeet. 2005. "The Varying Role of Information across Democratic Societies." Manuscript. University of California, Berkeley.

Serrano, Richard. 2011. "Obama Administration Won't Pursue Civilian Trials for 9/11 Suspects." *Los Angeles Times*, 5 April.

Shapiro, Robert, and Lawrence Jacobs. 2011. "Informational Interdependence: Public Opinion and the Media in the New Communications Era." In *The Oxford Handbook of American Public Opinion and the Media*, edited by Robert Shapiro and Lawrence Jacobs. New York: Oxford University Press.

Shaw, Daron. 2006. *The Race to 270*. Chicago: University of Chicago Press.

Shea, Daniel. 2013. "Our Tribal Nature and the Rise of Nasty Politics." In *Can We Talk?*, edited by Daniel Shea and Morris Fiorina. Upper Saddle River, NJ: Pearson.

Shepard, Kate. 2010. "ClimateGate: Officially a Fake Scandal." *Mother Jones*, 14 April. http://www.motherjones.com/blue-marble/2010/04/climategate-officially-fake-scandal.

Sherman, Gabriel. 2010. "Chasing Fox." *New York Magazine*, 3 October. http://nymag.com/news/media/68717/.

Silverleib, Alan, and Tom Cohen. 2011. "Obama Signs Debt Ceiling Bill, Ends Crisis." *CNN.com*, 2 August. http://articles.cnn.com/2011-08-02/politics/debt.talks_1_debt-ceiling-credit-rating-spending-cuts?_s=PM:POLITICS.

Skocpol, Theda, and Vanessa Williamson. 2012. *The Tea Party and the Remaking of Republican Conservatism*. New York: Oxford University Press.

Slater, Daniel. 2007. "Reinforcing Spirals: The Mutual Influence of Media Selectivity and Media Effects and Their Impact on Individual Behavior and Social Identity." *Communication Theory* 17 (3): 281–303.

Smith, Aaron. 2011. "The Internet and Campaign 2010." *Pew Internet and American Life Project*. http://pewinternet.org/Reports/2011/The-Internet-and-Campaign-2010.aspx.

Smith, Glen, and Kathleen Searles. Forthcoming. "Fair and Balanced or a Difference of Opinion? Why Opinion Shows Matter for Media Effects." *Political Research Quarterly*.

Smith, Robert. 2011. "The History of the Debt Ceiling." *National Public Radio*, http://www.npr.org/blogs/money/2011/05/17/136363196/the-history-of-the-debt-ceiling.

Sobieraj, Sarah, and Jeffrey Berry. 2011. "From Incivility to Outrage: Political Discourse in Blogs, Talk Radio, and Cable News." *Political Communication* 28 (1): 19–41.

Stanley, Alessandra. 2011. "The Republican Primary Campaign in Iowa is Right at Home on Fox News." *New York Times*, 10 December.

Starr, Paul. 2010. "Governing in the Age of Fox News." *The Atlantic*, January/February, 95–98.

Stasavage, David. 2007. "Polarization and Publicity: Rethinking the Benefits of Deliberative Democracy." *Journal of Politics* 69 (1): 59–72.

Steinberg, Jacques. 2007. "Cable Channel Nods to Ratings and Leans Left." *New York Times*, 6 November.

Stelter, Brian. 2012a. "At MSNBC, A Professor as TV Host." *New York Times*, 12 February.

———. 2012b. "The Anti-Fox Gains Ground. *New York Times*, 11 November.

Stewart, John. 2010. "Segment: Are You Ready for Some Midterms?" *The Daily Show with John Stewart*. http://www.thedailyshow.com/watch/thu-september-9–2010/are-you-ready-for-some-midterms—msnbc-s-political-narrative.

Stroud, Natalie. 2008. "Media Use and Political Predispositions: Revisiting the Concept of Selective Exposure." *Political Behavior* 30 (3): 341–66.

———. 2010. "Polarization and Partisan Selective Exposure." *Journal of Communication* 60 (3): 556–76.

———. 2011. *Niche News: The Politics of News Choice*. New York: Oxford University Press.

Sunstein, Cass. 2007. *Republic.Com 2.0*. Princeton, NJ: Princeton University Press.

———. 2009. *Going to Extremes: How Like Minds Unite and Divide*. New York: Oxford University Press.

Taber, Charles, Damon Cann, and Simona Kucsova. 2009. "The Motivated Processing of Political Arguments." *Political Behavior* 31 (2): 137–55.

Taber, Charles, and Milton Lodge. 2006. "Motivated Skepticism in the Evaluation of Political Beliefs." *American Journal of Political Science* 50 (3): 755–69.

Tajfel, Henri, and John Turner. 1979. "An Integrative Theory of Intergroup Conflict. In *The Social Psychology of Intergroup Relations*, edited by William Austin and Stephen Worchel. Monterey, CA: Brooks/Cole.

Tavernise, Sabrina. 2011. "Ohio Turns Back a Law Limiting Unions' Rights." *New York Times*, 8 November.

Tesler, Michael. 2010. "The Growing Cable News Divide in Midterm Vote Preference." *YouGov Model Politics*, 1 November. http://today.yougov.com/news/2010/11/01/growing-cable-news-divide-midterm-vote-preference/.

Thomas, Dan, and Larry Bass. 1996. "The Postelection Campaign: Competing Constructions of the Clinton Victory in 1992." *Journal of Politics* 58 (2): 309–31.

Torgerson, David, and Bonnie Sibbald. 1998. "Understanding Controlled Trials: What Is a Patient Preference Trial?" *British Medical Journals* 316 (360). DOI: 10.1136/bmj.316.7128.360.

Tormala, Zakary, and Richard Petty. 2002. "What Doesn't Kill Me Makes Me Stronger: The Effects of Resisting Persuasion on Attitude Certainty." *Journal of Personality and Social Psychology* 83 (6): 1298–313.

Tormala, Zakary, and Derek Rucker. 2007. "Attitude Certainty: A Review of Past Findings and Emerging Perspectives." *Social and Personality Psychology Compass* 1 (1): 469–92.

Turner, Joel. 2007. "The Messenger Overwhelming the Message: Ideological Cues and Perceptions of Bias in Television News." *Political Behavior* 29 (4): 441–64.

Turner, John. 1991. *Social Influence*. Pacific Grove, CA: Brooks/Cole.

Turow, Joseph. 1997. *Breaking Up America: Advertisers and the New Media World*. Chicago: University of Chicago Press.

———. 2012. *The Daily You: How the New Advertising Industry Is Defining Your Identity and Your Worth*. New Haven, CT: Yale University Press.

Valentino, Nicholas, Ted Brader, Eric Groenendyk, Krysha Gregorowicz, and Vincent Hutchings. 2011. "Election Night's All Right for Fighting: The Role of Emotions in Political Participation." *Journal of Politics* 73 (1): 156–70.

Verba, Sidney, Kay Schlozman, and Henry Brady. 1995. *Voice and Equality: Civic Voluntarism in American Politics*. Cambridge, MA: Harvard University Press.

Visser, Penny, George Bizer, and Jon Krosnick. 2006. "Exploring the Latent Structure of Strength-Related Attitude Attributes." In *Advances in Experimental Social Psychology*, edited by Mark Zanna. San Diego, CA: Academic Press.

Voorhees, Joshua. 2011. "Farleigh Dickinson Public Mind Poll Shows Fox News Viewers Less Informed on Major News Stories." *Slate.com*, 21 November. http://slatest.slate.com/posts/2011/11/21/fairleigh_dickinson_publicmind_poll_shows_fox_news_viewers_less_informed_on_major_news_stories.html.

Watts, Mark, David Domke, Dhavan Shah, and David Fan. 1999. "Elite Cues and Media Bias in Presidential Campaigns: Explaining Public Perceptions of a Liberal Press." *Communication Research* 26 (2): 144–75.

White, David. 1950. "The 'Gate Keeper': A Case Study in the Selection of News." *Journalism Quarterly* 27:383–90.

Williams, Bruce, and Michael Delli Carpini. 2011. *After Broadcast News: Media Regimes, Democracy, and the New Information Environment*. New York: Cambridge University Press.

Williamson, Vanessa, Theda Skocpol, and John Coggin. 2011. "The Tea Party and the Remaking of Republican Conservatism." *Perspectives on Politics* 9 (1): 25–43.

Wilson, Scott. 2011. "White House Orders Review of Energy Department Loans amid Solyndra Fallout." *Washington Post*, 28 October.

Wolf, Michael, J. Cherie Strachan, and Daniel Shea. 2012. "Incivility and Standing Firm: A Second Layer of Partisan Division." *PS: Political Science and Politics* 45 (3): 428–34.

Yzerbyt, Vincent, Muriel Dumont, Bernard Mathieu, Ernestine Gordijn, and Daniel Wigboldus. 2006. "Social Comparison and Group-Based Emotions." In *Social Comparison Processes and Levels of Analysis*, edited by Serge Guimond. Cambridge: Cambridge University Press.

Zakaria, Fareed. 2011. "The Gridlock We Can Fix." *Washington Post*, 21 July.

Zaller, John. 1992. *The Nature and Origins of Mass Opinion*. New York: Cambridge University Press.

———. 1996. "The Myth of Massive Media Impact Revived: New Support for a Discredited Idea." In *Political Persuasion and Attitude Change*, edited by Diana Mutz, Paul Sniderman, and Richard Brody. Ann Arbor: University of Michigan Press.

———. 2002. "The Statistical Power of Election Studies to Detect Media Exposure Effects in Political Campaigns." *Electoral Studies* 21 (2): 297–329.

Index